14.00

Please return on or before the date below.

2011-15 · 5 issues

Non-loan returns

−6 MAR 2017

/18

Clifton Library
Rotherham College of Arts & Technology,
Eastwood Lane, Rotherham, S65 1EG
Need to renew, book a PC or book a help session?
Call: (01709) 722869 or 722738

√19

√2)

This is Madness
A critical look at psychiatry and the future of mental health services
Edited by **Craig Newnes, Guy Holmes** and **Cailzie Dunn**
ISBN 1898059 25 X , 1999

This is Madness Too
Critical perspectives on mental health services
Edited by **Craig Newnes, Guy Holmes** and **Cailzie Dunn**
ISBN 1898059 37 3, 2001

Personality as Art
Artistic approaches in psychology
Peter Chadwick
ISBN 1898059 35 7, 2001

Spirituality and Psychotherapy
Edited by **Simon King-Spooner** and **Craig Newnes**
ISBN 1898059 39 X, 2001

Beyond Help
A consumers' guide to psychology
Susan Hansen, Alec McHoul and **Mark Rapley**
ISBN 1898059 54 3, 2003

The Gene Illusion
Genetic research in psychiatry and psychology under the microscope
Jay Joseph
ISBN 1898059 47 0, 2003

Violence and Society
Making sense of madness and badness
Elie Godsi
ISBN 1898059 62 4, 2004

Beyond Prozac
Healing mental suffering
Dr Terry Lynch
ISBN 1898059 63 2, 2004

Power, Interest and Psychology
David Smail
ISBN 1898059 71 3, 2005

www.pccs-books.co.uk

Making and Breaking Children's Lives

EDITORS

CRAIG NEWNES

AND

NICK RADCLIFFE

PCCS Books
Ross-on-Wye

First published in 2005
Reprinted 2008
Reprinted 2009

PCCS BOOKS
2 Cropper Row
Alton Road
ROSS-ON-WYE
HR9 5LA
UK
Tel +44 (0)1989 763900
Fax +44 (0)1989 763901
contact@pccs-books.co.uk
www.pccs-books.co.uk

Making and Breaking Children's Lives

British Library Cataloguing in Publication Data.
A catalogue record for this book is available from the British Library.

ISBN 978 1 898059 70 7

Cover design by The Old Dog's Missus

Printed by Cpod, Trowbridge, UK

CONTENTS

Part One: Constructing Childhood

Part Two: Problematising Children

Part Three: Appreciating Children

DEDICATED TO OUR CHILDREN

FOREWORD

OLIVER JAMES

It is not easy for professionals to find the time and energy to set out on paper what they do and how it helps to counter the toxins filling the emotional environment in which most children are now raised. I have the greatest admiration for such people. Donald Winnicott once argued that sanity is preserved in any society by the 10 per cent of the population who are emotionally mature; the ones who are not 'me, me, me' attention-seekers but who quietly get on with providing the sensible yet playful support which is so life-saving.

There are many such here. This book is chock-a-block with accounts of practical ideas and mindsets for neutralising the toxins in our social environment, as well as scientific evidence that there is nothing remotely inevitable about the breaking of children. Government ministers: Read, Learn and Inwardly Digest.

INTRODUCTION

The Destruction of Children

CRAIG NEWNES AND
NICK RADCLIFFE

Do you feel lucky? Are you a parent with productive, funny, creative children? If so, then you are one of millions. Do you celebrate your good fortune? The first author's mum used to say she thanked providence on a daily basis for her health. We do much the same for the health and happiness of our families and friends, well paid jobs and stimulating lives. Critically, we do feel lucky, having long ago learnt that almost everything that leads to what the world calls success is based on luck. For example, the first author was fortunate enough never to have been referred to a child psychologist, social worker or psychiatrist despite being pretty difficult at school. He has never been told he has a biochemically induced brain disorder leading to the demand for numbing drugs. His parents were never told that charging up and down the playground, staring out of windows and falling out of trees was due to hyperactivity. They were assured such behaviour was natural exuberance coupled with boredom in class and he would grow out of it—they're still waiting.

Importantly the village school he attended as an infant happened to have no shortage of open spaces to expend energy. That meant that pupils were relatively subdued in some lessons and teachers felt less harassed. Parents coped with their kids' conduct and only took them to general practitioners when they were actually ill or needed inoculations.

Of course the system has shifted: now parents or teachers take children to doctors who, quite naturally, view everything on a continuum of ill to well. So all conduct is viewed this way. Some children can be very challenging indeed. The GP will lean towards a diagnosis legitimising medication. A referral to a child psychiatrist may also lead to medication. Kids might even take it for a while. Then they might sell it on the streets.

The majority of children will benefit from being with adults who have emotional (social support and self-confidence) and financial means. This will include access to local knowledge and understandings about children passed down through parenting and between parents in their communities. Children will be loved and nurtured, their uniqueness encouraged and their behaviour generally tolerated. Importantly, the child's relationships with these adults will serve as a natural protective layer against many things including the potentially harmful effects of professional services.

Not all children are so lucky. Many children live in circumstances where one or more of the elements making up the protective layer are missing. They may live in poverty and debt brought on perhaps by family breakdown, loss, or by parents not keeping up with the pace of living. These adults may have struggled as children and now they struggle as parents. Their own children are now disadvantaged and, like the parents, they feel isolated. Many parents live with little emotional or financial support and increasing pressures from every angle. Being complained at by other adults to do something about their child's behaviour is a common experience. But they feel powerless to act. The stories told in the media about being a parent or adult are increasingly at odds with the actual lived experience of raising children. Raising a family is difficult at the best of times. If children are upset we find it hard to cope. If they are frightened and angry, one possible reaction from parents is fear and anger—hence the title of Dorothy Rowe's chapter: ADHD: Adults' fear of frightened children.

In such circumstances adults are less available to their children. They have less time, less energy and less curiosity. Their natural capacity for empathy and reflexivity might be temporarily disengaged. It is safer to seek the palliative of medicine than risk, on top of everything else, being told you are losing your mind.

Drugging children

Twenty years ago the journalist Matthew Parris attempted to live on unemployment benefit on an estate in Newcastle. When he returned recently he was aghast to find swathes of the population on antidepressants and their children on Ritalin. His findings are of course confirmed in the statistical evidence of the prescription of antidepressants and Ritalin: in the last ten years, prescriptions for psychiatric drugs to children and adolescents in the US have nearly tripled from pre-nineties levels.[1] According to the US Food and Drug Administration (FDA), 11 million prescriptions for antidepressants were written for children under 18 in 2002. Similarly, there has been an estimated 580 per cent rise in antidepressant use in the under-6 population.[2]

Before 1990 there were barely 5000 children in the UK diagnosed with Attention Deficit Hyperactivity Disorder (ADHD). There are now over 200,000. Ritalin remains the commonest treatment and, as Sami Timimi and Nick Radcliffe say in their chapter, there are increasing claims that children who are difficult to manage have a neuro-developmental disorder. Children that are in most peril are those that have lost the protection of familiar open-minded adults and find themselves in the care system. These children are five times more likely to have a psychiatric label and on all measures of development are disadvantaged when compared to their peers not in the care system.

What does all this mean? Has there really been an explosion of brain disorders in our children leading them to act in ways we find extremely challenging? There is a simple test of any such claim. If you were told that your child had a physical disorder, for example, cancer, you would ask for blood and other tests to confirm the diagnosis before risking potentially harmful chemotherapy. Applying this logic to any similar claim that your child's behaviour is due to a biochemical imbalance, ask this to be tested for. You will be offered no test. Like the overwhelming majority of psychiatric diagnoses the idea that challenging and downright odd behaviour is caused by faulty brain chemistry is just that, an idea. There are no tests for such faulty biochemistry but the claim does legitimise the use of psychiatric drugs. In her chapter, Grace Jackson explores the darker side of the impact of such 'dromospheric pollution'. The idea of faulty biochemistry also takes the focus off a host of other factors: the school, the neighbourhood where you live, parenting problems, and so on. In some ways, everyone benefits: child mental health professionals look like experts, schools can continue to increase class sizes as if this doesn't matter, parents can be reassured that difficult kids are not their fault and will be in the safe hands of the system. A diagnosis will also lead to much needed state financial aid for the family. As ever, psychiatry is being used to manage guilt and anxiety rather than have a serious look at the root causes of the problem: poverty, unemployment or soulless employment, the need for drug companies to maximise profit, and so on.

In recent years the general message from the child professional world has been 'children are problems'. Influential children's organisations like Young Minds make claims like 20 per cent of children will suffer from a mental disorder. These claims tend to reinforce the idea that 'the problem resides in the child'. This, again, is the discourse of individualism, which has been so crucial to the physical sciences' understanding and manipulation of our physical world; however it wreaks havoc in the world of the living where some of the most elementary understandings about psychology are being overlooked, for example, the crucial importance of relationships. The chapter by Baker and Newnes in this volume explores the discourse of individualism further with reference to the notion of personal responsibility.

Many users of mental health services liken their experience to entering another world—where their native experiences are re-described in a different language. A child in the clinic room for assessment for ADHD may repeatedly demonstrate positive and attentive behaviours but these behaviours are missed as the adults are talking about diagnosis. In a Pupil Referral Unit, the same child sits, works and achieves. Yet in the clinic room that child is given the diagnosis ADHD. The wholesale manufacturing of the neuro-developmental disorders branch of child psychiatry is leading to an almost exponential explosion in the use of drugs like Methylphenidate with children. It has also led to an impoverished form of inquiry into the relational and cultural meaning of behaviour.

The future

It is hard, in a world of profiteering and violence, to feel hopeful for the future of our children. It would appear that children have become another potential casualty in the war for big bucks. There are alternatives to labelling and drugging our children. There are alternatives to sitting on year-long waiting lists for professional therapy services. These alternatives have always been with us—neighbourliness, commitment and community action. For examples, look no further than the Family Well-Being Project in Birmingham or Imagine Chicago, both described in this volume.

Such options can take a long time. Our children deserve no less. They are, after all, the future.

Endnotes

1. Zito, J.M., Safer, S.J., dosReis, S., Gardner, J.F., Magder, L., Soeken, K. et al. (2003). Psychotropic practice patterns for youth: A 10-year perspective. *Archives of Pediatric & Adolescent Medicine, 157*(1), 17–25.

2. Zito, J.M., Safer, S.J., dosReis, S., Gardner, J.F., Boles, M., and Lynch, F. (2000). Trends in the prescribing of psychotropic medications to preschoolers. *Journal of the American Medical Association, 283*(8), 1025–30.

Part One

Constructing Childhood

CHAPTER 1

Constructions of Childhood

GERRILYN SMITH

In this chapter I have tried to focus on how my clinical work with Looked After Children (children who live away from their families of origin) is influenced by the thoughts and ideas that the notion of the destruction of children stirred up in me.

In preparing the references, I should, perhaps, apologise for the absence of sources in some cases. I have found it an interesting reflection of what we consider to be 'knowledge' and how we use 'knowledge' to support our views. Somehow my unreferenced collection of 'facts' could be seen as less compelling in the absence of complete references. However this has rarely stopped me from forming a view so I see no reason to be so constrained now.

Firstly it is clear that children and childhood are not synonymous. Children's lived experience is filtered through the socially constructed lens of childhood. Being a child is a transient state, one through which we all pass. Yet this period of biological immaturity is often seen as critical and sensitive to our understanding of our selves. Given my work with Looked After Children, I have often pondered on this notion of critical developmental phases especially as I am so often asked about the long-term prognosis for children who have experienced neglect, abuse or other traumatic events.

Let me begin by contextualising the world of children.

Children: Some figures

If we think about children in a global sense, then the socially constructed notion of childhood quickly emerges as bas-relief to the reality of their lives. The majority of the world's children are born to women under 20 years of age,[1] i.e. teenage mothers. Women having children in their teens is seen as a social problem here in

Britain. Within our culture there are unspoken values, legislation and ideas regarding the right age to have sex in the first place, (not before 16). Only recently was the age of consent for homosexual activity lowered so that it is now at the same age as heterosexual activity. One might wonder if much of the legislation about sexual offences was not more concerned with the potential outcome of heterosexual activity, (i.e. children) rather than the issue of the activity per se.

Worldwide, 150 million children work for wages, yet they are disenfranchised and have no real political voice. It is clear that their wages make a vital contribution to the economic survival of their families. It wasn't so long ago that the same was true in Britain. Many young boys received into care via the Approved School system in the 1960s came from poor families. The reasons for coming into care often involved so-called delinquent acts such as stealing milk off doorsteps, taking lead off roofs, not paying bus fares, coupled with not attending school. There was no recognition that their activities were a contribution to the overall financial survival of their families or that the education system was not equipping them for the lives they would lead.

State intervention often increased their delinquency and failed to provide a better education. In the worst cases like Bryn Estyn, Bryn Allen and Greystone Heath (to name but a few of the residential units known to have been corrupted by widespread abuse), the young boys were subjected to harsh regimes and many forms of abuse. This became their journey to manhood.

The majority of children in the world are parented by older children, often their siblings. We often do not take this into consideration when making assessments on attachments or considering psychological concepts like resilience despite the fact that sibling relationships are often the longest relationships of our lives.[2]

In Britain there are approx 61,000 children looked after by the state, 5 per cent more than in 2000.[3] The largest recorded category of need (reason for removal) was abuse and neglect (62 per cent).[4] To contextualise these figures, the level of abuse and neglect was so significant it came to the notice of statutory authorities who intervened and removed the children. Clearly these figures do not reflect all those children in the UK raised in poverty, or who suffer abuse and neglect.

Perhaps more shockingly, of this 61,000, only a small percentage is placed for adoption. The majority are in foster placements often facing uncertain futures or in some cases being returned to the families they were originally removed from. Not that this is in itself a bad thing if the necessary changes have occurred, but all too often it is merely passage of time and a failure by the state to provide a viable and 'better' alternative family context that leads to this return.

This is the domestic refuse of our society—the diaspora of children disconnected from family and community. Secularised and privatised notions of caring produce a state system for looking after children that is monitored through performance indicators. Looking after children who have been disconnected from their families of origin is big business.

In some cultural groups and/or ethnic minority communities the idea of having a child looked after by the state is incomprehensible. Rather than tapping this as a resource, already overburdened social service departments fail to notice this.

Recording of ethnicity is often inaccurate for Looked After Children. However, the overrepresentation of children from 'mixed marriages'[5] in the care system is generally acknowledged. For example, Liverpool figures for Looked After Children show 20 per cent identified as black compared to 5.7 per cent of the minority ethnic population of under 18s in Liverpool as indicated by the 1991 Census.[6]

State intervention into family life, whilst frequently triggered by issues of abuse and neglect, often becomes focused on 'poor parenting' without due regard to the social context of parenting in poverty. Whilst ostensibly it is both parents who are the focus of concern, in reality mothers bear the brunt of state scrutiny and fathers are ignored.

Looked After Children are often disconnected from their father's and paternal kinship networks. For example research on contact after adoption[7] found that for children under 5 who had contact, it was likely to be with their mothers or the maternal extended family. This research also included contact with siblings. Again if contact was happening it was most likely to be with the siblings produced by their mothers and not fathers.

While this may be the bleak side of childhood, here are some other interesting facts: children laugh on average 150 times per day compared to adults who laugh only 15 times. One suspects this could be plotted across the life-line with adult status conferred when your mean number of laughs per day falls below a certain number. Children's imaginative belief in fairies, angels, heaven (and of course trolls, monsters and devils) rapidly diminishes after the age of five.

A friend of mine repeated a story to me—telling me that when children come into the world they know everything but as they pass to the corporeal world, God leans forward and presses a finger to their lips saying 'Shh' leaving the imprint of the finger in the indent under our noses. And as we grow up, we lose this knowledge that is 'right under our nose'.

The number of questions a child asks prior to starting school, in the hundreds, diminishes to 20 after six weeks of school.

Based on American research,[8] by 4 years of age children from professional families will have heard 50 million words, working class children 30 million and welfare children 12 million. The ratio of encouraging words to discouraging words by the age of three also shows marked class distinctions—with children from professional families experiencing 700,000 positive words to 80,000 discouraging words whilst a welfare child experiences 60,000 positive words with the discouraging words outnumbering the positive.

Given words are how we construct our worlds, the implications of this inequitable system of language means the stories we live and tell will be bound by the words we have available to construct those stories.

This becomes the construction of childhood.

Constructions of childhood

Childhood is a political construction. Although rooted in a biological reality of immaturity, the meaning given to this immaturity varies widely—old enough to have sex, *not* old enough to drink alcohol, to get married, to vote, to join the forces, to collect benefit, to have your views considered, or to receive legal representation.

Much of social policy in relation to children is focused on 'what children would become rather than how they are ... at the time'.[9] This reflects a wider social construction of not 'being in the moment' if you like. Many young people have views on political issues that will directly impact on their lives, yet they are not able to vote. Educational priorities are set by adults for children. I am sure I am not the only parent of a child disaffected by constant examination and assessment or who feels an agent of state control in the constant battle over homework.

Children's needs can be treated as self-evident rather than informed by and reflecting socio-political preoccupations.[10] For example, a recent research study assessing the impact of the environment on *children*'s health in Europe, the first of its kind to specifically focus on children,[11] found that children bear a disproportionate burden of health consequences that are environmentally induced. There were marked variations across Europe with those children who were abused. Street children, for example, who were exploited or trafficked, lived in areas of armed conflict and were at highest risk of injuries, psychological distress, chronic infections and non-communicable diseases, impaired growth and death, i.e the children who are most vulnerable socially are also the most physically at risk.

Childhood as a concept is un-gendered, un-raced, un-cultured and un-classed. By this I mean it is used as a descriptor that hides salient aspects of self or of your group status. For example, figures on 'children' currently in care show the expected gender breakdown of 55 per cent male, 45 per cent female. Our attention is not drawn to the overrepresentation of children of mixed parentage within the care system or to the worrying pattern that boys become harder to place the older they get—from 5 years onward. The largest proportion of Looked After Children fall in the 10–15 age range. We are not given the gender breakdown for this age range.

In the same way that research on parenting is usually research on mothering—using the generic word 'children' reduces the complexity and the nuances of social intercourse and understanding to stereotypical pictures and patterns.

Our views of discourses on childhood are affected by our current position in relation to the material or indeed how we wish to position ourselves given the 'multiverse' we live in. Can I still remember how I felt as a child? How do I view childhood as a parent? As a mother? As a white woman?

'Discourses of childhood are central to the ways we structure our own and others' sense of place and position.'[12] In part I think this is because childhood is a state we all pass through so it is possible for us to form a view about childhood without, for example, having had children ourselves.

Childhood is a transitional stage itself further subdivided into stages. It is characterised initially by extreme dependency with a gradual move towards independence. Alice Miller[13] talks of our collective desire as adults to avoid remembering what it felt like to be a dependent child. She writes of the collusion of adults against the child's lived experience.

Children's views are only taken seriously when they are deemed sensible by adults. For example, children, when consulted about what they considered to be most important in their lives, put open and safe spaces to play at the top of their list with school at the bottom. Adults creating a similar list put school (or perhaps I should say education) at the top. Indeed the UK government's current targets for performance for Looked After Children focus quite heavily on educational attainment. In our desire to consult stakeholders, we can forget that repeated consultation without delivering services is a form of exploitation.

Children in the care system are consulted about their wishes and feelings. Their views when expressed should be given weight, however sometimes we are asking them to make decisions about issues that they do not fully comprehend. Or when they do express a clear view, it is disregarded because children lack the authority, not the imagination, to make their wishes come true.

The 'corporate parent' is an illusion. For example a child's residential placement can be terminated because it is too expensive in a cost-cutting exercise despite a child's wish to remain in that placement. A child's desire to stay with the foster family can be dismissed because the foster family is deemed short-term or the financial cost of long-term fostering is considered too great and the often hopelessly overly optimistic pursuit of a 'forever' family continues. Little respect is paid to the relational aspects of childhood. The corporate parent rarely has to explain such decisions directly to the child. Corporate accountability for such decisions is not to the child whose life is affected by it but up the managerial hierarchy. The task of explaining—if indeed this happens at all—is left to primary caregivers, usually foster parents.

The current construction of childhood emphasises the innocence of children, their proximity to nature and freedom from the contamination of the adult world. I only wish this were true. The study on the environmental burden of disease in children clearly shows how we are contaminating our children, significantly reducing their life chances. The study estimates 100,000 deaths and 6 million years of healthy life lost every year.[14]

On a less concrete note, many foster parents explicitly state they do not want to foster children who have been sexually abused—perhaps the biggest con-taminant of all. With incidence/prevalence figures for unwanted sexual contact before the age of 18 as high as 48 per cent in the general population, sexual abuse is an almost inevitable experience for children in the care system. It is currently subsumed under the general heading of abuse and neglect.

Children as consumer goods

Shocking as it may seem, children have become consumer goods. They are literally bought and sold. Intercountry adoption occurs in Britain despite at least 50,000 British children needing families. However, children and babies in the care system, clearly do not meet the constructed needs of would-be parents. They must be seen as damaged or 'shop-soiled' in some way. Yet by some strange imaginative leap, couples allow themselves to believe that the imported babies and toddlers, often from Third World countries, will be less tainted than the children waiting here for their 'forever families'. Pictures of Romanian orphanages or the idea of unwanted Chinese baby girls being left to die trigger for some the journey to parenthood.

Advances in fertility treatment have also transformed this journey. Predominantly heterosexual couples can 'try harder' to biologically procreate. The discourse of children as consumer goods clashes with this technology producing a new language around children. We have 'selective procreation' and 'designer babies'. Recently there was discussion about checking the backgrounds of would-be parents using certain fertility treatments to screen out unsuitable people. This is another step in the state regulation of the private personal world of procreation, which would focus predominantly on middle-class, heterosexual, would-be parents who can afford such treatments, rather than on the traditional poor and working-class parents whose procreative capacities have been traditionally regulated and monitored.

Many adults see having children as a right and a necessary part of the life process. This is often enacted in child care court cases where the issue of contact (with the biological parents) is often used as a lever to secure parental agreement for the child to live away from them. There is an unspoken assumption that contact with biological parents is in the child's best interest without real thought being given to significant others who may have far more to contribute to the child's mental health through the course of the child's life.

Having a child is not the same as wanting children to parent. The biological imperative often supersedes the desire to parent. As we begin the process of parenting we are often confronted by our preconceived (in its fullest sense) notions of how our child should be. This can be as basic as anticipating a son and having a daughter.

Motherhood in particular is built into the discourse of femininity. In my discussions with young women between the ages of 14 and 16 all were asked if, in their ideal world, they saw themselves as having children. Almost without exception they did. Many had quite elaborate and detailed ideas about the children they would have, including names. This was in stark contrast to the ideas they had, or rather did not have, about the father of their children. What was also interesting about these discussions was when asked if for some reason they were unable to have children how they would feel, many indicated that their desire to mother was so strong that they would adopt, foster or use whatever fertility treatment was available to them.

More attention needs to be paid to the differences between producing children and parenting them. In many black and minority ethnic communities the concept of collective responsibility for children—an inclusive approach to parenting—makes ideas of state care alien. The biological aspect of parenthood is not singled out over the collective responsibility of the community to raise children.

Moving away from a sense of ownership and recognising children's own agency helps to dispel cultural and psychological constructions of childhood as a state of innocence requiring the expertise of parents/adults to negotiate it. Indeed it is precisely such a construction that is exploited by child abusers who use this discourse of teaching children to introduce inappropriate sexual activity and extreme physical chastisement.

By focusing on children as goods, we pay little heed to childhood as essentially an interactive process. This interactive/relational process engages not only parents but also siblings, friends and other significant adults. The multiplicity of interactions and relationships in turn contributes to our psychological resilience.

For Looked After Children the singularity of their experience in terms of isolation from other ameliorating relationships is almost certainly what has triggered their removal. Part of the abusive system is to limit outside influences and relationships enforcing and heightening dependency on an authoritarian and controlling figure. Even the most neglectful parents frequently bind their children to them psychologically despite offering them inappropriate care.

Destruction of children

Given the idealised construction of childhood, it is not surprising then that child abuse and in particular sexual abuse of children not only hurts the child but also 'robs them of their childhood'. 'Childhood ... is not defined by age but by some set of qualities or experiences which are incompatible with being assaulted.'[15]

Only something as extreme as child murder punctuates the dominant discourse of childhood as a safe and playful interlude before the responsibilities of adulthood take hold. In Britain there are 50 child murders per year.[16] Only a few make national headlines. The reporting of those few serves to generate paranoia around child safety and to increase and escalate the regulation and legislation that surrounds children's lives instead of recognising the rarity of such events.

Awful as these child murders are, they need to be compared to hundreds of children killed in Honduras[17] or the thousands that die needlessly of starvation in Africa. Children and the quality of their lives are literally being destroyed daily.

Children who have been sexually abused can become demonised. It is not uncommon to meet foster parents who feel overly concerned about the possibility of false allegations being made against them, or teachers being unable physically to comfort children for fear of misinterpretation. This shift of responsibility to the child for 'making' adults uncomfortable demonstrates that the innocence of childhood will be conferred on the deserving child—deserving as deemed by adults. This is something parents of black boys have long been aware of as they experience the criminalisation process of their sons as they emerge into manhood.

There are other more subtle ways in which we destroy children. We compromise their psychological health. Children's behaviours—enacting their truth—can become defined or diagnosed as disturbed without due attention being given to their lived experiences. Looked After Children have found ways of coping with their adverse childhood experiences before the state 'rescues' them. Despite being received into care due to significant harm or the likelihood of significant harm (i.e. an action perpetrated against them) *they* quickly become pathologised. Their behaviours are seen as symptoms, not as adaptive to a previous context or as a form of protest to a current situation.

Interestingly it is often mothers who acknowledge children's agency more than anyone else. This is almost certainly a function of their proximity to the day-to-day reality of interacting with children.[18] The 'corporate parent' rarely acknowledges the agency of Looked After Children hence the need for advocacy services. Looked After Children are viewed as passive recipients of a state service and indeed many feel they should be grateful for what they receive. Compensation for abuses suffered within the care system is grudgingly given after long and protracted legal battles which directly attack the credibility of childhood accounts given by adults.

For example, Shy Keenan made repeated allegations as a child about her experiences of abuse. These were not taken seriously. As an adult, in her search for justice she tape-recorded her perpetrator confessing to his long term sexual abuse of her and others. This was presented as a television documentary[19] which in turn triggered a new police investigation into his criminal offences. He and others were convicted of serious sexual crimes against children and received long custodial sentences in March 2002.

Considerable attention has been paid to the mental health of Looked After Children with specific monies set aside to increase the services provided for them from Child and Adolescent Health. Estimates of clinically significant mental health problems for Looked After Children between the ages of 5 and 17 suggest a figure of 45 per cent as compared to 10 per cent for the general population. Conduct disorders are the most likely diagnosis at 37 per cent.[20] The gender distribution is along expected lines with boys showing higher rates of conduct disorders and girls showing higher rates for emotional disorders.

No specific mention is made of Post-Traumatic Stress Disorder in the research despite common knowledge that children coming into the care system will have been exposed to high levels of stress. Given children are received into care due to significant harm or environmental circumstances that are considered well beyond the threshold of acceptable stressors hence the need for statutory intervention, this seems a significant omission.

Diagnostic labelling is stigmatising and fails to acknowledge the very considerable part adults and the environment they have created for children have contributed to the presence of what is now deemed a 'psychiatric disorder'.

For example, the label 'Reactive Attachment Disorder' pathologises what can be seen as a perfectly normal reaction to repeatedly transient primary relationships. Statutory interventions in families where attachment issues are present often compound and exacerbate already fragile relationships. For example, separating a mother and child where there are serious concerns over risk but where rehabilitation is still being considered can exacerbate and paradoxically increase the risk of harm to the child. The concept of bridging placements is based on an idea that if a child can make attachments then we can move them on to their 'forever' family—expecting them to detach and re-attach as if they were spacecraft performing manoeuvres. This is part of the destruction of children.

Similarly Attention Deficit Hyperactivity Disorder (ADHD) as a diagnostic category is subject to much professional debate. Rarely is Post-Traumatic Stress Disorder considered as a differential diagnosis. The treatment pathway for ADHD (and other similar conditions) often involves the administration of psychotropic drugs such as Ritalin. For the Looked After Children population, where is the concerned parent who advocates other treatment interventions? Many foster parents feel compelled to administer drugs that they would not give to their 'own' (note the possessive case here) children. Figures do not appear to be readily available about the amount of prescribed drugs Looked After Children receive.

Deconstruction of childhood

The childhood transition to adulthood can be seen as a move from the feminine principles of relatedness and attachment to the masculine principles of action and detachment.[21] For the Looked After Children population, we can see that they are deprived of their childhood through systemic failures (an abusive, neglectful family of origin with no extended family available to mitigate these failures and a wider community that fails to step in to offer alternatives) and then received into state care where the possibility of reclaiming their childhood often seems a matter of chance.

Corporate parenting fails to unite both mothering and fathering. The paternal role of authority and financial provision[22] is privileged over the maternal role of caring and nurturing. This brings repeated clashes of epistemologies when trying to deliver a Child and Adolescent Mental Health Services Looked After Children (CAMHS LAC) service.

Additionally CAMHS services based on the use of psychiatric cases fail to challenge the wider political context of social failure that puts children at risk of disconnection from their families of origin. Psychological services aim at integrating the 'fragmented' child usually by focusing on specific aspects of the child's behaviour and development (note the singularity of the concept development).[23]

Recognising and valuing the role of alternative primary caregivers in the Looked After Child's life is more likely to generate both better service delivery and quality of life for the young person. For example, in one study alternative caregivers were found to intuitively predict relatively accurately the mental health of the child or young person they were caring for.[24]

The same study found both carers who thought there was a mental health need which psychometric measures did not confirm and from the researchers' point of view the more worrying scenario, 'false negatives', where a significant mental health problem as identified by psychometric measures was not intuitively recognised by carers. The carers included both foster caregivers and residential staff. This difference in role was not correlated with congruence between intuitive assessment and psychometric results. So for example we do not know if residential workers were more likely to miss clinically significant mental health problems than foster carers.

The study then suggests: 'These results provide evidence of the suitability of routine mental health screening of looked after young people, despite no statistical significance being found.'[25] The 'solution' of standardised mental health screening relies too heavily on individually focused models of service delivery rather than a more holistic approach that values the relationship between the child, their family of origin and their alternative carers. It is also another example of increased regulation and surveillance of Looked After Children's lives.

Only 9 per cent of the young people believed themselves to have mental health problems. This large discrepancy between self report and the views of carers of these young people diagnosed with mental health problems indicates a gap in the understanding between the looked after young person and those who care for them about what constitutes good mental health. If we fail to provide a healthy alternative model of family life, then the beliefs and behaviours consistent with the adverse family backgrounds Looked After Children are removed from will remain intact. In the absence of relationship, even a healthy alternative family model will not achieve a different way of constructing self.

Encouraging children and young people to talk about their lived experiences is a radical intervention. When they do so they often speak directly from their hearts—their truth. This can make us feel uncomfortable. Professional systems can deal with this discomfort in a number of unhelpful ways.

Firstly and perhaps most destructively is the denial of the child's lived experience. This formed a significant part of Alice Miller's work.[13] She helps us, as adults, to recognise how we deny children's realities because we become inducted into believing that growing up is about the power to control and construct children's lives through their experience of childhood. We believe we do this benevolently and in the child's best interest.

Similarly Freud's recantation of children's disclosures of abusive experiences was another denial of children's lived experience. This has spawned a number of other ways of dismissing adult cruelty to children—for example 'false memories'. Abuse experiences that challenge the adult's idealised view of childhood become construed as an intrapsychic phenomenon—an imaginary and secretly desired experience or possibly a false memory planted by another adult. Either way the lived experience in all its confusion becomes subjected to therapeutic discourse usually when we are adults or if as children, as an allegation and the subject of legal proceedings. Either way a child's effort to make sense of their world and by extension of their self is destroyed by well-intentioned adult intervention. Surely we can all remember the frustration of trying as children to get adults to understand our point of view.

In closing this article I decided to allow myself the freedom of wondering. Doesn't our experience of dependency/powerlessness as children teach us to be patient, endure and survive? How can we use our childhood experiences as resources rather than seeing them as the root of our problems? Maybe it is better to grow down rather than grow up? Maybe I am finally getting old enough to hear God's whisper again.

Endnotes

This chapter is based on an oral presentation to the Psychotherapy Section of the British Psychological Society. The title was given to me by Craig Newnes and so engaged my curiosity that I accepted both the invitation to speak and write without really knowing where it would take me—to play with it.

1. Phoenix, A. (1991). *Young Mothers?* Oxford: Polity Press.

2. Dunn J. and Kendrick, C. (1982). *Siblings, Love, Envy and Understanding*. London: Grant McIntyre.

3. National Statistics First Release SFR, 40/2000 (2004). DFES.

4. Office of National Statistics, November, 2003.

5. I considered a number of different ways to say this and in the end opted for 'mixed marriage' because children are the product of two people who may have thought the cultural-racial divide was not significant when they were in love with each other but somehow, when separated, those hidden or unspoken differences come into play.

6. Building Bridges (2003). *Hear Me Now!* Consultation on the views and needs of Black and minority ethnic young people in Liverpool.

7. Neil, E. (1999). The sibling relationships of adopted children: patterns of contact after adoption. *Adoption and Fostering, 23*,1.

8. Based on the work of Hart and Risley, 'Meaningful differences in everyday experiences of young American children' reported by Brooks in the *Guardian* January 2, 2004.

9. Burman, Erca (1994). *Deconstructing Developmental Psychology*. London: Routledge.

10. Woodhead, M. (1990). Psychology and the cultural construction of children's needs. In A. James and A. Prout (eds) *Constructing and Reconstructing Childhood: Contemporary issues in the sociological study of childhood*. Basingstoke, Hants: Falmer Press.

11. WHO (2004). Environmental burden of disease. Reported in FACT sheet EURO/05/04 Copenhagen, Budapest, 18 June 2004.

12. Burman, Erca (1994). *Deconstructing Developmental Psychology*. London: Routledge.

13. Miller, Alice (1983). *For Your Own Good: Hidden cruelty in child-rearing, the roots of violence*. New York: Farrar, Strauss and Giroux.

14. WHO (2004). op. cit.

15. Kitzinger, Jenny (1997). In Alison James and Alan Prout (eds) *Constructing and Reconstructing Childhood*, pp. 165–89. London: Falmer Press.

16. Cox, Judy (2002). Manipulation of a tragedy. *Socialist Worker,* 1815, 31 August 2002.

17. Reported by Casa Alianza 11 March 2003 and part of an Amnesty International Campaign.

18. Woollett, Anne (2004). Parenting: mothering, fathering and being parented. *Psychology of Women Section Review, 6*, 2, 3–14.

19. *A Family Affair,* BBC2 Newsnight Special, 20 November 2000.

20. Meltzer, Howard et al. (2004). The mental health of young people looked after by legal authorities in England. Department of Health, HMSO.

21. Dinnerstein D. (1978). *The Rocking of the Cradle and the Ruling of the World*. London: Souvenir Press. Gilligan, C. (1982). In *A Different Voice: Psychological theories and women's development*. Cambridge, MA: Harvard University Press.

22. Woollett, Anne (2004). Parenting: mothering, fathering and being parented, *Psychology of Women Section Review, 6*,2, 3–14.

23. I have adapted this idea from Anne Woollett's paper, op. cit.

24. Mount, et al. (2004). Identifying mental health needs, *Clinical Child Psychology and Psychiatry, 9*, 3, 363–82.

25. Ibid, p. 376.

CHAPTER 2

Histories of Child Abuse

JONATHAN CALDER

Ten years ago I was earning my living by sub-editing psychology newsletters during the day and spending my evenings studying for a Masters degree in Victorian Studies.

By day I was reading articles that shared a particular view of child abuse. Psychologists believed that it had been discovered recently, they believed that this discovery had been made within the academy or the clinic by doctors and psychologists, and they believed that wider society had been unwilling to accept the truth of their discovery.

In my studies I was coming across a very different story. Charles Dickens was the most popular novelist of his day: people queued for periodicals containing the next instalment of his novels in just the way that later generations tuned in to see who had shot JR or who had been evicted from the Big Brother house, and contemporary critics remarked on the way that his novels were popular right across the social scale. And, of course, the maltreatment of children is a central theme in Dickens' work. Not only that, but it is central to just those novels of his—*Oliver Twist, David Copperfield, Great Expectations*—that have most entered our culture and are most familiar to modern-day readers or to those who know them through films or television adaptations.

Nor, incidentally, is this subject matter unique to Dickens or to Britain. In *The Brothers Karamazov*, when Ivan is seeking to challenge Alyosha's religious faith, it is examples of cruelty to children that he uses to clinch his case.

So this is the conflict I was faced with. According to one view, child abuse was a frightening new discovery, made by professionals and fighting for acceptance in the wider world. According to the other, it was something that the wider world had always known about and has always discussed.

Ten years on, this conflict persists. A search of the Internet soon turns up an article[1] that, whatever its limitations, presents a succinct summary of the former view—that knowledge about child abuse began in and is largely confined to the Clinic and Academy. It begins by saying:

> Public awareness of all forms of child abuse has changed considerably in the last 30 years. Before the 1960s there was little or no mention of it, either in publications or in the media.

and continues:

> It was not until the mid 1960s that Dr Henry Kemp [*sic*] referred to the 'Battered Baby Syndrome', but it took many years for it to be widely accepted that parents, particularly mothers, could inflict such injuries upon their children.[2]

In this chapter I argue that this view is simply wrong. By means of a brisk journey through a variety of published sources, I attempt to show that child abuse is not a recent discovery and that it has always been known about and talked about beyond the walls of the Clinic and the Academy. This journey, incidentally, also reveals that professionals have not always been on what now appears to us to be the enlightened side of the childcare debate.

I am not chiefly concerned with offering a correct history of child abuse myself, though I believe the alternative I suggest is a better one and that this is an area, above all, where the truth matters and where tricksy, postmodern approaches are likely to strike us as morally questionable. What I hope to do is help to release people working in the field from the grip of a faulty view and to open up the space in which a more accurate, more nuanced account can be written.

Abuse: a new discovery?

The author most often cited in support of this view is Lloyd deMause, who writes as follows:

> The history of childhood is a nightmare from which we have only recently begun to awaken. The further back in history one goes, the lower the level of childcare, and the more likely children are to be killed, abandoned, beaten, terrorized and sexually abused.[3]

This view has certainly been influential, if one takes into account the number of citations deMause's work has received, but is it correct?

Evidence for the truth of a different view comes from Linda Pollock's *Forgotten Children: Parent-child relations from 1500 to 1900*.[4] While conducting the research for this book, Pollock found 85 cases of child abuse reported in *The*

Times between 1785 and 1860, including 19 cases of incest. The defendants were found not guilty in only seven per cent of the cases, and in a further 24 per cent were sent for trial in a higher court, presumably because more severe penalties were available.

These reports make it clear that the existence of child abuse was recognised during this period. To give some examples: in a case in 1787 an ill-treated child's appearance in court 'drew tears from almost everybody'.[5] In 1809 'a case of the most unparalleled barbarity' was described in which a girl's parents said they had punished her for lying: 'The magistrate, however ... expressed a becoming indignation at their brutal conduct.'[6] And in 1810 a trial 'exhibited a picture truly shocking to every feeling of humanity'.[7]

As Pollock says:

The fact that the majority of cases were ... found guilty meant that the law and society had condemned child abuse long before the specific Prevention of Cruelty to Children Act appeared in 1889. Parents who abused their offspring were generally considered 'unnatural' and the cruelty as 'horrific' or 'barbaric'.[8]

And, one might add, on the strictest interpretation of the deMause thesis, even the passing of such an act in 1889 is inexplicable.

If people who believe that it is only recently that the wider public has become aware of child abuse were asked to date that awareness, it is likely that many would point to the death of Maria Colwell in 1973. Certainly, when journalists report the death of a child through abuse and assemble a list of previous, similar cases, this is generally the earliest example they come up with.

How then to account for the opening words of the book *A Place Called Hope*[9] by Tom O'Neill who, when it was published in 1981, had just retired from his career as a residential social worker with Kent County Council?

The book begins:

On 9 January 1945 my brother, Dennis O'Neill was beaten to death by his foster-father in a lonely farmhouse in Shropshire. Twenty-eight years later, on 6 January 1973, Maria Colwell was beaten to death by her step-father in a council house in Brighton. Both deaths resulted in a public outcry about the standards of official supervision of the children.[10]

Studying *The Times* from 1945 one finds that the trial of Dennis O'Neill's foster-father for manslaughter received prominent coverage—so prominent that it took precedence over reports of the progress of the War. Not only that: on a strangely contemporary note, there was an outcry about lenient sentencing when Dennis O'Neill's foster-father was convicted. Following the trial there was an inquiry, presided over by Sir Walter Monckton, an influential figure, who must have been diverted from important war work to conduct it.

In short, there is nothing in these two cases to say that people were any less concerned about child abuse in 1945 than they were in 1973. The evidence for a step-change in awareness some time in the 1960s is simply not there.

I do not want to go on piling up counter-examples indefinitely, but there is one further aspect of the theory that child abuse is a recent discovery that needs to be commented upon. For this theory asserts that there is one exception. In the words of the Internet article I quoted earlier:

> Of course, Freud had 'discovered' the existence of child sexual abuse many years earlier. However, in response to peer pressure at that time he completely repudiated his theory, claiming reports of abuse were merely incestuous fantasies.[11]

This idea stems, of course, from Jeffrey Masson's book *The Assault on Truth*.[12] Yet reading Masson again today, one is struck by his insistence that the sexual abuse of children was already well known when Freud was training as a doctor. Indeed, Masson goes to some lengths to establish that works by nineteenth-century French doctors who wrote about it—Brouardel, Bernard, Tardieu—were in Freud's personal library.

Whatever the rights and wrongs of Masson's claim that Freud's reasons for abandoning his seduction theory were ignoble, it is clear from a reading of his own book that the popular account of Freud that it has given rise to is simply wrong. The sexual abuse of children was already known before Freud; indeed, Masson seems just as indignant that Freud ignored it for so long as he is that he later changed his views to talk about fantasies.

Nor will this idea come as any surprise to a student of French history. One of the charges against Marie Antoinette at her trial was that she had sexually abused her own young son. Again sexual abuse is seen, not as something unimaginable, but something that, just as today, might be produced as a charge at a revolutionary show trial. Robespierre, incidentally, is reported to have responded to this charge by complaining of his fellow revolutionary Hebert: 'It's not enough that Antoinette should be a Messalina. That idiot must make her an Agrippina.'[13]

Agrippina, of course, was Nero's mother, which reminds us that incest was known in classical times and, more importantly, its existence was known to anyone in more recent centuries who had received a classical education. Again, what we have been told is unimaginable turns out to have been widely known and widely talked about.

Are professionals the ones who care?

Another aspect of the claim that child abuse is a recent discovery is the idea that, while the public has generally proved resistant to the concept, professionals have taken a more enlightened view.

The accounts of the various trials discussed above show that there is ample evidence that the public was aware of abuse and as outraged by it as any professional, so I shall devote this section to looking at some of the ideas that circulated in radical circles in the 1970s. These do not fit easily with the idea of professionals as an enlightened vanguard and form an interesting byway that is in danger of being written out of history.

This discussion begins with another book. Philippe Ariés first published his *Centuries of Childhood* in 1960.[14] Its thesis was not that child abuse is a recent discovery, but something altogether more radical. He argued that childhood itself is a recent concept; as he would have put it, not a recent discovery but a recent *invention*.

Ariés held that the concept of childhood did not exist at all in the medieval period, arose among the upper classes in the sixteenth and seventeenth centuries, became fully established in the eighteenth century upper classes, and did not become common to all social classes until the twentieth century. He based this work on a study of art history, arguing that medieval artists depicted children as miniature adults not because they lacked technical skill but because they *saw* them as miniature adults. They lacked the concept of childhood. He also studied a range of texts from earlier periods, making a great deal, for instance, of an account of the infancy of the future Louis XIII.

Whether right or wrong, Ariés' view of the history of childhood was extremely influential for some years. If we return to Linda Pollock's *Forgotten Children*— and this book was conceived as an answer to Ariés, not to deMause—we shall find evidence that this influence is hard to justify.

Pollock argues, a little fiercely, that the sources Ariés and his followers use to support their view that childhood is a recent invention are 'suspect and are certainly not a secure enough base to warrant the dramatic generalisations derived from them'.[15] In response, she offers her own study drawing, not only upon the newspaper reports discussed earlier, but also upon 496 published diaries and autobiographies from Britain and America. Of the diaries, 98 were written by children or were started when the diarists were children.

Her conclusion from this wider range of sources is that there were:

> ... very few changes in parental care and child life from the 16th to the 19th century in the home, apart from social changes and technological improvements. Nearly all children were wanted, such developmental stages as weaning and teething aroused interest and concern and parents revealed anxiety and distress at the illness or death of a child. Parents, although they may have found their offspring troublesome at times, did seem to enjoy the company of their children.[16]

And she lists some examples of this enjoyment:

> Clifford (1590–1676) and Wallington (1598–1658) enjoyed talking with their young children and Jefferay (1591–1675) described the long forest

rambles he and his children took; Blundell (1669–1737) made toys for his daughters and helped them to make a garden.[17]

If Ariés was right, it is hard to see how these mundane examples of happy childhood experience could exist.

Pollock's case is not that nothing ever changes. She suggests, for instance, that there was an intensification of adult demands for obedience and conformity, particularly in schools, in the early nineteenth century, which had been relaxed by the end of that century. But her work, with its close attention to contemporary sources, is a valuable corrective to Ariés' theories quite as much as it is to deMause's.

For a while Ariés' theory was very influential. If one looks at *Changing Childhood*,[18] a self-consciously radical collection of short articles, one sees his influence everywhere. The art historian Peter Fuller talks about artists' 'denial of childhood',[19] but for most writers in the collection Ariés' central idea is liberation.

This is an era in which books with titles like *Escape from Childhood*[20] were written. John Holt's work contains chapters on, among other subjects, 'The right to vote', 'The right to work' and 'The right to drive'. Reading him today it is hard to resist the idea that Holt was not so much calling for a change in our attitude towards children as calling for the abolition of the very concept of childhood. See for evidence his rather stern chapter on 'How children exploit cuteness'.

The chapter that reads most strangely today is the one entitled 'The law, the young, and sex'. One would not, I think, come across a passage like the following in any current book.

> Some people have voiced to me the fear that if it were legal for an adult to have sex with a consenting child, many young people would be exploited by unscrupulous older ones. The image here is of the innocent young girl and the dirty old man; few worry about the young boy having sex with an older woman. Here, too, we are caught with the remains of old myths—in this case, that only men were sexual, that women were pure and above it— from which it follows that any young girl having sex with an older man must necessarily be his victim.[21]

This is not a simplistic call for the 'sexual liberation' of children; if anything, it is an anguished examination of Holt's own internal conflicts on the idea. But such ideas were in the air in the 1970s. When I worked in Birmingham, which dates it as late as 1981 or 1982, pamphlets from the Paedophile Information Exchange could still be found among a tableful of literature from other municipally approved good causes in the Central Library.

There is some coverage of this period in Christian Wolmar's book on childcare scandals, *Forgotten Children*,[22] but he treats it largely as a plot by a few paedophiles to infiltrate more respectable movements. This approach tends to underestimate the extent to which a broader strand of educated opinion was prepared at least to entertain the idea of something like the sexual liberation of children. And if this fact does not fit the picture of professionals discovering child sexual abuse and then informing an incredulous public about it, what are we to make of the following?

In *The Best Kept Secret*, Florence Rush describes an international conference held at Swansea University in 1977, and sponsored by the University and the British Psychological Society. She quotes a report from the *Guardian*'s women page written by Polly Toynbee:

> When paedophiles at the Swansea conference advocated the legalisation of sex between children and adults and the reduction of the age of consent to four, the cooks, porters and caretakers of the University of Swansea threatened to strike.[23]

It seems that those cooks, porters and caretakers were in the vanguard of what we would today regard as enlightened thinking, not the professionals. And those paedophiles were also offering a *reductio ad absurdum* of Ariés' view. For, if there is no such thing as childhood, it follows that there can be no such thing as child abuse.

Why is this faulty view held?

If child abuse is not a new discovery, and if the professional world has not always taken an unhesitatingly condemnatory view of it, why do so many professionals believe that it is and that they have?

One answer lies in the way that the history of the professions is generally written. We have all been raised to recognise the foolishness of the Whig view of history—the idea, common in nineteenth-century writing, that the whole of English history was a logical and inevitable progress towards the perfect constitution that Englishmen then enjoyed.

The same idea was current at the start of the twentieth century. The poet Stephen Spender describes his own boyhood in a family at the heart of the Liberal establishment thus:

> Through the books we read at school, through the Liberal views of my family, it seemed that I had been born on to a fortunate promontory of time towards which all other times led.[24]

And he went on to say:

> History seemed to have been fulfilled and finished by the static respectability, idealism and material prosperity of the end of the nineteenth century. This highly satisfactory, if banal, conclusion was largely due to

the Liberal Party having found the correct answer to most of the problems which troubled our ancestors. [25]

Today we probably laugh at such a view, but something very similar often holds sway in the professions and social sciences. Here is David Philips writing about the way the history of crime and law is written in Britain:

> It was assumed that events moved towards their 'proper' modern end: the historians' task as simply to supply the narrative and explain why there were so many culpable delays and hesitations in the coming of this inevitable and desirable state of affairs.[26]

A trawl of shelves of long-unborrowed books on childcare in a university library reveals a similar pattern. Time and again, the founding of a particular experimental school or the passing of a particular piece of legislation is treated as the end to which all history has been working.

DeMause strikes us at first as a bold, radical figure, far away from such conventional Whig thinkers, yet he has much in common with them. Indeed, it is hard to see how one could go further in privileging the present over the past than his description of the 'history of childhood' as nightmare cited earlier.[27]

Further, deMause offers a 'periodisation' of modes of parent-child relations. It begins with the Infanticide Mode (antiquity to fourth century AD), and then runs through the Abandonment Mode (fourth to thirteenth centuries AD), the Ambivalent Mode (fourteenth to seventeenth centuries), the Intrusive Mode (eighteenth century), the Socialisation Mode (nineteenth to mid-twentieth centuries) to the Helping Mode, which began in the mid-twentieth century and is still presumably still going on today.

Given the unrelenting emphasis on abuse in deMause's work, we are not standing on sunlit uplands or on Spender's 'fortunate promontory of time', so much as standing on a low hillock above a foul swamp. But there is no doubt that, for deMause, the more recent, the better. It is not surprising that professionals find it hard to learn from the past when they are encouraged to take such a bleak view of it.

This Whig view of history reinforces a pronounced stress on novelty in the professions. I recall, again in my role as a sub-editor, coming across a review of a book on psychology and some aspect of public policy that complained that some of the references given were five years old. This struck me at the time as odd. One would not find such a complaint made about a book on the arts, nor even in a book about the physical sciences if the only grounds for it was that the material quoted was five years old. This emphasis on recency again makes it hard to learn from history.

A good example of this process at work comes from the blurb on the back cover of another book:

In 1986 the author, an ordinary Nottingham social worker and mother of two received a letter from a woman asking for help to trace her parents. She claimed that at the age of four she had been put on a boat to Australia by the British Government. Margaret Humphreys replied that she must be mistaken, yet curiosity drove her to investigate the case.[28]

And eventually she wrote *Empty Cradles*, an excellent and moving book which, when it first appeared in 1994, won such reviews, the same cover tells us, as 'The secrets of the lost children of Britain may never have been revealed if it had not been for Margaret Humphreys, from the *Sunday Times*. The *Independent* said it was 'a story that defies belief'.

Yet this was not new knowledge at all. For a little research, or even a moderately good memory, reveals that same story had been told in Philip Bean and Joy Melville's *Lost Children of the Empire*,[29] published in 1989, and Gillian Wagner's *Children of the Empire* from 1982.[30]

Not only that. Another search study of those long-unborrowed books will reveal that the sending of children to the Empire was not a secret at all. It was an aspect of public policy like any other, and was discussed in government reports; and it was a controversial policy. Horatio Bottomley, the publisher, politician and fraudster, who had himself grown up in the workhouse, campaigned against the policy and, aided by a succession of murders and suicides in Canada, kept the subject in the headlines both there and in Britain.[31]

If professionals do not have the time or the inclination to read history, the same might be said of their approach to literature. Take, for instance the question of the abuse of children in institutions. In 2003, Margaret Hodge's appointment as Minister for Children proved controversial because of her handling of allegations of abuse in children's homes in Islington when she led the council in 1992. Defending her, one of her colleagues said that we should not judge her too harshly because we *all* knew little about such abuse in those days.[32]

This did not seem a convincing argument when it was made, if only because there had been a high-profile abuse trial in Leicestershire in 1991.[33] Nor is discussion of the abuse of children in institutions a recent political phenomenon. One of the more attractive figures in the Edwardian Liberal government, Charles Masterman, was asked to investigate an alleged scandal on a training ship as long ago as 1909. Horatio Bottomley, the defender of the orphan children sent to Canada, regarded Masterman's report as a whitewash and as a result hounded him for the rest of his career.[34]

But then we have never had any trouble in believing in the existence of abuse in institutions for children when it comes to literature. It occurs, of course, in such acknowledged classics as *Oliver Twist* or *Jane Eyre*, but when we read of an orphanage in children's literature it is almost invariably a place of horror—a place to run away from. Not only do we have no difficulty in entertaining the idea of institutional abuse, we positively expect it. The rather alarming conclusion here seems to be that professionals find it *harder* to accept the reality of professional abuse than the rest of us. It may be that we should look to the exalted educational and social status of the professional as a partial explanation of this, and that their lack of contact with the general public on equal terms makes it hard to tap into the knowledge of abuse that has always existed in wider society.

Other histories

The history of childhood, like the history of much else, has developed and relies more upon chance and the actions of particular individuals than the theorists allow. Take, for instance, the genesis of the 1948 Children's Act. If you read the Barnardo's website, you are told:

> Evacuation brought 'charity children' and 'ordinary' middle- and upper-class families into contact with each other and they gained a greater understanding of their circumstances. The disruption of war also improved understanding of the impact of family break ups and effects on children brought up away from home.[35]

No doubt these factors did play a part, but the history of the Act is more complex than that and two often-neglected actors were involved in its inception.

On 15 July 1944 *The Times* published a letter from Marjory Allen—Lady Allen of Hurtwood—calling for an inquiry into the condition of children living in state and charity homes. She wrote that 'many thousands of these children are being brought up under repressive conditions that are generations out of date and are unworthy of our traditional care for children'.[36]

Marjory Allen worried that her timing was wrong—'Our armies were fighting their way through France; London was enduring bombardment by a new missile, the sinister low-flying buzz-bomb; and 30,000 children had been evacuated from London the previous day'[37]—yet her letter met with an extraordinary response.

Sir William Haley, in the 1958 Haldane Memorial Lecture on the development of public opinion, described it as follows:

> Day after day and week after week the letters poured in. Many came from leaders in social work and others who had also first-hand experience. Even after the normal correspondence had been closed, *The Times* had to publish no fewer than six round-ups of further letters.[38]

Not everyone agreed: the Secretary-Superintendent of the Southern Railway Servants' Orphanage wrote to say that large orphanages were just like public schools and asked why the orphan should be treated differently from the child of the rich man.[39]

It would be easy to present Allen as a heroine of common sense standing up against professional theorising and vested interests. Certainly, when you read the comments of the Secretary Superintendent, there was an element of that about her activism. In the pre-War period the children's charities saw themselves as the experts on institutional care and they insisted on running vast, barrack-like homes. Set against this background, it is hard not to have sympathy for the cottage home or family model of care that Allen promoted.

Yet the picture is more complex than that. Marjory Allen was not Lady Bountiful: when she wrote her letter she was chairman of the Nursery School Association and well connected in the professional world. In her memoirs she takes issue with those who read her letter as a simple plea for less professionalism. She complains that Nancy Astor 'seemed to think that training actually destroyed what she valued most: "love for children and a sense of vocation".'[40] And though she enjoys the comments of George Bernard Shaw,

> who contrasted the terrifying effects of the hygienic Kaiserin Augusta's House in Berlin, where all the children 'died like flies', with the beautiful results of slapdash methods in the west of Ireland where, he asserted, all the children survived happily, nurtured by 'maternal massage' ...[41]

she remarks that:

> I am all in favour of maternal massage, but I like the masseuses to have some training as well. Shaw, too, recommended a combination of both the systems he described.[42]

While Allen does mention a later meeting with John Bowlby, the name of Winnicott is missing from her memoirs. Yet Marjory Allen's actions in questioning the institutional childcare practices of her day, if not inspired by these two figures, were quite in line with their insights. Today there seems to be an expectation that lay and professional opinion will differ markedly on childcare, but to Allen there was no conflict between advanced professional thinking and what one might call her familial, maternal or common-sense approach.

Indeed, this approach held sway in institutional care for a good two decades after the War. Christian Wolmar comments that:

> As late as 1967, the service was very female dominated and the staff largely lived in the homes. The Williams Committee, reporting on the staffing of residential homes that year, noted 'two thirds of people at present employed in residential homes are single women and one third of all staff are over 50 years of age'. All but seven per cent of workers in the survey lived on the premises, which provided an important but hardly noticed safeguard for the children.[43]

Wolmar links the influx of male staff into the childcare system with the later scandals that arose in children's homes. It might be more accurate to see the problem as an influx of new theory as part of the cause too.

The breakdown of the family view

Though Ariés' claim that childhood is a recent invention cannot be sustained, it has to be acknowledged that he in many ways was a positive influence. Certainly, the talk of liberation in the air in the 1970s reflected an insight that traditional concepts of childhood could be cloying and should not be immune from examination. The idea that childhood was not a given but a human construct opened up all sorts of interesting questions about, for instance, the ways that schools have traditionally been organised.

There was an analogous movement in writing *for* children. Humphrey Carpenter's *Secret Gardens*[44] is chiefly a study of Edwardian children's literature but he includes an epilogue on books of the post-War era. He writes of one popular work:

> *The Borrowers* is largely an account of a child rejecting parental protection and asserting her independence. Childhood is equated not with a Golden Age of special perceptions and visions, but with a state of imprisonment. Mary Norton's book suggests that, however terrible the consequences may be … the child must break the parental bonds if it is to grow up.[45]

Equally, if the concept of childhood had a beginning then it can also have an end, and many books have been written along these lines. Most have been expressions of horror at modern trends in the media—whether the video nasties of the 1980s or, more quaintly to us today, imported American horror comics in the 1950s.[46]

Neil Postman's *The Disappearance of Childhood*,[47] with its subtitle *'How TV is changing children's lives'* and approving Malcolm Muggeridge quotation on the cover, sounds like one more of them. In fact, it is a more interesting work than that. Postman sees the invention of literacy as the key to the invention of childhood. A child, pre-eminently, was someone who could not read and write, and it was this difference, and the educational institutions that grew up around it, that formed the modern concept of the child. Now, Postman argues, as literacy is declining in importance in the face of the expansion of other media, our concept of childhood is bound to change with it.

Conclusion

It seems that the simple answer to the conflict of views I came across ten years ago is that the Clinic's view of child abuse as a recent discovery is wrong. The chastening truth is that child abuse has always been known about and talked about, that the willingness amongst the public and professionals to do something about it has waxed and waned through the years, and that it is by no means clear that the professionals have always been on the more admirable side of the argument.

This chapter aimed to clear away these misconceptions to allow a better history of our attitudes to child abuse to be written. Once this more subtle appreciation of the route by which the Clinic and Academy have arrived at their current understanding is in place, we shall be more aware of the curious twists and dead ends it has incorporated.

This awareness, in turn, may encourage a degree of scepticism amongst professionals. If they are less certain that they stand upon Spender's 'fortunate promontory of time towards which all other times led', they may be more inclined to adopt a critical stance towards both their own practice and government policy.

Endnotes

1. Anonymous (2005). Sexually abusive young people. Retrieved from http://freespace.virgin.net/jeffnmag.highlands/sexually.htm on 22 February 2005.

Though this article claims 'to offer guidance for social workers working with adolescents who sexually abuse other children and to be based on knowledge gained from training provided by various named eminent people, backed by extensive reading and casework practice', a search of the site does not yield the name of an author. Perhaps its anonymity makes this article more qualified to serve as a typical example.

2. It is worth noting that this article rules out one obvious solution to my puzzle. One cannot say that the psychologists I was reading were discussing sexual abuse while the Victorian novelists were writing about physical abuse, because it insists that physical abuse is also a recent discovery.

3. DeMause, L. (1976). The evolution of childhood. In L. deMause (ed) *The History of Childhood* (p. 1). London: Souvenir.

4. Pollock, L. (1983). *Forgotten Children: Parent-child relations from 1500 to 1900.* Cambridge: Cambridge University Press.

5. Ibid., p. 93.

6. Ibid., p. 93.

7. Ibid., p. 93.

8. Ibid., p. 93.

9. O'Neill, T. (1981). *A Place Called Hope: Caring for children in distress.* Oxford: Basil Blackwell.

10. Ibid., p. ix.

11. Anonymous.

12. Masson, J.M. (1985). *The Assault on Truth: Freud's suppression of the seduction theory.* Harmondsworth: Penguin.

13. Stove, R.J. (2003). Death in the Temple. *Quadrant Magazine, 47*, 6. Retrieved from www.quadrant.org.au/php/archive_details_list.php?article_id=382 on 22 February 2005.

14. Ariés, P. (1973). *Centuries of Childhood*. Harmondsworth: Penguin.

15. Pollock, p. 263 op.cit. (see above, n. 4).

16. Pollock, p. 268.

17. Pollock, p. 268.

18. Hoyles, M. (ed) (1979). *Changing Childhood*. London: Readers and Writers Publishing Cooperative.

19. Ibid., p. 83.

20. Holt, J. (1975). *Escape from Childhood: The needs and rights of childhood*. Harmondsworth: Penguin.

21. Ibid., p. 208.

22. Wolmar, C. (2000). *Forgotten Children: The secret abuse scandal in children's homes*. London: Vision.

23. Rush, F. (1980). *The Best Kept Secret: Sexual abuse of children*. Englewood Cliffs, NJ: Prentice-Hall (p. 188).

24. Spender, S. (1951). *World within World: The autobiography of Stephen Spender* (p. 1). London: Hamish Hamilton.

25. Ibid., pp.1–2.

26. Phillips, D. (1983). A just measure of crime, authority, hunters and blue locusts: The 'revisionist' social history of crime and the law in Britain 1780–1850. In S. Cohen and A. Scull (eds) *Social Control and the State* (p. 51). Oxford: Martin Robertson.

27. DeMause, op. cit. (see above, n. 3).

28. Humphreys, M. (1996). *Empty Cradles*. London: Corgi.

29. Bean, P. and Melville, J. (1989). *Lost Children of the Empire*. London: Unwin Hyman.

30. Wagner, G. (1982). *Children of the Empire*. London: Weidenfeld and Nicolson.

31. Middleton, N. (1971). *When Family Failed: The treatment of children in the care of the community during the first half of the twentieth century*. London: Gollancz.

32. Hall, S. (2003). The Guardian profile: Margaret Hodge. *The Guardian*, 21 November. Retrieved from http://politics.guardian.co.uk/labour/story/0,9061,1090151,00.html on 22 February 2005.

33. D'Arcy, M. and Gosling, P. (1998). *Abuse of Trust: Frank Beck and the Leicestershire children's homes scandal.* London: Bowerdean.

34. Masterman, L. (1968). *C.F.G. Masterman.* London: Frank Cass and Co.

35. Barnardo's (2004). *Who We Are: History 1945–60.* Retrieved from www.barnardos.org.uk/whoweare/history/history3.jsp on 22 February 2005.

36. Allen, M. (1944). Letter: Children in 'Homes'. *The Times*, 14 July. Cited in M. Allen and M. Nicholson (1975). *Memoirs of an Uneducated Lady: Lady Allen of Hurtwood.* (pp.178–9). London: Thames and Hudson.

37. Allen and Nicholson, p. 180.

38. Cited in Allen and Nicholson, p. 180.

39. Allen and Nicholson, p. 182.

40. Ibid., p. 181.

41. Ibid., p. 181.

42. Ibid., p. 181.

43. Wolmar, p. 121 op. cit. (see above, n. 22).

44. Carpenter, H. (1987). *Secret Gardens.* London: Unwin Hyman.

45. Ibid., p. 217.

46. Sringhall, J. (1994). Horror comics: The nasties of the 1950s. *History Today, 44,* 10–13.

47. Postman, N. (1985). *The Disappearance of Childhood: How TV is changing children's lives.* London: W.H. Allen.

CHAPTER 3

The Discourse of Responsibility

ELINA BAKER AND
CRAIG NEWNES

This chapter examines the assumptions underpinning the concept of responsibility (in particular, moral responsibility) and how power shapes and sustains the construct as an internal attribute. We ask how education and social care professionals construct or challenge the idea of taking responsibility as no more than a form of being seen to act in socially desirable ways.

Our own position is that responsibility, though a legal and linguistic construction, is frequently taken to be an internal characteristic or attribute of any given individual. We believe that those who wield power are likely to talk of the irresponsibility of *others*. Relational power thus becomes the key factor in any discourse of responsibility, whether that power be legal, physical or economic.

Some stories

A young woman is asked to meet the head teacher of her son's primary school because he has been consistently not attending. The boy, she is told, has Attention Deficit Hyperactivity Disorder and has no sense of responsibility. She is told that she may find herself facing criminal charges unless he attends school regularly. She must learn to act more responsibly as a parent. A 14-year-old spends a morning in the park instead of at school. She and her mother are visited by an education welfare officer who writes a report suggesting that the family has 'responsibility issues' that may lead to a care order. A young psychiatric patient, already a father of three, punches a nurse in the face because he thinks she is trying to poison him with medication. He is placed in seclusion and told that he must take responsibility for his behaviour. Discharged from a psychiatric unit, a young woman repeatedly contacts her key worker in a state of distress; she has a crisis over money, her boyfriend, her housing and her children. Her key worker tells her that she must start taking responsibility.

We have often heard the term of 'responsibility' used in such situations and have felt troubled by it. In this chapter we hope to further explore what it means when we ask someone to take responsibility and what the alternatives might be.

The nature of responsibility

We want to address the construction of responsibility by first examining two assumptions within which the concept of responsibility might nest: the idea that persons (and their various characteristics) are continuous and the related notion that people can be meaningfully described in terms of stable (and internal) attributes.

The second author has recently written about some of the consequences of a closed head injury and other injuries resulting from a car accident. The change in consciousness resulting from the accident raises questions about the confidence with which we assume that persons (and to a lesser extent, identities) are continuous from day to day, whatever the interruptions. He had previously considered himself both reasonably concerned about his family, his work and the world around him and similar in this concern to others. Subsequent to the accident, things appeared to change:

> The wider picture evaporates. Global warming? Neither here nor there. Weapons of mass destruction? Irrelevant. British politics? *Love Actually* is more interesting. Sport? Who cares (especially about motor racing)? In this new world, environment is everything. People close at hand must be kind ... trains as timetabled, traffic wholly safe and stimulation not too complex. Health professionals must be on time or fear and self-doubt mount. Noise must be controllable (hypersensitive hearing is quite something in conjunction with spinal injury: scraped chairs and certain pitches of voice send the body into spasm, legs and arms twitching like lightning conductors). ... And life, even getting out of bed, is exhausting ... A lifetime's assumptions about similarities between you and other people are shattered. The whole idea of consciousness, let alone shared consciousness, is challenged. One wonders how the world functions at all.[1]

Assumed continuity (of the self, personhood, memory, day-to-day life, and so on) is a given within much philosophical discourse.[2] Change too is, of course, fundamental to existence. Bereavement, loss or a major change in someone's circumstances through assault, domestic violence, educational assessment or admission to a psychiatric unit can, however, be perceived as not affecting this essential continuity. Even when direct physical harm is sustained by an individual, any damage is made sense of (by the individual and others) by reference to the ways in which the individual's continuous personal characteristics have been affected or interrupted. Damasio[3 4] sees these as an aspect of extended consciousness (his term) that he calls the autobiographical self. Many people working in human services do not easily admit to major personality change (selves are seen as, more or less, intact across time and place). We almost never consider the possibility that the changed person is so different as to make the notion of taking responsibility for previous action the equivalent of being responsible for someone *else*.

We wonder what our discipline, psychology, would look like in a world in which the self was not assumed to be continuous. Therapy would struggle to survive as people would not need to be psychologically accountable for the self they were seen to be yesterday, even though they could be positioned as morally and legally accountable. Sadness or fear would be met with assertions that there is no need to face saddening or fearful events or relationships from one day to the next; parenthood, marriage and friendship would have to face the lack of commitment inherent in the notion of the discontinuous self. We suspect there would be anarchy. Certainly, practices in the prison system and child and family psychiatric system would be hard pressed to maintain all but a legal and moralistic role if the idea of contingent behaviour was made irrelevant by the loss of any individual psychological accountability for that same behaviour across time.[5]

At least one novelist, Carol Shields, has no difficulty in challenging the assumption of continuous personhood. She opens *The Box Garden* thus,

> ... we change hourly or even from one minute to the next, our entire cycle
> of being altered, our whole selves shaken with the violence of change.[6]

Such a position is rare indeed in the numberless texts on family life, counselling, self-improvement and the more academically-inclined psychology end of the market. Systemic thinkers would have some advantage, though systems-thinking and those schools emphasising the newer narrative approaches are still in a minority.

Further, we would wish to criticise the view that responsibility is an individual attribute. Our position is essentially Strawsonian;[7] that you cannot separate something called responsibility from the various attitudes and responses from which we infer that someone is responsible (Strawson's 'reactive attitudes'). This position owes much to Ryle:[8] see, for example, his discussion of other mental predicates such as 'understanding' as public displays. Embodied emotions such as guilt, shame, pride, enthusiasm, indignation and so on are subject to change as contexts change. Even allowing that persons are continuous across time, these responses will surely change with circumstances; such as parental divorce, the death of a sibling, childbirth, domestic violence or assessment by a mental health professional leading to incarceration. To expect that young people's sense of responsibility and display of what would typically be described as responsible conduct remain undiminished or unaltered seems, to us, to expect too much. We might, in postmodernist vein, challenge the idea that what are described as internal characteristics are immutable, be they courage, intelligence or responsibility. We could even, somewhat mischievously, suggest that power hierarchies are sustained, not because people at the top have superior *internal* attributes but because our rulers *define* the characteristics to be praised and promote the notion that internality is crucial (rather than luck, environment or money, i.e. context).

Further, social workers, individually focused psychologists and psychiatric staff might be seen as, implicitly, taking a position that emotions do not affect will, and thus, responsibility. For the psychiatric system, one can be responsible or otherwise, however one feels.[9] Emotional reaction to, for example, being sectioned under the Mental Health Act, is not, in everyday practice, seen as relevant to responsibility and moral culpability. People who are devastated after being sectioned under the Act are thus still urged to 'take responsibility' even though their legal accountability for their actions has been suspended. Further, children and adolescents are urged to be more responsible despite the remarkable complexity of the strictly legal interpretation of the expression (a child can be found guilty of murder aged 10, but cannot drive until 17).

Analytically inclined thinkers might go further. Riker,[10] for example, suggests that people should be held accountable for all that they do on the basis that their actions might be unconsciously motivated—and as it is their own unconscious, Jungian ideas on the universal unconscious notwithstanding, they can be held responsible. Riker's position might be seen as extreme. Nonetheless it informs a view that positions responsibility as entirely an individual matter.

If the social service and education professionals involved in the examples given above were to be asked what they had meant by taking responsibility they are likely to have talked about accepting the consequences of actions, feeling sorry and trying to find more constructive ways of solving problems. They tacitly assume that the person is still *capable* of these things despite their changed circumstances. Such capabilities are seen (conveniently) to be continuous and internal. Such a discourse is shared by service recipients who might be motivated to comply with professional demands, perhaps partly to make amends for their conduct.

Even within the definition typically used by social care and educational professionals, it is entirely possible that someone could engage in antisocial and similar behaviours and yet still be described as acting responsibly. When someone self harms, for example, it seems likely that they have found a behaviour that provides a singularly powerful solution to the problem of expressing or coping with overwhelming feelings.[11] They may also, at least at the time, be prepared to accept the consequences, such as loss of blood, permanent scarring and even alienation from others. It is only when they come into contact with a system that attempts to control their behaviour that its consequences create such concern in others and becomes unacceptable. The psychiatric response, through removing power and control, then creates 'the very circumstances that are likely to have led to the need to self injure'.[12]

A teenager who avoids school for fear that her parents might separate if she is not around can be seen (in functional terms) as having made a decision based on a higher order need: if her behaviour has the desired effect at home, a few detentions given by the school authorities are a price worth paying. There may also be times when violence represents a solution whose consequences are acceptable both to the individual and also to a wider society, in particular in resistance to oppression. For a soldier being tortured in a prisoner of war camp or for a member of an oppressed minority, the consequences of violent resistance may be aversive but they may accept them, given the already aversive conditions of their life. Their resistance may also be approved or even applauded by the rest of their society or culture of origin. For many living in degrading or other oppressive circumstances the experience is one of despair: disrespect for what appear to be irrelevant social strictures or at least a reordering of priorities will be the result.[13] It is not too difficult a leap of logic to wonder if a young parent, as in our third example, surrounded by images of war and finding themselves in an oppressive environment (however benignly intended) might see some kind of aggressive action as a responsible way of dealing with troublesome emotions. So he lashes out at the most immediate symbol of that oppression: the psychiatric nurse.

Diagnosis, disorder and the discourse of responsibility

One might infer, then, that in order to be judged to have taken responsibility, what people must do is simply what the system wants. Although they may not be responsible for their behaviour, they can take responsibility for it by engaging with the system, through taking medication or participating in therapy or, after swallowing hard, to just go to school. The subtext of the phrase taking responsibility is thus 'do what I as the more powerful person expect of you'. The apparent desire to get someone to take responsibility (or to do what they are told) can thus be more about conformity or punishment than helping them to lead a more fulfilling life. The second author, for example, has six children. Does this make him responsible or irresponsible? Some would say that if he can afford it, good luck to him. Others would say that his family is burdening the state's resources and will have a wider impact on global well-being through its increased consumption of natural resources so he should have acted more responsibly. In his mid-twenties he ran away from his Lincolnshire home, friends and professional job because he couldn't bear to watch his ex-partner make a new life for herself with someone else. Does this make him a responsible person who shows bouts of irresponsibility or a fundamentally irresponsible person? If the latter, what are we to make of the fact he is director of a National Health Service psychological therapies service employing 85 people? One solution to this conundrum, within psychological discourse, is to separate the act from the actor, a position we find less common in individualistic mental health services.

In our first example, a young woman potentially faces a prison sentence if her young son continues to refuse to go to school. The child is warned of this possible outcome of his conduct in terms of showing more responsibility. No doubt he recognises this exhortation as a version of something all too familiar—when angry, his mum's partner invariably yells, 'Why don't you grow up?' Both the school and the adult at home are saying, 'Do what you are told.'

In our second example the family's difficulties are constructed as 'responsibility issues'. They are positioned as (essentially internal) problems to be solved. This allows the social worker to help the family with financial and other needs and at the same time ignore the glaringly obvious fact that three such families live within a hundred yards of each other on the same socially deprived housing estate—an estate the social worker has chosen not to live in, if at all possible.

In our third opening example, the young man expected to take responsibility is detained under the Mental Health Act. In other examples some part of the Act may well still apply, such as a guardianship order. This seems to imply that as a result of their mental disorder, people are unable to control their behaviour, and cannot thus be responsible for it. Indeed, had the man killed someone because of his belief that they were poisoning him he would be found not guilty of murder on the grounds of diminished responsibility. Under these circumstances a service user might well ask 'How can I take responsibility when you won't give me any?' This is an example of what has been called the 'paradox of responsibility': being told to change and, simultaneously, that you cannot do so.[14]

In the last opening example a woman is told to 'take responsibility' for her problems rather than contacting her community mental health nurse to ask for help every time something goes wrong. Contacting a key worker at times of crisis can of course be seen as taking responsibility, by turning to the people who (apparently) are employed to help. There seems to be an attitude in a number of Community Mental Health Team (CMHT) workers that their job is to 'make themselves redundant' by promoting self-sufficiency, rather than just being supportive: at all costs, workers must never promote dependency. It seems to us contradictory to dissuade people from asking for help at times of crisis and to encourage them to solve their own problems. In describing what they found helpful about involvement from professionals, psychiatric service survivors have identified the importance of continuity and developing a strong relationship (often with fellow patients) as well as ongoing accessibility and availability.[15] Especially for service users with informal support networks that are themselves sources of stress, turning to professionals for help seems an appropriate and constructive problem-solving strategy, rather than a way of 'avoiding responsibility'.

Smail[14] further suggests that a positive correlation exists between position in the power hierarchy, sense of personal virtue and a belief that the less powerful need to be more responsible. For children this might translate into: 'Teachers, social workers, family workers know best; so do what you're told.'

The expansion of psychiatric practice and language into everyday life and discourse accelerated during the last century. Early examples of the *Diagnostic and Statistical Manual of the American Psychiatric Association* included far fewer categorisations of conduct than the latest *DSM-IVR*. In recent legislature put before the US Senate there are proposals for the mental health assessment of *all* US citizens, with a special focus on young people. It is unlikely that the numbers of diagnosed individuals will fall after such screening.

The numbers of children diagnosed with Attention Deficit Hyperactivity Disorder (ADHD) have increased from less than 10,000 in the UK before 1990 to over 200,000 today. Social commentators may use such an increase to justify claims that society, schooling and modern life in general is bad for children. Our position would be that the change in discourse is simply that—a change in the dominant language used to describe conduct. To Rowe,[16] the behaviour looks the same as it ever did, the feelings and reasons for it easily discerned but medical hegemony and the language of the dominant medical discourse ensures that children are labelled and drugged.

This kind of labelling has implications for the discourse of responsibility. A parent told she must spend more time with her wayward children might be simultaneously labelled depressed (within the medical discourse) and irresponsible (from a moralistic position). Similarly a child distracted during lessons or challenging to the school order in other ways may be initially thought of as irresponsible or naughty but later labelled ADHD. Such labelling and accompanying practices appear to shift the locus of the difficulty from the wider context to the person, but in such a way that the person somehow 'can't help it' due to a psychological disease state over which they have little control. This *should* return our gaze to the environment—the way to stop tigers endlessly pacing zoo cages is to allow them much more room to roam—but what happens is a further concentration on the individual, specifically the individual's biochemistry. The gift of blame removal through diagnosis is rapidly balanced by an insistence that the consequences of that blame removal (the exchange of 'bad' for 'mad') involve a possible lifetime at the hands of mental health professionals and their medicines.

Ironically the irresponsible mother is seen as sufficiently responsible to remember her prescribed medication (she doesn't, not least because she knows it is not the answer to her problems). The child may not be so fortunate and will receive the medication from a school nurse or mixed into the school dinners. Thus, we arrive at a position whereby some notion of responsibility (or lack of it) is embedded in the diagnostic system and maintained in the treatment methods but could be summarised exclusively by a dictum that people (children or adults) should do what the wider system wants.

Additional financial benefits, via various social care and disability funds, may accrue to a family once a diagnosis is given. We can only conjecture that this may be insufficient reward for living life as part of a drug company's profit margin.

Responsibility, social control and power

A psychologist working with older children might set taking responsibility for their own distress and its expression as a therapeutic goal. In achieving this they would also achieve the internalisation of the normalising gaze which seeks to identify and correct deviance, as a form of social control.[17] When a school publicly rewards particular kinds of conduct which will make classrooms more manageable or a therapist teaches a client self-control, both practices can be seen as promoting a highly efficient form of social control: conformity that is imposed upon the individual by themselves.[18]

It has been argued that concepts like responsibility (used to describe the internal psychological operations of individuals) function to divert attention from the way in which distress is caused by the operation of power in the social environment.[19] It is thus impossible for someone to take responsibility for thoroughly addressing their distress, as its origins are beyond the limit of their power. At best we play the cards dealt, in the full knowledge that the dealer is a hustler and the game changes automatically to roulette if it looks as though we may win.

The proximal powers surrounding children are such that they must strive hard to be noticed, let alone be seen as important in any given school or family. Despite this, even quite young children can be frequently urged to 'be more responsible', criticised for not 'taking responsibility' and so on. It has been suggested that what is needed in mental health services is a 'rights-based' approach, involving policy changes to provide the support, public attitudes and access to allow people to live the lives they choose. The challenge such a position presents psychiatric, social service and family services is considerable.

In the opening examples there is a tacit assumption that the professional procedures do not affect the ability to learn (or practice taking responsibility as defined by the educational and social care systems). Thus, being observed by educational psychologists in classrooms, diagnosed as mad or otherwise labelled, or being visited by strangers from social services are experiences not seen as changing the person, or at least only as having socially desirable consequences. The extraordinary lack of power experienced by targeted individuals is likely to mean that the social care and educational systems will impact on them in both intended and unintended ways. How does one protest about terrible classrooms and teachers, psychometric testing, ward rounds or hospital food? These circumstances can add fear to an already constant sense of confusion. Gazing out of the window, talking and distracting others, self harm and staying off school may well seem the only means of protest—and entirely responsible means—if the forces countering opposition seem overwhelming. If the consequences of actions are some reduction in privileges or an insistence on attending therapy sessions with the family, these are likely to feel insignificant if compared to the already experienced loss of freedom, autonomy and simple, plain fun.

It seems that what people need to take is not responsibility, but power. A limited number of ways have been identified in which professionals can promote this empowerment. These seem relatively weak when set against the forces of the established order: they include working with individuals, communities and schools, enabling user-led research and taking political action.[20][21] A professional working with the young people described at the beginning of this paper could at least help them to become aware of the distal influences on their experiences and provide 'compassionate acceptance of who they are.'[22] Notably, some professional services do just this. They can refer them to a peer group, where they could experience support from and solidarity with others with similar experiences or they could encourage them to go on the Internet,[23] talk with children and families in a similar position and otherwise engage in conversation with potential allies. Equally they could write to the local paper to try and raise awareness of the issues involved. Trying to alert politicians to the plight of many families with a diagnosed child *may* be a way in which the more powerful can take responsibility for the lives of the less powerful.[24]

If those positioned as powerful have some control in the system (for example, as psychologists working in schools), then recognition of Strawson's point is vital: if we expect young people to take responsibility we must make the experience of their environments as conducive to familiar 'reactive attitudes' as possible. Children used to caring for other members of the family need to have their continuing role of carer respected even when acting in ways teachers find challenging. (Teachers, in turn, need stronger support, less emphasis on targets and smaller class sizes.) Adults used to being treated *as* adults must receive the same respect when assessed by social workers or in their new surroundings when admitted to hospital. Condescension, criticism and worse will not provoke responses construed as 'responsible'. Simply telling people to be more responsible won't help at all.

Endnotes

1. Newnes, C. (2004). Diary. *Journal of Critical Psychology, Counselling and Psychotherapy,* 4, 2, 112–13.

2. Murdoch, I. (1992). *Metaphysics as a Guide to Morals.* Harmondsworth: Penguin.

3. Damasio, A. (2000). *The Feeling of What Happens.* London: Vintage.

4. Damasio, A. (2004). *Looking for Spinoza.* London: Vintage.

5. For a further discussion of ways of re-conceptualising the practice of psychology, see Hansen, S., McHoul, A. and Rapley, M. (2003). *Beyond Help—A consumer guide to psychology* (pp. 227–46). Ross-on-Wye: PCCS Books.

6. Shields, C. (1977). *The Box Garden* (p.1). London: Fourth Estate.

7. Watson, G. (1987). Responsibility and the limits of evil. In F. Schoeman (ed) *Responsibility, Character and the Emotions*. Cambridge: Cambridge University Press.

8. Ryle, G. (1949). *The Concept of Mind*. London: Hutchinson.

9. Arguments for and against this position can be found in Sabini, J. and Silver, M. (1987). Emotions, responsibility and character. In F. Schoeman (ed) *Responsibility, Character and the Emotions*. Cambridge: Cambridge University Press. Such arguments take up much of Oakley, J. (1992). *Morality and the Emotions*. London: Routledge.

10. Riker, J.H. (1997). *Ethics and the Discovery of the Unconscious*. New York: SUNY.

11. Babiker, G. and Arnold, L. (1997). *The Language of Injury: Comprehending self mutilation*. Leicester: BPS Books.

12. Johnstone, L. (1997). Self injury and the psychiatric response. *Feminisim and Psychology*, 7, 421–6: p. 425.

13. In the psychiatric system, it has been suggested that violent resistance is the understandable response to oppressive practice. See, Coleman, R. (1999). Hearing voices and political oppression. In C. Newnes, G. Holmes and C. Dunn, (eds) *This is Madness: A critical look at psychiatry and the future of mental health services* (pp. 149–63). Ross-on-Wye: PCCS Books.

14. Smail, D. (2003). *Power, Responsibility and Freedom*. Retrieved March 25, 2004 from the World Wide Web: http://www.davidsmail.freeuk.com/pubfra p.48.

15. Faulkner, A. and Layzell, S. (2000). *Strategies for Living: The research report*. London: Mental Health Foundation.

16. Rowe, D. ADHD—Adults' Fear of Frightened Children. Chapter 7, this volume.

17. Foucault, M. (1977). *Discipline and Punish: The birth of the prison*. London: Penguin.

18. See also: Rose, N. (1999). *Governing the Soul*. London: Routledge.

19. Smail, D. (1993). *The Origins of Unhappiness*. London: Robinson.

20. Harris, C. The Well-being Project. Chapter 13, this volume.

21. See also: Smail, D. (2003). Endnote 14.

22. Ibid., p. 58

23. The Internet suggests innumerable opportunities for sharing information with the general public, simultaneously improving informed consent for prospective service users. See, for example, www.shropsych.org and Radcliffe, N. and Newnes, C. (In press) Welcome to the future of liberal family therapy working. *M/C A Journal of Media and Culture*. A version of this paper is also available in a non-cyber publication: *Clinical Psychology, 47,* 33–35.

24. A cynic might suggest that the links between government and big business are already too strong: politicians, driven by self-interest, are all too well aware, what is being done to citizens for the sake of profit.

CHAPTER 4

ADHD and the
Philosophy of Science

FREDDY JACKSON BROWN

> What we see is not reality in itself, but reality exposed to our method of questioning.
>
> Werner Heisenberg, 1901

As the prevalence of the Attention Deficit Hyperactivity Disorder (ADHD) diagnosis continues to rise in the Western world, there is a growing discussion about what it actually is. For some researchers ADHD is a behavioural disorder that is caused by some kind of as yet undiscovered neuropathology or dysfunction.[1] For others it is a label of social control that allows powerful and addictive psychotropic drugs to be administered to children in order to manage aspects of their behaviour.[2] Whether ADHD is a valid medical diagnosis or instead a label for social control is a keenly joined debate with little sign of resolution. However, the controversy that surrounds ADHD is more than just an ontological dispute, it stems in part from often unexamined philosophical assumptions about medical diagnoses and about science in general. This chapter will look at some of the philosophical commitments that underpin views about science and in turn how we think about ADHD.

Scientific narratives and ADHD

What is ADHD? First and foremost, of course, ADHD is a diagnostic label and as such it has acquired a certain scientific status and legitimacy. But unlike a traditional medical diagnosis, it does not refer to a set of biological symptoms that are the product of a distinct pathological process. Rather, a diagnosis of

ADHD is simply the label for a particular cluster of behaviours (as in fact are the majority of psychiatric diagnoses). That is quite straightforward, except that there are lots of different behavioural clusters that don't attract diagnostic labels. Stamp collectors, politicians and hairdressers all exhibit distinctive behavioural repertoires, but you are unlikely to hear them talked about in terms of a 'diagnosis'. Neither will you hear causal explanations in terms of underlying neurology, healthy or otherwise.

Why do some behavioural clusters attract diagnostic labels while others do not? Closer examination reveals that it is only problematic behaviours that are talked about in diagnostic terms. Positive behavioural clusters are more typically called hobbies or jobs. Of course, not all negatively perceived repertoires are given diagnostic labels; some are termed criminal or antisocial. But leaving aside the wider issue of how we label different behaviours, one reason some negative behaviours are labeled with diagnostic terms is that currently Western society patrols many of its social boundaries with the sanction of medical/mental illness.[3] From the nineteenth century onwards, society has increasingly sought to control unwanted behaviours by medicalising them.[4] The rationale behind this is that just as bodily disorders are caused by underlying biological diseases, so likewise behavioural disorders are the product of a diseased or dysfunctional mind/brain.

Like other diagnoses, ADHD has come to be seen as some kind of biological disorder that disrupts our behavioural functioning, even though there is no clear evidence for this. Conventionally, medical diagnoses refer to particular biological diseases that underlie bodily ill health. ADHD is conceptualised in the same way even though its 'symptoms' are behaviours and not bodily signs. As a formal diagnosis, it has acquired a standing in our society that is afforded to all medical terminology. The status of an ADHD diagnosis is further bolstered by its scientific basis of modern medicine. Medicine is a science and traditionally science is said to provide us with objective facts about the world. After all, science gives us 'in its theories a literally true story of what the world is like'.[5] As an accepted medical and thereby scientific term, ADHD is frequently seen as a real entity that causes a child's disorganised behaviour. But while science is often thought to give us a 'literally true' picture of the world, is this actually what science does?

To understand what science is, how it functions and what it achieves, we have to examine its philosophical foundations. Unfortunately, and in spite of its importance, philosophy has often had a bad press. Henry Brook Adams, for instance, once quipped that it gives us nothing more than 'unintelligible answers to insoluble problems'. But in truth it offers more than that. It functions to describe and then in turn shape the different ways by which we view the world and make sense of our experiences. In that sense it is fundamental to any explanatory discourse.

Today, science is dominated by two distinct and competing narratives—discovery and invention.[6] A narrative is a story or model by which we make sense of the world. The discovery narrative holds that science is the process by which we discover (literally 'un-cover') real things about the real world. It is underpinned by the assumption that it is possible to produce absolute and objective 'truths' about how the world actually is. Although this narrative dominates the lay view of science, it is often not held by scientists themselves. Albert Einstein, for example, argued that theories arise by means of invention (*durch Erfindung*), rather than by discovery (*nicht durch Entdeckung*). And his great contemporary, Niels Bohr wrote, 'There is no quantum world. There is only abstract quantum description.'[7] Clearly for many scientists, science is not simply about discovery.

In contrast, the invention narrative views science as a process (one of many) by which we produce useful ways of talking about our experiences. There is no assumption of a singular reality that can be objectively known. Instead science is seen as simply a way of organising our experiences in ways that solve certain problems. The criterion by which we judge a theory to be true or accurate is not its presumed objectivity or its correspondence with 'reality', rather it is the extent to which it allows successful working.[8] From this perspective science is about practical utility, not ontology. That is, a theory is said to be 'true' if it works. Simple, except that what works depends on what you are trying to do. This means that two opposing theories can both be true if they are successful by their own criteria. For instance, both Ptolemaic and Copernican views of our solar system can be 'true' as they set out to achieve different things. In simple terms, the former produces an account that is consistent with Holy Scripture and thereby maintains religious hegemony and the latter accounts for planetary movements more accurately. While a Ptolemaic view would have been no good for getting satellites into space, this was not something its advocates wanted to do and so it is irrelevant to judge it by this criterion.

But surely scientific experiments 'discover' new things about the world. While it is certainly the case that experiments produce new data, the invention narrative holds that what sense we make of them depends on what we are trying to achieve. This does not mean that science invents data. To do so would be fraudulent and would lead nowhere.

Rather, while new observations can be made via experimentation, the theories by which we organise these data depend on the problems we are trying to solve. And when the problems change, then so do our theories by which we understand the world and the so-called 'reality' in which we live.

Unfortunately science is littered with examples of individuals who have put their personal ambitions above the goals of science and invented data. The most infamous example of this in relation to psychology was the discovery that Sir Cyril Burt had fabricated or at least 'adjusted' data on his research with identical twins.[9] There was also his mysterious research assistant Miss Conway whose existence was never verified. In the end, of course, fraudulent acts are nearly always found out and their perpetrators ridiculed and then forgotten.

The invention narrative arises from the tradition of philosophical pragmatism as outlined by the likes of William James, Charles Pierce, John Dewey and more recently Richard Rorty.[10] For some,[11] pragmatism is deeply unpalatable. This may in part be because its perceived 'relativism' suggests that anything can be true if you set the right criteria. While it is possible that there could be as many different 'true' theories about the world as there are humans on the planet, in practice people tend to find common cause and agree on particular goals and the criteria by which to measure success. It follows then that in order to evaluate a theory we need to understand what it is trying to achieve and for this we need an analysis of the values, hopes and ambitions of its advocates. Again some are uncomfortable with the notion that science is a values-based process, although this has long been appreciated by philosophers.[12][13]

In psychology today, one of the foremost proponents of pragmatism, and the invention narrative of science in particular, is the field of behaviour analysis. This is the branch of behaviourism influenced by the work of B. F. Skinner. It is a curious irony that even though throughout his career Skinner argued consistently for pragmatic principles and the view that science was a process of invention,[14] his work was often misunderstood to represent the opposite. However, from a behaviour analytic perspective, science does not discover 'reality', rather it is simply a process (one of many) by which we find useful ways to talk about the world.[15][16] For a behaviour analyst, the traditional distinctions between objectivity and subjectivity are irrelevant. Every observation, every data point and indeed every theory is subjective in the sense of being personal and the idea that an observation can be truly objective is rejected. As Skinner noted, no one can 'step out of the causal stream and observe behavior from some special vantage point, "perched on the epicycle of Mercury"'.[17] But if everything is ultimately subjective, then what do we mean when we use the term objectivity? Objectivity is 'not as a property of the external world, but as a description of the effectiveness of scientific activity'.[18] That is, we call something objective when it is effective and not because it matches with a presumed underlying 'reality'.[19]

The medical sciences in general and psychiatric diagnoses like ADHD in particular, are typically underpinned by the discovery narrative. Our knowledge and understanding of psychopathology is likewise said to grow as we isolate ('discover') new diagnostic categories. Within this framework ADHD is seen as a real clinical entity that somehow affects (even infects) children's lives. Although the neurological pathology presumed to underlie it has yet to be identified, in an echo of the general disease model, it is common to hear that children 'have' ADHD, just as they might 'have' chicken pox or the flu. Of course, it is nonsense to say that ADHD causes the problematic behaviour from which it is inferred, but unfortunately the reification of diagnostic labels into causal entities is an all too common linguistic practice.[20] It seems that psychiatric nosology (i.e. terms such as depression and schizophrenia) is particularly prone to this error.[21][22]

From within the invention narrative, ADHD is seen as simply a useful way of talking about a set of problematic childhood behaviours that commonly go together. However, for a term to have validity it has to be of practical use and whatever may be thought of ADHD, it certainly has its uses. What are they? In my experience of working in the field it regularly serves the following functions:

1. as a (pseudo) medical explanation so the child's behaviour is not seen as 'naughty or 'willful';
2. to place the 'cause' within the individual rather than their context and thereby to remove responsibility (blame?) from the parents or care systems;
3. to select the appropriate drug/treatment regimes to reduce problem behaviours;
4. to control the access to resources; and
5. to maintain professional status and authority via expert/technical language.

While there remain many questions about the value of an ADHD diagnosis, it could be argued that at least the first four functions above bring some benefits for the child. The question remains, however, whether there is another way forward that delivers a better outcome. For instance, there may be times when it is more therapeutic to refer to contextual 'causes' (i.e. functional relations) for the behaviour than to see it as the product of an internal pathology. Similarly, although damping down ADHD behaviours with psychotropic drugs might help with short-term management, it may not be in the child's long-term best interests. One of the difficulties we face when raising questions such as these relates to the challenge of getting valid data upon which these issues can be resolved. Without data, all we are left with is rhetoric and in our 'evidence-based' world this is rarely enough.

The inclination for internal explanations of behaviour

It is common to hear a person's behaviour explained by a diagnosis without any recognition of where the diagnosis came from; that is, because a behavioural diagnosis is inferred from the presence of a distinctive set of behaviours it cannot also explain them. This type of pseudo-explanation is pervasive even in professional circles. For instance, the question 'Why does a person feel hopeless about the future and stay in bed all day?' is often followed by 'Because they're depressed'. How do you know they are depressed? Because you know they feel hopeless about the future and stay in bed all day. Likewise with ADHD. Why does a child 'fail to give attention to details and make careless errors?' (This is the first criterion of inattention taken from the *ICD-10* ((International Classification of Diseases)) definition of ADHD.) Because they've got ADHD. But how do you know they have ADHD? Because they 'fail to give attention to details and make careless errors'. This is a basic logical error and should have no place in a discussion about the origin of any human behaviour.

The medical model explains observable bodily symptoms by identifying the internal disease processes, disorders or pathologies that cause them. The model works because there is a close relationship between individual diseases and their consequences in the body. The advent of microscopes and related technologies has allowed medical researchers to isolate the bacteria, viruses or other disease processes that lead to particular bodily symptoms and in turn to develop effective treatments. The presence of a particular pattern of bodily symptoms therefore enables a diagnosis to be made and this tells us what the underlying disease is (or might be) and subsequently what treatments will be effective. This model has been tremendously successful in treating disease processes in the human body. However, such an approach is unlikely to work for behavioural diagnoses because there is not a similarly close relationship between behaviours and either biological or contextual events; that is, behaviours just don't map one-to-one with either internal or external events. The functional relationship between behaviour and its historical and current context is much more complex and hence the use of diagnostic labels for understanding behaviour is simply inappropriate.

It is interesting that ADHD behaviour is often assumed to be the result of some kind of underlying neurological disorder or pathology.[23] The tendency to look inside something in order to understand it is deep-seated within Western thinking[24] and may partly account for why many researchers make no or little mention of the context in which ADHD behaviour occurs—a surprising omission bearing in mind that behaviour is largely a context-dependent phenomenon. That human behaviour has a neurological correlate is undoubted, but whether we can usefully reduce human activity to this level is another matter. Indeed it is likely that complexities of organisation will make such reductionism impossible,[25] though in our current medical era, this probably won't stop people trying.

Research undertaken by attribution theorists may shed some further light on why diagnoses continue to be seen as explanatory concepts. Attribution theory has extensively researched how people explain observable behaviour.[26][27] Broadly speaking it has been found that people either explain behaviour in terms of internal/ personal factors (e.g. traits, attitudes, intelligence, etc.) or external/situational factors. Interestingly, people typically have a strong bias to explaining other people's behaviour in terms of assumed internal factors and yet their own behaviour in terms of external or situational factors. Kelly called this bias the 'fundamental attribution error' as once a behaviour has been explained by either internal or external factors, other explanations tend to be discounted even when there is strong evidence for them.

One important implication of attribution theory is that internal attributions 'tend to become a license or justification for treating people differently based on their inner entities that are taken to cause their behavior'.[28] This tendency can account in part for why behavioural diagnoses (i.e. those based on behaviours, not biological symptoms) are seen as explanations for the behaviour from which they are inferred. That is, due to the strong attributional bias to explain other people's behaviour in terms of internal factors, diagnostic labels have come to be seen as explanations of the behaviour. But as above, to turn a descriptive label derived from the presence of a particular set of behaviours into an explanation of those same behaviours is simply tautological nonsense. ADHD, therefore, should not be seen as the cause of a child's problematic behaviour, rather just a descriptive summary label.

Finally, it is worth considering whether ADHD behaviour really is a 'disorder' at all. Perhaps from the outside it may appear so, but what about for the child? It may be simply how they have learned to interact with the world. In fact there is a growing data-set which indicates that far from being a context-independent neurological disorder, ADHD behaviour can be seen as a child's attempt to adapt to their environment. For instance, it is now well established that in some situations children diagnosed with ADHD can behave as effectively as non-diagnosed children.[29][30] Therefore whether a child's behaviour is consistent with a diagnosis of ADHD depends on the situation in which they are observed. Some researchers[31] have theorised that ADHD behaviour emerges as genetically predisposed children develop an impulsive or ADHD behavioural repertoire in response to their early learning environments. If this is the case, what these children need is new learning experiences to adjust their repertoires to be more generally effective, not drugs to dull down or reduce the problem behaviours. Indeed this is just what many psychology therapies try to do[32] and research data show that in some cases this can be more effective than drug treatments.[33]

Summary

In spite of its rapidly increasing prevalence, ADHD remains a disputed term. For some it refers to a neurological disorder, while for others it is a label for social control. But to understand ADHD, we need in part to go beyond ontological arguments about its validity and look at the philosophical commitments that underpin more general views about medical science. Science is informed by two competing narratives—discovery and invention. According to the discovery narrative, ADHD is the label for a real (probably biological) entity that affects some children. As such it is often erroneously used as an explanation for the behaviour from which it was inferred. One of the limitations of the discovery narrative is that once a theory or term has been accepted, it can then be taken to represent how the world really is (or at least a close approximation of it). This can hinder the consideration of different ideas, as they can either challenge 'reality' too much or seem irrelevant.

Seen from the invention narrative perspective, ADHD is just one way of talking about a particular set of problematic childhood behaviours. While currently this diagnosis serves a number of functions, we should be aware that there are other ways of talking about the behaviours to which it refers. Indeed, unless you believe we are at the pinnacle of our scientific understanding, it is almost certainly the case that we can come up with better ways of construing ADHD. Of course, the question remains, what do we mean by 'better'? From a pragmatic perspective the answer to this will vary depending on what people agree needs to be done. So it is down to us. If we are happy to continue to use drugs to contain the behaviours associated with ADHD and to continue to look for presumed underlying neurological pathologies, then ADHD will be with us for some time yet. If we have an alternative vision for children diagnosed with ADHD, then we need to work towards it. The choice is ours.

Endnotes

1. Durston, S. (2003). A review of the biological basis of ADHD. *Mental Retardation and Developmental Disabilities Research Reviews, 9*, 184–95.

2. Baldwin, S. and Anderson, R. (2000). The cult of Methylphenidate: Clinical update. *Critical Public Health, 10*, 81–6.

3. Foucault, M. (1965). *Madness and Civilization.* New York: Random House.

4. Scull, A. (1984). *Decarceration.* Cambridge: Polity Press.

5. Van Frassen, B.C. (1980). *The Scientific Image.* Oxford: Clarendon Press.

6. Follette, W.C., Houts, A.C. and Hayes, S.C. (1992). Behavior Therapy and the New Medical Model. *Behavioral Assessment, 14*, 323–43.

7. Herbert, N. (1985). *Quantum Reality: Beyond the new physics.* New York: Anchor Press.

8. Roche, B. and Barnes-Holmes, D. (2003). Behavior analysis and social constructionism: Some points of contact and departure. *The Behavior Analyst, 26*, 215–31.

9. Hearnshaw, L.S. (1979). *Cyril Burt, Psychologist,* (p. 73). London: Hodder and Stoughton.

10. For an excellent history of the origins of pragmatism, see Menand, L. (2002). *The Metaphysical Club: A story of ideas in America.* London: Flamingo.

11. For example, Fodor, J. (2003). Is it a bird? Problems with old and new approaches to the theory of concepts. *Times Literary Supplement*, January 17th, 3–4.

12. Chalmers, A.F. (1983). *What is This Thing Called Science?* Milton Keynes: Open University Press.

13. Kuhn, T.S. (1962). *The Structure of Scientific Revolutions.* Chicago: University of Chicago Press.

14. Skinner, p. 253, op. cit. (see above n. 14).

15. Barnes-Holmes, D. (2000). Behavioral Pragmatism: No place for reality and truth. *The Behavior Analyst, 23*, 191–202.

16. Leigland, S. (2003). Is a new version of pragmatism necessary? A reply to Barnes-Holmes. *The Behavior Analyst, 26*, 297–99.

17. Skinner, B.F. op. cit.

18. Roche, B. and Barnes-Holmes, D. (2003). Behaviour analysis and social constructionism: Some points of contact and departure, (p. 220). *The Behavior Analyst, 26*, 215–31.

19. Much has been written on this subject, but for a general summary, see Chiesa, M. (1994). *Radical Behaviorism: The philosophy and the science.* Boston: Authors Cooperative.

20. For an account of why this occurs, see Hineline, P.N. (1980). The language of behavior analysis: Its community, its functions and its limitations. *Behaviorism, 8*, 67–86.

21. Boyle, M. (1993). *Schizophrenia: A scientific delusion?* Oxford: Taylor and Francis.

22. Mirowsky, J. and Ross, C.E. (1989). Psychiatric diagnosis as reified measurement. *Journal of Health and Social Behaviour, 30*, 11–25.

23. Swanson, J.M. (2003). Role of executive function in ADHD. *Journal of Clinical Psychiatry, 64*, 35–9.

24. Onians, R.B. (1988). *The Origins of European Thought*. Cambridge: Cambridge University Press.

25. Stewart, I. (1990). *Does God Play Dice? The new mathematics of chaos*. London: Penguin.

26. Heider, F. (1958). *The Psychology of Interpersonal Relations*. New York: Wiley.

27. Kelly, H.H. (1967). Attribution theory in social psychology. In D. Levine (ed) *Nebraska Symposium on Motivation, 15*, 192–238.

28. Moore, J. (2003). Behavior Analysis and Social Justice, (p. 185). *The Behavior Analyst, 26*, 181–93.

29. Sonuga-Barke, E.J.S., Taylor, E., Sembi, S. and Smith, S. (1992). Hyperactivity and delay aversion – I. The effect of delay on choice. *Journal of Child Psychology and Psychiatry, 33*, 2, 387–98.

30. Sonuga-Barke, E.J.S. (2002). Interval length and time use by children with AD/HD: A comparison of four models. *Journal of Applied Child Psychology, 30*, 257–65.

31. For example, Taylor, E. (1999). Developmental neuropsychology of attention deficit and impulsiveness. *Developmental Neuropathology, 11*, 607–28.

32. For example, Neef, N.A., Bicard, D.F. and Endo, S. (2001). Assessment of impulsivity and the development of self-control in students with Attention Deficit Hyperactivity Disorder. *Journal of Applied Behavior Analysis, 34*, 397–408.

33. For example, Gulley, V., Northup, J., Hupp, S., Spera, S., LeVelle, J. and Ridgway, A. (2003). Sequential evaluation of behavioral treatments and methylphenidate dosage for children with Attention Deficit Hyperactivity Disorder. *Journal of Applied Behavior Analysis, 36*, 375–8.

CHAPTER 5

ADHD, Diagnosis
and Identity

GERALDINE BRADY

A limited amount of research has directly sought to establish the views of children and young people who have the diagnosis of Attention Deficit Hyperactivity Disorder (ADHD). This chapter, based on a larger empirical study, focuses directly on children's own understanding of ADHD diagnosis and treatment and the effect on developing self-identity. The explanations and frameworks of understanding which practitioners provide to children play a vital role in shaping children's understanding of their difficulties. An overwhelming emphasis on biomedical, individualised explanations may negatively influence the developing self-identity of children. A more multi-modal approach may help to give children an alternative view of themselves and locate their difficulties within a broader context. Children and young people should be given space to share their views and concerns in order to shape the development of 'joint working' within the context of Child and Adolescent Mental Health Services (CAMHS).

Defining the research focus

Debates about the concept of Attention Deficit Hyperactivity Disorder (ADHD) have brought to the fore professional and disciplinary differences which exist between medicine, psychology, education and social services. Within the dominant biomedical discourse ADHD is understood as an objective condition in existence long before its scientific categorisation.[1] Alternatively, ADHD can be seen as socially and culturally constructed [2] [3] [4] [5] in that explanations for any 'abnormal' behaviour are more likely to be found in children's social environment rather than in an underlying pathology. Despite the current emphasis on the need for 'joint working'[6] [7] both with outside agencies and within CAMHS teams, practitioners who hold diverse and competing views regarding terminology, diagnosis and treatment may find it almost impossible to work together. My contention in this chapter is that Child and Adolescent Mental Health Services (CAMHS) and other agencies may be able to ameliorate a focus on pathological explanations by providing a more multidisciplinary assessment and treatment approach. In turn, I argue that the lay voices of children and young people have an important story to tell of the experience and meaning of the diagnosis of ADHD. The provision of a safe, internal forum for regular professional debate regarding the 'evolving concept'[6] of ADHD would be of benefit to some practitioners and may ultimately be of benefit to children.

Research design

Access to a busy Child and Adolescent Mental Health Service, based in a Midlands city, was gained in October 2000. The findings presented here form part of a larger doctoral study which explored how children/young people, parents and clinicians experienced ADHD. The seven children (six boys and one girl) who took part in the in-depth interviews were selected from the 125 children and young people with a diagnosis of ADHD who were registered CAMHS clients at the time. The ages of the group of seven ranged from 6 to 15. Five were white British, one black British and one North American. Three families were owner-occupiers, one was in private rented accommodation and three rented their homes from the Local Authority. The family format of parents included four reconstituted families, one single parent and two biological two-parent families. Four of the children already had a diagnosis of ADHD and three were diagnosed during the fieldwork period. The children were visited three times over twelve months to talk about how their life was affected by ADHD through in-depth, qualitative interviews.

A 'social studies of childhood' perspective regards childhood as socially, culturally and historically variable[8] and is keen to emphasise the competence of children, their abilities within relationships, their wish to participate in decision-making and their drive towards social life. As understandings of childhood have shifted, sociological research has begun to give credence to children's own accounts, focusing on the meanings which children and young people attach to their lives, their knowledge of the social order, their experiences, and their opinion on the childhoods they are asked to live.[9] In order to understand children we need to access their own accounts, rather than gathering information from parents or professionals, research *for* rather than *on* children.[10] Sensitive ways of engaging children were used in this study to discover how young people felt about their diagnosis of ADHD; a combination of oral, written and artistic contributions gave children the chance to express their feelings and opinions. A useful starting point for a sociological analysis of children's experiences of ADHD is to conceptualise children as competent, active contributors to society, coupled with a view of ADHD which recognises it as arising from simultaneously biological and social processes, accepting that there is an underlying reality to the experience whilst acknowledging that what we know as ADHD is socially constructed.

Children and young people's accounts of ADHD as 'deficit'

The diagnosis of ADHD has both practical and social consequences, but also a deeper, symbolic significance. It provides a legitimated framework from which to understand behaviour, and the opportunity to receive practical help. Yet medical discourse dominates all other descriptions, marginalising explanations provided by other professionals, parents and children. The terminology of ADHD was common parlance within the medical locales frequented by the children and young people in this study, but what did ADHD mean to the children themselves? Sean, aged 12, offered this medicalised explanation:

That it's, it's something that's not working in your brain, or something like that, and it makes you want attention and that. (Sean)

Asked how he felt about having it Sean replied, 'Not bothered', yet when asked if any of his peers ever made derogatory comments towards him he said 'No, cos I'd punch them'. This seems to indicate that at some level he was affected by the negative association with the diagnostic label. Emma (aged 11) also offers a medicalised explanation for her difficulties:

ADHD? It's sort of, erm, it's like an illness you react to ... I think that as I'm growing up I've come to terms with what I've got, so it's easier for me now. (Emma)

Sean and Emma appear to accept the way in which their difficulties with concentration, restlessness and paying attention have been medically defined. Marcus (aged 10), however, was keen to assert his personal identity rather than accept a purely medicalised definition. He resisted association with the stigma of the medical label and did not wish anyone outside his family to know about the diagnosis of ADHD. Marcus's mother recalls her son's reaction to her sharing information with friends:

When he was first diagnosed, it was such a weight off my shoulders, both mine and my husband's shoulders, cos you just blame yourself, your parenting skills, everything. So I was telling people that he was going to be on this drug, but he was cross, 'You haven't told, have you? I don't want them to know! You haven't! You promised me!' (Marcus' mum)

The invisibility of ADHD means that children can decide who to disclose the diagnosis to. Sometimes this was an unwelcome burden of responsibility and young people would rather not have to make that decision. Emma was particularly affected by the way in which she felt she was perceived by her peers. She had discussed with me the name-calling which she was subject to at school, the most frequent and hurtful of which was 'psycho' and she seemed to have internalised the message that she was not 'normal'. When I asked whether Emma's life would be easier if more people understood about ADHD she replied:

> Yeah, cos then they could understand how I feel and how they would feel
> if it happened to them … If you don't tell your friends that you've got it it
> can end up in an argument cos they'll say 'I thought I was meant to be your
> best friend!' (Emma)

When asked what she would like to happen in the future Emma said, 'I would like to be normal and popular.' Revealing the diagnosis to others can lead children to be discriminated against but equally peers may already perceive the young person to be strange in some way. Weinbren and Gill's[11] study of childhood epilepsy discovered that 'felt stigma may be influenced not only by societal and parental beliefs but also by a feeling of difference and personal insecurity'.

The above examples serve to illustrate the ways in which young people regard ADHD as having a physical reality; it affects their life in a myriad of ways. In conceptualising the behaviours related to ADHD as problematic young people's views are likely to have been affected by family and friends, their peer group, wider society, various forms of media and the practitioners who have provided explanations. The majority of young people in this small-scale study had received some limited educational and social support, but the medical definition of their difficulties remained dominant and was the explanation most often to be reproduced. That is not to say that respondents were unable or unwilling to change their life view. After attending a number of sessions with an educational psychologist Emma provided an altogether different explanation of ADHD:

> It's just like having, well, everybody's different and I'm just different and
> my friends are different to me, so it's easier to think of it like that instead
> of an illness and thinking that I'm ill. (Emma)

It might be naïve to assume that counselling therapy had directly influenced Emma's view of her difficulties but such a statement does indicate that Emma appeared to prefer this more positive and less stigmatising explanation. Emma feels that she benefits from her regular meetings with the educational psychologist:

> … cos like I can tell someone about things that have happened during the
> week, and I don't have to worry about it … people don't understand why I
> react the way I do and why I'm this sort of person. (Emma)

Emma clearly finds this 'talking therapy' to be helpful, but in many cases access to a psychologist was not made available to children once they had received a psychiatric diagnosis. Medical diagnosis itself is not necessarily a negative outcome for children and young people and respondents indicated that there were benefits to having their difficulties recognised by the medical profession. In terms of practical help, sources of support included regular appointments with a psychiatrist, in some cases help in securing a statement of special educational need or Disability Living Allowance, and some positive accounts of the significance of pharmacological treatment, usually with Methylphenidate.[9] Access to such resources often made a difference to the lives of children and young people.

The ADHD label also had a symbolic quality, in that it provided an explanation for the 'difference' which they had often felt and an element of legitimation, although this appeared to be of more importance to parents who had often felt 'blamed' for their child's behaviour. Significant others sometimes related to young people with more understanding and empathy once they were aware that their behavioural difficulties were linked to ADHD. This often led to the development of more positive relationships, particularly within the family.

The effect of medication on developing self-identity

There were also some reported disadvantages of having a medical diagnosis and being treated with medication, apart from the much discussed side-effects.[12] As suggested in the examples given above, believing that they 'had' ADHD young people internalised the notion that they were damaged and that only medication could fix them. However, not everyone adopted this view and accepted the diagnosis or the treatment offered. Frank (aged 12) had been taking medication daily for three months under the supervision of his mother but no change in his behaviour had been observed. It was suspected that Frank might be avoiding the medication in some way; at his CAMHS appointment the psychiatrist suggested that his mother leave the room and she asked Frank directly how often he 'skipped' a tablet. He replied:

> Every day. My mum brings it up with a drink and I swallow it, keep it at the back of my throat and sick it up out of the window when she's gone. (Frank)

The doctor attempted to discover the reasoning behind this decision and asked whether Frank knew of anyone else who had ADHD and was prescribed Ritalin (MPH):

> Yeah, Tyrone Patrick, he's a psycho, a little fire starter—he comes up behind you if you stand still and sets fire to your trousers—he goes to a special school, and he's tried to kill himself seven times. (Frank)

Clearly, Frank does not wish to associate himself with this boy and if he is the only other person he knows with a diagnosis of ADHD he is going to feel negatively about it. He does not want to be regarded as either 'ill' or 'different' and does not accept that he needs this form of treatment. The stigma associated with the ADHD label impacts on the identity of young people and can affect compliance or adherence to the medication regimen. Parents sometimes cannot comprehend their child's world view; if medication is associated with improved behaviour and academic success it is difficult for parents to understand why their child would not want to take it. Non-compliance is often associated with irrational behaviour or ignorance, but in this situation it appears to be a rational choice when the social context is taken into account.[13]

Young people's attitudes towards diagnosis and medication are complex and multi-layered. Whilst exploring Sean's feelings regarding medication he eventually tells me:

> I don't like feeling different, it's boring sitting still in class and it doesn't feel right—it's like, it's like it's not the 'real me'. (Sean)

Sean draws attention to the way in which taking medication has an effect on who he perceives himself to be; he actually feels different. It appears that one of the consequences of taking psycho-stimulant medication can be an 'altered personality' or, as Sean says, 'it's not the real me'. The young people who raised this issue tried to explain how medication had an effect on their self-identity, and on the way others perceived them, notably their peer group. Having cultivated the role of 'class clown', a fun but quite volatile character, Sean associates medication with being 'ordinary'. He acknowledges that he behaves in a more socially acceptable way when he complies, which pleases his mum and teachers, but ultimately it is more important to him to maintain popularity amongst his peers. Cooper and Shea's[14] empirical study of the perceptions and attitudes of children with ADHD to their condition found that students perceived the 'real me' to be their non-medicated self, and this person was sometimes associated with enjoyment and fun. This finding was borne out in the data collected from young people in this study; clearly this has implications for clinical practice in that children and young people often have very valid reasons for not taking medication, reasons which do not always come to light during their visit to CAMHS. The complexity of the decision-making process in treatment with psycho-stimulant medication is discussed elsewhere.[14] [9] [15] Young people are seeking social acceptance; above all they want to identify with their peers and not be perceived as 'different' or 'mental'. Thus, although medical diagnosis of a condition may allow access to resources and practical support and an element of legitimation,[16] [17] [18] there are some unforeseen consequences to a reliance on medical diagnosis and treatment.

Listening to children's voices: relevance for practice

ADHD is both a medical diagnosis and a social label. The way in which the difficulties of respondents in this study were conceptualised by professionals was of relevance to the way young people thought of themselves and the way in which they were regarded by others. The data suggest that an overwhelming emphasis on medical diagnosis and treatment leads young people to regard themselves as 'damaged' and can contribute to a negative view of the self, particularly when young people are constantly reminded by parents of what a 'nightmare' they have been as a baby, toddler and child. More importantly, the implication that deficits exist in individual children may have an unhelpful impact on children's developing self-identity. Radcliffe, Sinclair and Newnes[19] indicate that:

> locating the 'problem' within the young person may exacerbate their difficulties—labelling a young person as having a psychiatric disorder may give them a sense of self as being 'different' from others and negatively impact upon their confidence and self-worth.

Diagnostic labels can be constraining, limiting our view of children's competencies. Defining children's levels of attention, activity and impulse as a medical problem draws attention to what children have difficulty doing rather than the things they do well. Although doctors/psychiatrists at the CAMHS observed in this study were keen to explain the condition carefully, answer any questions, and try not to cause concern, they did not place an emphasis on distancing the 'problem' from the child.[20] As Hughes[21] notes, we cannot always know what children were told by the professionals and practitioners that they have encountered, we can only know how they interpreted the information and many of the children and young people in this study appeared to regard their difficulties as biologically determined.

Treatment with Methylphenidate had an immediate effect on activity levels, attention and empathy in all six children in the in-depth interview sample who were taking medication. Some young people enjoyed aspects of this change, but also drew attention to the less desirable aspects of the medication, namely changes in the way in which they perceived their own identity. The value of medication is in enabling relationships to develop more positively, but the tendency to rely on medication alone to treat ADHD can be criticised. In addition, some individuals are not yet ready to relinquish their 'ADHD identity'; they are invested in that identity, and know no other experience. Such an identity may be perceived, at least in part, to be positive by young people themselves, such as Sean's expressed sense of loss at no longer being regarded as fun, the 'class clown'. We need to acknowledge that the new persona provided by the application of medication may in some way be less than the non-medicated identity.

Being regarded as 'disabled', rather than naughty, can be assumed to lead to improved relationships at both home and school but once a child has a label it becomes difficult to lose it, whether it attends to disability, special educational needs, emotional and behavioural difficulties or mental health difficulties and all labels affect children's self-perception and the perception of wider society. These particular children are affected by the general stereotyping of 'the ADHD child' and, as in Schneider and Conrad's [22] study of the stigma potential of epilepsy, children choose to conceal or disclose their ADHD diagnosis depending on the situation and the people involved. Children and young people would benefit from an understanding of the interaction between psychosocial and biological factors and this could be achieved through the formation of a therapeutic relationship with professionals outside of medicine. Increased understanding of the wider social and environmental influences on behaviour may lead to raised self-esteem amongst young people.

In four cases the ADHD label and medication were responsible for young people re-evaluating their lives; they were now able to refer to two separate selves—namely the non-medicated and the medicated person. Children and young people may require support which is non-medical in order to come to terms with such changes. As Williams and Bendelow[23] note '… our relationship to our bodies is, for the most part, a largely taken-for-granted one' but conditions such as ADHD can call into question this previously unquestioned reference point.

Implications for practice and further research

Resisting the dominance of the biomedical definition of ADHD will inevitably involve various professions and agencies engaging in joint work to facilitate constructive debate and practice. The mental and emotional health needs of children should be met through the coordinated efforts of health, education and social services, and multidisciplinary networks.[6] Government initiatives which advocate practitioners and services working in partnership often fail to take account of the differing underpinning philosophies of the professions concerned and how interdisciplinary tensions can affect the delivery of services. The *National Service Framework for Children* (2004)[24] identifies factors that facilitate joint working within CAMHS, including understanding of and respect for the different roles and expertise of members of staff. This research suggests that such engagement is crucial to the improved treatment of those who have the diagnosis of ADHD.

Moreover, CAMHS need to engage users in developing services, directly asking children and parents what would be helpful and how CAMHS can better support. Children and young people have complex needs which vary over time; they need to be supported holistically—their body, mind and self cannot be split into convenient 'bits' that various practitioners deal with.[6] Ways of resisting the dominance of medical definition will inevitably involve engaging in joint work which allows for constructive debate, and does not involve either giving in to the dominance of biomedicine, or refusing to engage: both positions are untenable and do not help children and their families to cope with daily life.

In research debates and in practice, the voices of young people have been somewhat neglected. The 'lived experience' of children and parents is coming to be regarded as essential experiential evidence within social research into illness and disability.[25] It is crucial that these views are perceived to be as important as those of medical practitioners or medicine will be practised on the basis of assumptions made about the place of children in society, the relative passivity of their designated role, and the expectations which adults have of them, rather than on a body of knowledge which has been actively contributed to by children themselves.

My research suggests that professional approaches influence children and young people's identity. Examples from the data provide an illustration of the profound impact of ADHD on the lives of children and young people and suggest that their contribution should be central to any attempt to understand ADHD. Young people wish to be accepted and to live a 'normal' life but the medical diagnosis carries a stigma. I contend that the development of a more multi-modal approach to assessment and treatment will help young people to gain an alternative view of themselves and to locate any difficulties in a broader context; this suggests that further attention needs to be paid to the psychosocial consequences of diagnosing children and young people with ADHD.

Acknowledgements

I wish to thank the children and young people who took part in this study and CAMHS staff for allowing me to observe their practice. I also wish to thank Dr Andrew Parker and Dr Gayle Letherby for helpful comments on earlier drafts of this chapter.

Endnotes

1. Tait, G. (2003). Free will, moral responsibility and ADHD. *International Journal of Inclusive Education, 7,* 4, 429–46.

2. Ideus, K. (1995). Cultural foundations of ADHD: a sociological analysis. In P. Cooper and K. Ideus (eds) *Attention Deficit/Hyperactivity Disorder: Educational, medical and cultural issues.* Kent: The Association of Workers for Children with Emotional and Behavioural Difficulties.

3. Slee, R. (1995). *Changing Theories and Practices of Discipline.* Brighton: Falmer.

4. Prior, P. (1997). ADHD/Hyperkinetic disorder: How should educational psychologists and other practitioners respond to the emerging phenomenon of school children diagnosed as having ADHD? *Emotional and Behavioural Difficulties, 2,* 1, 15–27.

5. Baldwin, S. (2000). Living in Britalin: Why are so many amphetamines prescribed to infants, children and teenagers in the UK? *Critical Public Health, 10,* 4, 453–62.

6. British Psychological Society (1996). *Attention Deficit Hyperactivity Disorder: A psychological response to an evolving concept.* Leicester: British Psychological Society.

7. British Psychological Society (2000). *Attention Deficit/Hyperactivity Disorder (AD/HD): Guidelines and principles for successful multi-agency working.* Leicester: British Psychological Society.

8. James, A. and Prout, A. (eds) (1997). *Constructing and Re-constructing Childhood: Contemporary issues in the sociological study of childhood* (2nd ed). London: Falmer Press.

9. Bendelow, G. and Brady, G. (2002). Experiences of ADHD: children, health research and emotion work. In G. Bendelow, M. Carpenter, C. Vautier and S. Williams (eds) *Gender, Health and Healing: The public/private divide.* London: Routledge.

10. Mayall, B. (1996). *Children, Health and the Social Order.* Buckingham: Open University Press.

11. Weinbren, H. and Gill, P. (1998). Narratives of childhood epilepsy: have I got epilepsy or has it got me? In T. Greenhalgh and B. Hurwitz (eds) *Narrative Based Medicine: Dialogue and discourse in clinical practice,* (p. 68). London: BMJ Books.

12. Breggin, P. R. (1998). *Talking Back to Ritalin: The hidden dangers of stimulants for children.* Monroe, ME: Common Courage Press.

13. Wirsing, R. and Somerfeld, J. (1992). Compliance—A medical anthropological re-appraisal. In D.J. Trakas and E.J. Sanz (eds) *Studying Childhood and Medicine Use: A multi-disciplinary approach.* Athens: ZHTA Publications.

14. Cooper, P. and Shea, T. (1999). ADHD from the inside: An empirical study of young people's perceptions of the experience of ADHD. In P. Cooper and K. Bilton (eds) *ADHD: Research, practice and opinion.* London: Whurr Publishers.

15. Brady, G. (2004). Children and ADHD: A sociological exploration. Unpublished PhD thesis, University of Warwick.

16. Bury, M. (1982). Chronic illness as biographical disruption. *Sociology of Health and Illness, 4,* 2, 167–82.

17. Kohler-Reissman, C. (1989). Women's medicalisation: A new perspective. In P. Brown (ed) *Perspectives in Medical Sociology.* California: Wadsworth.

18. Broom, D.H. and Woodward, R.V. (1996). Medicalisation reconsidered: Towards a collaborative approach to care. *Sociology of Health and Illness, 18,* 3, 357–78.

19. Radcliffe, N., Sinclair, S. and Newnes, C. (2004). Editorial. Carl and the Passions: 'so tough'. *Clinical Psychology, 40,* August, 2004. Special Issue: Children and ADHD: Sharing untold stories.

20. White, M. and Epston, D. (1990). *Narrative Means to Therapeutic Ends.* London: WW Norton and Company.

21. Hughes, L. (1999). How professionals perceive ADHD. In P. Cooper and K. Bilton (eds) *ADHD: Research, practice and opinion*. London: Whurr Publishers.

22. Schneider, J. and Conrad, P. (1980). In the closet with illness: Epilepsy, stigma potential and information control. *Social Problems, 28,* 32–44.

23. Williams, S.J. and Bendelow, G. (2000). Recalcitrant bodies? Children, cancer and the transgression of corporeal boundaries. *Health, 4,* 1, 51–71.

24. Department of Health (2004). *National Service Framework for Children, Young People and Maternity Services*. London: Department of Health.

25. Shakespeare, T., Barnes, C., Cunningham-Burley, S., Davies, J., Priestley, M. and Watson, N. (2000). *The Lives of Disabled Children*. ESRC 5–16 Research programme, research briefing http://www.esrc.ac.uk

Part Two

Problematising
Children

CHAPTER 6

The Rise and Rise of ADHD

SAMI TIMIMI AND
NICK RADCLIFFE

This chapter offers an overview of the rise in diagnosing ADHD and the use of stimulants in children and is presented in the context of the cultural discourses and power hierarchies that exist in contemporary Western society.

Something's happening here

Something strange has been happening to children in Western society in the past couple of decades. The diagnosis of Attention Deficit Hyperactivity Disorder (ADHD) has reached epidemic proportions, particularly amongst boys in North America. The diagnosis is usually made by a child psychiatrist or paediatrician with advocates of the diagnosis claiming that children who present with what they consider to be over-activity, poor concentration and impulsivity are suffering from a medical condition which needs treatment with medication. The main medications used for children with a diagnosis of ADHD are stimulants such as Ritalin, whose chemical properties are virtually indistinguishable from the street drugs, speed and cocaine. Boys are four to ten times more likely to receive the diagnosis and stimulants than girls, with children as young as two being diagnosed and prescribed stimulants in increasing numbers.[1]

By 1996 over 6 per cent of school-aged boys in America were taking stimulant medication[2] with more recent surveys showing that in some schools in the United States over 17 per cent of boys have the diagnosis and are taking stimulant medication.[3] In the UK prescriptions for stimulants have increased from about 6,000 in 1994 to about 345,000 in the latter half of 2003,[4] suggesting that we in the UK are rapidly catching up with the US. Concerned professionals and parents are increasingly vocal in their criticism of the excessive use of stimulants and there are debates among clinicians proposing that ADHD is better regarded as a 'cultural construct' than a bona-fide medical disorder (e.g. see [5] [6]).

Despite the assertion from ADHD industry insiders that 'ADHD' is a medical disorder,[7] even they have to concede that despite years and millions of dollars spent on research (it is the most thoroughly researched child psychiatric label— from a biological perspective that is) no medical test for it exists, nor has any proof been forthcoming of what the supposed physical deficit is, and so diagnosis is based on the subjective opinion of the diagnoser.[8] Indeed its validity as a distinct diagnostic entity is widely questioned as it cannot reliably be distinguished from other disorders in terms of aetiology, course, cultural variation, response to treatment, co-morbidity and gender distribution.[9] [10] [11] [12] [13] Furthermore there is no evidence that treatment with stimulants leads to any lasting improvement.[14] Indeed a recent meta-analysis of randomised controlled trials showed the trials were of poor quality, there was strong evidence of publication bias, short-term effects were inconsistent across different rating scales, side effects were frequent and problematic and long-term effects beyond four weeks of treatment were not demonstrated.[15]

In the absence of objective methods for verifying the physical basis of ADHD, we also conceptualise ADHD as primarily a culturally constructed entity. The cultural dynamics of this label cannot be understood without first understanding the cultural discourses and power hierarchies that exist in contemporary Western society. It is a very compelling and dominating story invented and perpetuated by those whose interests are served by its telling and retelling (ADHD was literally voted into existence in the 1980s by the American Psychiatric Association when drawing up the third edition and third edition-revised versions of the Diagnostic and Statistical Manual). By focusing on within-child explanations for presenting behaviours, ADHD divorces a child from their context, and real life experiences, including traumatic ones, become clinically less important. In this article we explore how ADHD manages to occupy and hold onto such a dominant position despite the growing criticism and lack of evidence supporting its alleged medical origins.

The claim that ADHD is a medical disorder

To believers, ADHD is a diagnosable neuro-developmental disorder. Its identification is based on the observation of a constellation of behaviours that must be found across different settings and that are said to reveal abnormalities in children's activity levels, impulsiveness and concentration. Commonly, when a child is diagnosed the first-line treatment of choice is a stimulant such as Methylphenidate. Stimulants are portrayed as safe and effective and children that are diagnosed and treated in this way are said to show vast improvements in their behaviour, activity levels, concentration and achievements. In the real world the picture is not so straightforward.

ADHD in practice

In practice, the diagnosis of ADHD relies on adults in varying caring relationships with the child, reporting the above behaviours to a medical diagnostician. As diagnosis is based on the observation of behaviours alone, this has led to a kind of 'open season' where anyone can 'have a go': teachers, parents, school doctors, welfare officers, and so on. As the construct becomes more widely known within any community, confidence in making provisional diagnoses grows too. What is alarming is the apparent lack of awareness of the self-fulfilling nature of this process.

This self-fulfilling process occurs at many levels. For example, when a parent and child meet a specialist medical practitioner, the meeting is likely to be organised to elicit the type of information needed to fulfill predetermined diagnostic criteria. The relationship between the people's beliefs, expectations and subjective reporting will shape and inform the questions asked, responses given, and of course the child's behaviour in the room. Basically, some observable behaviours in children (such as inattention and hyperactivity) change in status from behaviours containing no more or less information (in isolation) than the inattention or hyperactivity as described by an observer, to becoming the basis of a primary diagnosis. The biomedical template is applied and the behaviours are interpreted as a sign of a physical disorder. This leaves out several layers of experience and context that could contribute to any observed behaviour as well as alternative meanings that could be given to that behaviour. This also denies the participant observers an opportunity to witness the child demonstrating exceptional behaviours.

This medical explanatory model has enormous cultural power. Naturally, most of the population will assume that once doctors have named these behaviours as a disorder, such a categorisation must have a natural and scientific basis. This leads to the huge differences in the experiences of children with the label being interpreted as of lesser importance when compared to the assumed similarities children with a disorder are felt to possess.

Behaviour rating scales have become a key part of the diagnostic process and are presented as an objective tool. Critics point out that agreeing a cut-off point for the behaviours in question is a culturally and subjectively driven process which is reflected in the fact that epidemiological studies (using rating scales) have produced very different prevalence rates for ADHD (in its various forms), ranging from about 0.5 per cent of school age children to 26 per cent of school age children.[8] The criteria used for rating behaviours are based on Likert-type frequency descriptors (for example, often, seldom, never, and so on), thus reliable diagnoses depend on how consistently raters share a common understanding of the behaviours to be rated. Despite attempts at standardising criteria and assessment tools in cross-cultural studies, major and significant differences between raters from different countries,[16] as well as between raters from different ethnic minority backgrounds,[17] continue to be apparent.

If trained professionals cannot agree on how to rate behaviours relative to some sort of agreed (all be it arbitrary) 'norm', it is not surprising that non-professional observers and informants have different thresholds. For example, Reid et al.[11] cite several studies reporting that specialist teachers tend to be more tolerant of misbehaviour and judge students' behaviours as less deviant than general class teachers.

ADHD is thus ideally placed as a convenient diagnostic 'dumping ground' allowing all of us (parents, teachers, doctors, politicians) to avoid the messy business of understanding human relationships and institutions and their difficulties, and our common responsibility for nurturing and raising well-behaved children. Loose, subjective diagnostic criteria with no established medical basis lend themselves to the 'elastic band' effect of ever stretching boundaries as the drug companies help themselves and the medical professions develop new markets. This has resulted in stimulants being prescribed for their perceived performance enhancing properties and with more children in classrooms taking stimulants many parents end up feeling their child is at a disadvantage if they do not.[18] Stimulants are also being prescribed to children without them even fulfilling broad diagnostic criteria. This trend has now become so established that in some areas of the United States, less than half the children prescribed stimulants reach even the broad formal criteria for making a diagnosis of ADHD.[19 20] In the UK you can now get a diagnosis via a 25-minute telephone consultation, without the child concerned being seen.[21 22]

So why such a strong belief in ADHD?

ADHD exists as a concept because it has been positioned within the empiricist tradition of medical and psychological research. Writing on schizophrenia, Boyle[23] draws attention to some of the devices that psychiatry uses to create the impression of a brain disorder despite the absence of supporting evidence. Firstly, she points out that by using their powerful status doctors can simply assert that it is a medical disorder, in such a way as to minimise opposition. In the case of ADHD, the Barkley et al.[7] consensus statement would be a good example of such rhetoric. Here a group of eminent psychiatrists and psychologists produced a consensus statement to forestall debate on the merits of the widespread diagnosis and drug treatment of ADHD. Secondly, to support the assertion of a medical disorder, apparently meaningful associations with biological processes are created. For example, funding research that supports claims of biological or genetic causes (whether this delivers results or not), leads to the construct implicitly being regarded as if it is part of a larger field (in the case of ADHD, neuro-developmental psychiatry). Thirdly, the medical discourse prevails by ignoring or rejecting other non-biological accounts of (in this case, children's) behaviour, or by co-opting them as peripheral or consequential rather than antecedent.

Privileged social groups, who hold important and influential positions, have a powerful effect on our common cultural beliefs, attitudes and practices. Child Psychiatry in the UK does appear to have re-invented itself in the last ten years. Having struggled with a crisis of identity about being doctors, influential child psychiatrists successfully influenced the UK's professional discourse convincing it that there were more personal rewards for the profession by it adopting a more medicalised American style approach (e.g. see [24]). ADHD has, along with a string of other so-called disorders, helped construct the field of neuro-developmental psychiatry, which the public, trusting such high status opinions, has come to view as real.

The development of diagnostic categories such as ADHD is of course of huge interest to the pharmaceutical industry. Indeed some argue that ADHD has been conceived and promoted by the pharmaceutical industry in order for there to be an entity for which stimulants could be prescribed.[25][26] It is after all a multi-million dollar industry, with the US National Institute of Mental Health[27] and the US Department of Education and the Food and Drug Administration[28] all having been involved in funding and promoting treatment which calls for medicating children with behavioural problems. The situation with drug companies controlling the agenda of scientific debate has become so prevalent that it is virtually impossible to climb up the career ladder without promotional support from drug companies. Most senior academics have long-standing financial links with drug companies inevitably compromising the impartiality of their opinions.[29]

Similarly the impartiality of patient support organisations has to be questioned. In recent years it has become apparent that drug companies are using such consumer lobbying groups to their advantage not only by (often secretly) generous donations, but also on occasion by setting up patient groups themselves.[30] The main pro-medication pro-ADHD consumer support group in North America is CHADD, which receives substantial amounts from drug companies, receiving an estimated $500,000 in 2002.[31] There are other support groups: for example, in the United Kingdom the parent support group 'Overload' have been campaigning for prescribing doctors to provide more information to parents about the cardiovascular and neurological side effects of stimulants, believing that many more parents would be likely to reject such medication if they were being properly informed about it by the medical profession. However, without the financial support of the multinational giants, their message rarely gets heard.

ADHD is now also firmly entrenched in the cultural expectations of our education system. The defining of a disability requiring special needs help at school is now shaped by the disciplines of medicine and psychology.[32] The adherence of these two fields to measuring physical and mental competence in order to determine normality inevitably conveys assumptions about deviance and failure and these labels then become attached to both individuals and groups who have failed to measure up or conform. Special needs practice in schools rests on within-child explanations.[33] Psychiatric diagnoses have thus become an acceptable device for raising funds to meet children's perceived special needs. Increasing experience of children rendered less troublesome (to a school) by taking a stimulant, when coupled with a belief that these children's non-compliant behaviours were caused by a medical condition has also increased demand from teachers for children to be diagnosed and medicated.

Effects of this new category of childhood

What are the effects of embracing practices that impose descriptions such as ADHD onto children's behaviour? Children quickly become objects of such descriptions. Their creativity, capacity for 'exceptional behaviours' and diversity go unnoticed. ADHD pushes teachers, parents and medical practitioners into self-doubt about their capacity to teach and care for children. The opportunities for developing reflexive, appreciative child management practices and skills are lost.

In mental health settings, the chance to build a repertoire of therapeutic skills and practices that might facilitate people to talk about their experience in ways that can create more empowering meanings that build on their own knowledge is also lost. Instead children are persuaded to take highly addictive and potentially brain disabling drugs for many years and may well be cultured into the attitude of 'a pill for life's problems'. Children and their carers risk developing 'tunnel vision' about their problems rendering them unnecessarily 'disabled' and dependent on 'experts'. The effect this has not only on the physical health of our children in the West, but also on our ways of viewing childhood is incalculable. Behind the rise in diagnoses and the liberal prescription of such dangerous medicines lurks a deep malaise that is infecting Western culture—hostility to children—for in our modernist, hyperactive, individualistic lifestyles children 'get in the way'.

Endnotes

1. Zito, J.M., Safer, D.J., Dosreis, S., Gardner, J.F., Boles, J. and Lynch, F. (2000). Trends in prescribing of psychotropic medication in pre-schoolers. *Journal of the American Medical Association, 283,* 1025–30.

2. Olfson, M., Marcus, S.C., Weissman, M.M. and Jensen, P.S. (2002). National trends in the use of psychotropic medications by children. *Journal of the American Academy of Child and Adolescent Psychiatry, 41,* 514–21.

3. LeFever, G.B., Dawson, K.V. and Morrow, A.D. (1999). The extent of drug therapy for Attention Deficit Hyperactivity Disorder among children in public schools. *American Journal of Public Health, 89,* 1359–64.

4. Wright, O. (2003). Ritalin use and abuse fears. *The Times* (UK) July 28th, p. 3.

5. Timimi, S. and Taylor, E. (2004). ADHD is best understood as a cultural construct. *British Journal of Psychiatry, 184,* 8–9.

6. Baldwin, S. and Cooper, P. (2000). How should ADHD be treated? *The Psychologist, 13,* 598–602.

7. Barkley, R. A. et al. (2002). International Consensus Statement on ADHD. *Clinical Child and Family Psychology Review, 5,* 89–111.

8. Timimi, S. et al. (2004). A critique of the international consensus statement on ADHD. *Clinical Child and Family Psychology Review, 7,* 59 –63.

9. Rutter, M. (1983). Behavioral studies: Questions of findings on the concept of a distinctive syndrome. In M. Rutter (ed) *Developmental Neuropsychology* (pp. 259–79). New York: Guilford.

10. Taylor, E. (1989). On the epidemiology of hyperactivity. In T. Sagnolden and T. Archer (eds) *Attention Deficit Disorder: Clinical and basic research* (pp. 31–52). Hillsdale, NJ: Lawrence Erlbaum.

11. Reid, R., Maag, J.W. and Vasa, S.F. (1993). Attention Deficit Hyperactivity Disorder as a disability category: A critique. *Exceptional Children, 60,* 198–214.

12. Koriath, U., Gualtieri, M.D., Van Bourgondien, M.E., Quade, D. and Werry, J.S. (1985). Construct validity of clinical diagnosis in pediatric psychiatry: Relationship among measures. *Journal of the American Academy of Child Psychiatry, 24,* 429–36.

13. Timimi, S. (2002). *Pathological Child Psychiatry and the Medicalization of Childhood.* Hove: Brunner-Routledge.

14. Joughin, C. and Zwi, M. (1999). *Focus on the use of stimulants in children with Attention Deficit Hyperactivity Disorder. Primary evidence-base Briefing No.1.* London: Royal College of Psychiatrists Research Unit.

15. Schachter, H., Pham, B., King, J., Langford, S. and Moher, D. (2001). How efficacious and safe is short-acting methylphenidate for the treatment of attention-deficit disorder in children and adolescents? A meta-analysis. *Canadian Medical Association Journal, 165,* 1475–88.

16. Mann, E.M., Ikeda, Y., Mueller, C.W., Takahashi, A., Tao, K.T., Humris, E., Li, B.L. and Chin, D. (1992). Cross-cultural differences in rating hyperactive-disruptive behaviors in children. *American Journal of Psychiatry, 149,* 1539–42.

17. Sonuga-Barke, E.J.S., Minocha, K., Taylor, E.A. and Sandberg, S. (1993). Inter-ethnic bias in teacher's ratings of childhood hyperactivity. *British Journal of Developmental Psychology, 11,* 187–200.

18. Diller, L.H. (1998). *Running on Ritalin.* New York: Bantam.

19. Wasserman, R.C., Kelleher, K.J., Bocian, A., Baber, A., Childs, C.E., Indacochea, F., Stulp, C. and Gardner, W.P. (1999). Identification of attentional and hyperactivity problems in primary care: A report from pediatric research in office settings and the ambulatory sentinel practice network. *Pediatrics, 103,* E38.

20. Angold, A., Erkanli, A., Egger, H.L. and Costello, E.J. (2000). Stimulant treatment for children: A community perspective. *Journal of the American Academy of Child and Adolescent Psychiatry, 39,* 975–84.

21. Curtis, T. (2004). Doctor in child drug treatment row to face GMC. *Scotland on Sunday,* 18th January.

22. Baldwin, S. and Anderson, R. (2000). The cult of methylphenidate: Clinical update. *Critical Public Health, 10,* 81–6.

23. Boyle, M. (2002). It's all done with smoke and mirrors: Or how to create the illusion of a schizophrenic brain disease. *Clinical Psychology, 12,* 9–19.

24. Goodman, R. (1997). An over extended remit. *British Medical Journal, 314,* 813–14.

25. McGuiness, D. (1989). Attention Deficit Disorder, the Emperor's new clothes, Animal 'Pharm' and other fiction. In S. Fisher and R. Greenberg (eds) *The Limits of Biological Treatments for Psychological Distress: Comparisons with psychotherapy and placebo.* Hillsdale, NJ: Lawrence Erlbaum Associates.

26. Breggin, P. (2002). *The Ritalin Fact Book.* Cambridge, MA: Perseus Publishing.

27. Karon, B.P. (1994). Problems of psychotherapy under managed care. *Psychotherapy in Private Practice, 2,* 55–63.

28. Breggin, P. (1994). *The War Against Children: How the drugs programmes and theories of the psychiatric establishment are threatening America's children with a medical 'cure' for violence.* New York: St Martin's Press.

29. Burton, B. and Rowell, A. (2003). Unhealthy spin. *British Medical Journal, 326,* 1205–7.

30. Herxheimer, A. (2003). Relationships between pharmaceutical industry and patients organizations. *British Medical Journal, 326,* 1208–10.

31. O'Meara, P. (2003). Putting power back in parental hands. *Insight Magazine,* 28th April 2003.

32. Hey, V., Leonard, D., Daniels, H. and Smith, M. (1998). Boys' underachievement, special needs practices and questions of equity. In D. Epstein, J. Elwood, V. Hey and J. Maw (eds) *Failing Boys? Issues in gender and underachievement.* Buckingham: Open University Press.

33. Ainscow, M. and Tweddle, D.A. (1988). *Encouraging Classroom Success.* London: Fulton.

CHAPTER 7

ADHD:
Adults' fear of frightened children

DOROTHY ROWE

In the early 1960s I worked as an educational psychologist in Sydney, Australia. My title was Specialist Counsellor for Emotionally Disturbed Children. If school principals were concerned about a particular child they would ask me to visit the school. I didn't have an office. I kept my files and my tests in the boot of my car. I interviewed the teachers and children at school and I often saw families in their own homes.

My first visit to a child's home may have been arranged through a phone call but after that I often just dropped in because I happened to be passing. This may have been convenient for me but it also provided me with an understanding of the family that formal meetings in an office or an arranged meeting in the child's home could never have given. There was a 9-year-old boy, Peter, who persistently refused to go to school. He would set off for school each morning only to get as far as the school gates when he would panic and flee home. Nowadays he would be given a diagnosis of school phobia but, as I discovered, school had very little to do with his fear. It was not until I went to his home that I found that there were more people in the family than Peter and his parents. In the back bedroom was Peter's aged grandmother. She seemed to be very fond of Peter and he of her. I made a number of visits to Peter's home and he and I got to know one another very well. He talked to me about school and told me that he liked studying, he liked his teachers and he had some good mates there. One day when neither his parents nor his grandmother were nearby he said to me, 'When I'm getting ready for school Grandma always says to me, "If you go to school today I'll die.".'

For Peter's parents and teachers the problem was that Peter would not go to school. All they could see was Peter's refusal to go to school. They may have noticed that on approaching school Peter became quiet, his face went white, he began to tremble, and then he turned and ran home; in short, he showed some of the outward signs of being frightened. Even if they did notice this they were mistaken in thinking that the object of his fear was the school.

Many adults are unable to see that a child is afraid. All that they are aware of is that the child's behaviour is a problem to adults. Attention Deficit Hyperactivity Disorder (ADHD) is a prime example of how adults see children only in terms of whether the children are a bother to adults.

The so-called symptoms of ADHD can be summarised as: difficulty in paying attention, difficulty in concentration and in staying with and completing a task, difficulty in keeping things in order, being easily distracted, often forgetful, restless, fidgety, unable to rest or relax, active for activity's sake, impatient, impulsive, sometimes talking excessively but unable to engage in a dialogue, unable to consider other people.

Every person, adult and child, knows this state of being extremely well. It is the state of being afraid. Adults are well aware of their own fear, and of how they feel and behave when they are afraid, but they hate to acknowledge that a child is afraid because a frightened child is showing that some adults are failing to look after that child properly. Parents want to believe that they are good parents, teachers want to believe that they are good at their job, and doctors and psychologists want to believe that they are experts on how children ought to behave. Instead of looking critically at themselves and at the society which adults have created, adults locate the problem within the child and then blame the child. Instead of noticing that the child is afraid and then finding out what the child is afraid of, adults label the child with a fictitious diagnosis, ADHD, and then treat that disorder by putting the child into a drug induced torpor.

Before the invention of ADHD and the vast array of disorders described in the Diagnostic and Statistical Manual, adults simply saw children whose behaviour did not please adults as being either mad or bad. Parents and teachers, then as now, wanted children to be quiet and obedient. I discovered that only the most discerning of teachers were aware that a child could be 'too good'. I came across children in school whose behaviour was impeccable but who were quietly sliding into psychosis. It was not until their good behaviour became noticeably odd that their teachers thought to consult me. One teacher discovered that a young girl in his class waited until he specifically gave her an order even though he had already given the same order to the class. One evening he returned to his classroom to collect something and found the girl still sitting at her desk. He had forgotten to tell her to go home. A high school principal asked me to see one of the school's best pupils who had become very quiet and withdrawn. I gave her a Rorschach test and was shocked to find that all her responses were full of bizarre images of penises. When I saw the girl's mother I tentatively suggested that the girl had had some very unpleasant sexual experiences. The mother nodded and half under her breath said, 'Her grandfather'. She had known and had said nothing.

The type of child who was referred to me most frequently was an 8- or 9-year-old boy who was a great trouble to his teacher because he could not sit still and pay attention. In those days the major part of an educational psychologist's work was in administering group intelligence tests. If there was anything unusual about a child's score on these tests the child was given a Wechsler Intelligence Test for Children (WISC) as this was considered to be the best measure of intelligence. Even in the early 1960s we knew that all these tests were useless at predicting the child's academic progress but nevertheless we continued. After all, we were the experts in intelligence. Whenever a child was referred to me I was required to give the child a WISC, no matter what degree of emotional distress the child was in. Accordingly I gave each of these inattentive boys a WISC. For once this test was useful for it showed that these boys fell into two distinct groups.

The WISC gives two IQs (intelligence quotients), a Verbal IQ and a Performance IQ which aims at measuring abilities which do not involve language and verbal reasoning. The first group of boys scored significantly higher on Performance IQ than on Verbal IQ. There is nothing unusual in this. Many men find it much easier to think and reason in terms of space and patterns than in terms of language. However, the school curriculum then as now required children to draw on the abilities measured by the Verbal IQ tests rather than on the Performance IQ tests. Thus children whose Performance IQ is significantly higher than their Verbal IQ are at a great disadvantage at school. Unless they are good at sport they have no opportunity to shine at school and be rewarded in ways which made them feel valuable and acceptable. Instead they receive constant criticism and pressure to produce what they are unable to produce. Many of the boys I saw had failed to absorb the basics of reading, writing and mathematics and consequently had to find ways of hiding these deficiencies from their teachers and fellow pupils. If the boys came from families indifferent to education their life at home may have been peaceful, but, if the boys came from families where educational attainment mattered, the boys would have been aware that they were a disappointment to their parents. They may also have been punished at home as they were at school.

All adults should be able to remember the experience of being punished as a child. They should be able to remember the feeling of being small, helpless and trapped while the adult, big and powerful, inflicts pain by words and blows. Once experienced, the fear of being punished never goes away. This is why most adults are very law-abiding.

The second group of boys were also being punished but for more than not being able to settle in class and pay attention. Their WISC scores showed no particular pattern that would make studying difficult. The source of their fear lay in their home.

World War II ended in 1945 but the effects of that war were felt in families for decades afterwards. This group of boys had parents or grandparents who had had what we used to call then 'a bad war'. Many of them had fathers who had been involved in the fighting. I went to university in 1948 where the majority of my fellow students were ex-service men and women. I married one of them. Being involved in the fighting during a war changes people, and not for the better. The experience of war leaves people more prone to extreme habits, extreme reactions and extreme ideas. Some of these boys had parents or grandparents who had been in Japanese prisoner of war camps, and some were survivors of the Nazi concentration camps. Some of the boys were the children of migrants who, having lost everything during the war, were now struggling to survive in a strange country while mourning all that they had lost. These parents may have loved their children but they could not parent them. Many of the boys worried about their parents and felt responsible for them, just as Peter felt responsible for his grandmother. All of these boys were frightened of their parents. Some of them saw school as a haven, but their fear did not let them take advantage of what the school had to offer.

All this was happening in a society which was recovering economically from the war and becoming prosperous. Jobs were plentiful and secure, even for those who left school with no qualifications. The country was peaceful, there was little crime, and the only drugs were alcohol and nicotine. It is a nonsense to say that all these boys had an unrecognised disorder, ADHD — which has now grown to epidemic proportions. Society has changed, and there are now even more frightened children. No longer can a boy leave school without an academic qualification to his name and get an apprenticeship which leads to a secure and respected job for life. Education has become a regulated process of turning out the kind of child of which adults approve. Children who cannot fit the approved pattern are shown by the school system that they are useless and worthless. Many children are born to parents as little able to parent them as were the war-survivor parents of the 1960s, not because parents now have survived a war but because they have been defeated by drugs or poverty. In the 1960s we believed in progress, that our lives would get better and better. Now we know that progress is possible only for the rich, and even they can fall victim to terrorism and climate change. Children in the 1960s saw terrible images of death and destruction only in the ten-minute newsreels at the weekly cinema. Now those images are presented daily on television. Some of these images are of real events, some manufactured for the television or computer screen. I can still see with my mind's eye many of the images of war that I first saw as a child. How do today's children deal with the terrible images they have in their heads? By being restless and inattentive? How can frightened children be helped to deal with their fear if the adults who should know better do not recognise when a child is frightened?

Fortunately some stories do end happily. I had said to Peter that when he felt ready to return to school I would go with him. I played no part in how Peter's parents dealt with what Peter finally felt able to tell them but it seemed that they recognised their responsibility in the matter. Early one morning Peter's phone call woke me from a deep slumber. I had been to a very enjoyable party the night before. When later that morning Peter and I approached the school gates one of us was white-faced and trembling. It wasn't Peter. It was me.

CHAPTER 8

The Effects of Domestic Violence on Children: Trauma, resilience and breaking the cycle of violence

ARLENE VETERE AND JAN COOPER

Any act or omission committed within the framework of the family, by one of its members that undermines the life, the bodily or psychological integrity, or the liberty of another member of the same family, or that seriously harms the development of his or her personality.

(Definition of physical violence in the family)[1]

Children are at greatest risk of harm in their own homes, either at the hands of their parents and carers, or through the effects of knowing about, overhearing and watching other family members behave violently. Moffitt and Caspi[2] in their review of the effects of domestic violence on children, estimate that children who witness domestic assault are four to nine times at greater risk of being physically assaulted themselves. Further, they go on to estimate that over two-thirds of domestic assaults are witnessed by children. In our practice, we assume that the children always know.[3] Children do not believe that their mothers walk into doors.

The British Crime Survey[4][5] estimates that one-third of reported violent crime is domestic assault. Gender differences are reported in the frequency and severity of domestic assaults, with 90 per cent of women reporting attacks from their male partners, and 48 per cent of men reporting attacks from their female partners. Given that the man knows the effects of his violent actions will be greater, this changes the analysis and assessment of the intent of male violence. Browne and Herbert[6] point out that women are at increased risk of physical assault from their male partner during pregnancy and, during the process of separation and divorce, at times of contact handover for their children. Writing in the USA, Straus and Gelles,[7] estimate that one in three women will be physically assaulted by their male partner over the course of their relationship. As therapists, we would note that most researchers do not enquire about the duration of a physical assault, nor about behaviours such as pushing and shoving, and their short- and long-terms effects on well-being. All researchers estimate that under-reporting is a problem in their data collection procedures.

More research attention has been paid to men's assaults on their women partners. Recently however, Renzetti[8] and Lie et al.[9] estimate similar high levels of victimisation in their samples of lesbian women, with about half of the women reporting sexual, physical and verbal abuse from their intimate partner. Given that we are all socialised within dominant discourses of patriarchy and entitlement, we need to explain why some men and some women behave abusively to their intimate partners, and many more do not. One conclusion might be that there is some felt experience in couple and family intimacy that may play a role in generating abusive behaviour.

It has been estimated[10] that in the UK approximately 34,000 children spend some time in women's refuges each year. Rennison and Welchans[11] have estimated that 40 per cent of households where domestic abuse occurs, contain children under the age of 12 years. The figures for the British Crime Survey map the extent of the problem for women, men and the children for whom they are responsible. This chapter addresses the problem of domestic violence for children, and examines the extent to which children's services can be expected to respond alone. In the UK, children's services have paid less attention to developing policy and services directed at understanding and ameliorating children's distress, despite the amendment to the Children Act[12] to include witnessing domestic violence as a child protection concern. In our view, the problem is too big for any one service on its own.

Trauma and its effects

> People are more likely to be killed, physically assaulted, hit, beaten up, slapped or spanked in their own homes by other family members, than anywhere else, or by anyone else, in our society.[13]

Osofsky[14] defines trauma in children as an 'exceptional experience of powerful and dangerous stimuli that overwhelm the child's capacity to regulate emotions'. Domestic violence as trauma can be a discrete event, it can be continuous and it can be transgenerational.

When children live with parents and carers who are frightened and/or frightening, in households where coercion, intimidation and fear are used to control others and get one's own way, when children watch the people they love assault and hurt other people they love, their anxieties are raised and they are not safe.

In this chapter we shall consider the effects of aggression on children's adaptation to their emotional and relational context, in terms of their physiological, cognitive and emotional development, and the development of attachment systems in the family. Attachment behaviour in family groups is thought to be a developmental process of social regulation of emotion and behaviour. For example, if a child gets too excited, a parent calms them down. Thus when parents and carers are frightened or frightening, or both, they may find it harder to be mindful of their children, they may be volatile or inconsistent in their caring responses, and the child's signals of distress and fear might go unnoticed. If the child cannot trust reassuring communication from a parent because the parent is not safe, it puts the child in a terrible double bind. In attachment terms, children are biologically impelled to seek comfort and security, yet they find they cannot trust it.[15] Living constantly in such a paradox might restrict a child's ability to explore and play, to regulate their own emotional arousal, and to learn constructive ways of resolving conflict. This lack of mental safety may be expressed as constant moving about. The child learns 'to dodge' and cannot stay still for long. It is no surprise to us that some researchers have suggested that the occurrence of domestic violence is associated with environmental suppression of IQ in young children.[16]

The development of reflective functioning in a child is likely to be harder in an atmosphere of family violence, when they struggle to contemplate others' ill intentions towards their family members and towards them.[17] Much of what socialises young children often takes place in a family context, where adults filter wider cultural messages about childhood, family life, gender expectations, and so on. Young children have not yet developed a basis for comparison, and adapt to their family environment as best they can. However, some children may be protected from the traumatic effects of witnessing violence by the development of secure attachments, which helps them understand the representational nature of mental states and think about what lies behind others' actions. This could be protective for older children especially, whose developmental abilities will enable them to think in a prepositional or 'as if' manner. Conversely, children who develop insecure or disorganised attachments in homes where violence is witnessed have been found to be at higher risk of a diagnosis of conduct disorder later in childhood, for relationship problems, for depression, and for school readiness.[18 19]

Resilience can be fostered within a secure attachment with someone outside the violent household, if security is not to be found at home, or within the immediate family. The securely attached child is helped to think about thinking. This has a protective function in the face of frightening events and people. The child can think about intentions and motives that may lie behind others' actions in an empathic way.[20] This could serve to reduce the catastrophic nature of witnessing, or being caught up in a parent's or carer's violence, and paves the way for a child to engage in positive relationships within social institutions outside the family, such as school. School life, and later on, employment, can offer social experiences of belonging and the development of a sense of personal competence. It is our view that we need to continue to raise awareness of the effects of domestic violence on children. In terms of prioritising prevention and early intervention, we still have a long way to go.

Osofsky[21] in her review of the effects of family-wide violence on children, concludes that children show the same signs of distress when they are exposed to violence as when they are physically abused. The effects of domestic violence on children are well documented. Young children can experience sleep difficulties, show emotional distress (such as crying, withdrawal, irritability and difficulty settling), appear to 'lose' learned skills, and develop new fears. Older children can experience sleep problems, act in a more 'clinging' way as if they were a younger child, complain of stomach or headaches, show a decline in their school performance, with attention and concentration problems, and act in aggressive ways. Adolescents can engage in risk-taking behaviours, report sleeping difficulties, sadness and depression and mood swings, report conflict at home, and show a decline in school performance, with attention and concentration problems. Any gender differences in children's responses might show in girls tending to develop more internalising problems, and boys tending to develop more externalising problems. Thus younger children are more likely to 'lose' skills, such as toileting and the use of language, whereas older children may be more likely not to show their feelings about anything, such as an apparent lack of emotion sometimes described in teenagers. The major defence a child may use is not to want to talk about it!

Patience and persistence is sometimes needed to understand children's responses in a culturally attuned way. The psychological and social effects of a child's exposure to family violence can be masked and may depend on a range of mediating and interacting factors, such as:

a) the characteristics of the violence (a single event or chronic violence, which can have the worst effects, and where the post-traumatic effects model as analogy breaks down, as the violence is continuous);

b) the developmental phase of the child and other resources and supports available to the child as a result of their age;

c) the child's proximity to the violence;

d) the child's familiarity with the victim and perpetrator (in our work we have noticed that when the child has a more meaningful relationship with the man who hurts their mother, the effects on the child can be more harmful);

e) the availability of family and community support; and

f) the responses to violence exposure by the family, the school and wider community groups, including mental health services for children and families.

These factors need to be made visible in our assessments of the behaviour of troubled children in their immediate social and familial contexts. They show why the effects on children of domestic violence are so devastating. Service providers need to consider the implications of risks and protective factors when planning and delivering mental health services to children and their families.

Therapeutic responses

Screening for the effects of domestic violence is not routine within Children and Adolescent Mental Health Services (CAMHS) in the UK. Thus we have no way of knowing how many of these children come into the CAMHS service and how many therapeutic interventions are designed to help reduce children's distress. No distinct treatment approaches have been developed within the UK for these children, other than the more open-ended approaches advocated by Hague et al.[22] The open-ended approaches grew out of the refuge movement and refuge workers' attempts to help children by encouraging them to talk about their experiences at opportune moments. Such an approach, whilst worthwhile, could not be expected to lead to a more structured look at children's needs and specific ways to help. The North American approach to helping children who witness violence has been based around group work, that attempts to: (a) challenge children's views about domestic violence; (b) encourage them to talk about their experiences; (c) support the development of a range of coping responses; and (d) to help them with safety planning. Although there is little empirical support for the effectiveness of these approaches, much of the work done by the children's charities in the UK is group based.

Safety

Our most important response as practitioners is to prioritise safety in our work with children and their families. Our first task is to help the child feel safe. This can be achieved in a number of ways. We can help the child and their carers to return to normal routines as soon as possible, after a traumatic event. The pacing and timing of interventions is important. We can support relationships and help strengthen new relationships, for example, in post-adoption consultation work, where the adopted child has come from a family of origin context of domestic assault, helping the new family settle down into its routines. The intensity of a one-to-one therapeutic relationship may be too threatening for a traumatised child at this time.

If however we suspect a child might be living in a context of domestic abuse, Hester et al.[23] suggest we can ask questions about who gets angry in the home, about what happens when people disagree, whether the child has ever seen anyone hurting anyone else, what makes them worried, frightened or unhappy? If the child is willing to talk with us, we can ask more detailed questions about the most recent episode of violence, whether weapons were used, whether anyone was prevented from leaving the house, whether the police have ever come to the house, what does the child do at these times, and where were their siblings at the time? When developing a personal safety plan with a child, it needs to offer support that is consistent with the child's cultural needs, and reflects their age and understanding. Identify a safe place for the child to go to if there is repeat violence; make sure there is someone they can go to if necessary; make sure they know how to contact emergency services; and be clear with them that it is neither safe nor their responsibility to intervene directly to protect their mothers.[23]

Cultural attunement

Knowing *how* to talk to young children and their parents affected by exposure to family violence, even though we may not always know the answers, is important. Patience and cultural attunement is needed to understand children's responses and to help people cope.

We work in a part of the UK that has an ethnically diverse community, with people more settled and more recently migrated. We are concerned that children from some ethnic minority groups may be receiving a different quality of professional care than other children. Our observation fits with patterns observed by others that secondary and tertiary referral services are more used by majority ethnic children.[24] After all, the expression of psychosocial problems and patterns of healthcare usage for children are likely to be affected by complex interactions between family, social structures, beliefs and available healthcare provision. In addition, the lack of a common language, despite the use of translators, may make it much harder to communicate and express concerns about well-being, both for parents and carers and the children themselves. We might predict that these issues are more formidable for younger children than adults, because of their reliance on adults to access services for them. Children born in the UK of parents born elsewhere have experience within two cultural and language systems, which may act as a resource for communication. However, if family communication is disrupted as a result of the effects of violent behaviour this may further serve to create barriers between the child and their parents/carers, the family and service providers and between children and other concerned adults, such as teachers.[25]

In practice, we have approached these dilemmas around children and their families in a number of ways. Routinely we include discussion of cultural and religious issues in our work and in our notes. We make efforts where we can to include and involve extended family members, including older siblings, in our assessments and sometimes in our therapeutic work. Where possible, we help family members choose their own translators, because of the repercussions within small communities of having translators who 'know' the family. Finally, we seek regular consultation from professional members of the same cultural and religious communities. These consultations are a means of both staying aware and thinking creatively around the various ways different people approach some common dilemmas of living with, and raising children in contexts of family violence.

Children's coping responses

> It matters a great deal to children that they can tell their story at their own pace and voice their fears.[26]

Audrey Mullender and her colleagues[26] make a strong plea for including children's voices in the development of child care policy and practice around domestic violence, arguing that the marginalisation of children as a source of information about their own lives hampers the development of relevant professional practices. Their research with nearly 1400 ethnically diverse junior and secondary school children in England challenges whether adults always make the right assumptions and decisions around children's needs in situations of domestic violence. In particular, two issues emerged from their research conversations with children and young people that had an important bearing on children's ability to cope, namely, being listened to and having their views taken seriously, and being actively involved in making decisions and helping to find solutions. This finding highlights in a striking fashion, the importance of children's agency in relation to decisions taken for them and the people they love. In Mullender et al.'s study, the children seemed most impressed by those professionals who knew about domestic violence and were prepared to do something constructive in response to it. In particular they expressed a desire to be helped by people who had 'gone through it'.

Mullender et al.[26] noted that children's coping strategies seemed to divide into immediate adaptation and longer-term coping and adjustment. Immediate coping included seeking safety and help, use of distraction and strategies for blocking out what was happening, supporting and being supported by brothers and sisters, and trying to protect their mothers. Mullender et al.[26] grouped the reported longer-term coping strategies into outward looking and inward looking. Outward looking coping was active and problem focused, and involved talking to others, such as friends, extended family and community figures, having a safe and quiet place to go, calling the police, supporting family members, and being involved in finding solutions. In our view, this is an awesome list of decision-making responsibilities that many children regularly take. Inward looking strategies were emotion focused, and included crying, emotional withdrawal, watchfulness, and hiding their emotions.

How can we help? When children talk to us, they need to know our anxieties are both contained and containable. Osofsky[21] recommends that our therapeutic responses are developmentally attuned to the needs of children. For example, young children need reassurance, protection, simple answers to questions, and understanding for 'clingy' behaviour. Older children need realistic answers to questions, help with maintaining their routines and structured, non-demanding tasks, and gentle, firm limits for their behaviour. Adolescents need factual answers, discussion opportunities, help with linking thoughts to feelings, encouragement to take up community-based activities, and some involvement in emergency issues and decision making. Families need practical and/or faith-based support, help in resuming their routines, and therapeutic help with longer-term adjustment problems.

Such a list, whilst admirable, presents a daunting challenge for UK-based public and voluntary agencies to work in partnership, across the lifespan needs of children and parents.

Parental trauma

We may question to what extent children's services unwittingly overlook how and whether children's mothers and fathers may be traumatised, either by the effects of chronic domestic assault, or by a legacy from their own childhoods. If parents themselves are traumatised, they may struggle to listen and respond to their children because it re-evokes their own traumatic experiences. Onyskiw and Hayduk[27] review research that explores how parenting can become disrupted and/or diminished as a result of men's violence to women in families with children. Jouriles and Norwood[28] suggest that effects on parenting can include less time to listen to children, emotional withdrawal from children, and coercive and harsh discipline practices. These findings emphasise how children can be affected even when they are not present.

Families need us to put safety first in our assessment and management of risks of further violence.[29] Our task is to help perpetrators of violence acknowledge responsibility for their behaviour, for their family members' right to live in safety and without fear of them, and to help victims of violence take steps to prioritise their own safety. When working with intergenerational violence and family trauma, we can join with parents and carers in the places where things go well, supporting family strengths and relationships, whilst acknowledging the awfulness and distress. Families need pragmatic and community support, support and encouragement to maintain routines, and help with long-term adjustment problems.

Parents and carers need to trust the information we give them. This points to the need to collaborate with other disciplines and other agencies, in a coordinated community response to the problems of domestic violence for adults and children. In Child and Adolescent Mental Health settings, a child-focused approach may well miss the effects of trauma on the parent/s. We can support parents and others in listening to children, and our multidisciplinary colleagues can create a context of support for us in this difficult work. We all value talking and listening. For some children living in a context of domestic violence, most support may be offered through their schools. As community practitioners we can help raise awareness of the effects of domestic violence on children and help parents and caregivers pay attention to the effects on children in developmentally appropriate ways. As child and family mental health practitioners, we bring an understanding of people's sensitivities, of how people communicate, how things can go wrong in family relationships, and the development of resilience, which may be helpful to other professionals who come into contact with children who witness domestic assault.

In our practice as therapy supervisors, we need to be more proactive, directive, flexible and visible than we might ordinarily be, in response to the complexity and difficult emotional demands made on the supervisee when working with violence in family systems.[30]

An example of therapeutic work

In our therapeutic work with children who have been exposed to violent behaviour at home, we have two major challenges: (a) to help them cope with their overwhelming thoughts, feelings and anxieties; and (b) to help them and their families resume daily routines and activities that help and support their psychosocial development. As practitioners, we try to develop our relationships with the child and their household and extended family members in a way that promotes advocacy and safety, as well as using our relationships within the professional networks to develop collaboration and trust. Once we can be assured a child is safe, we may undertake therapeutic work to help children resolve any traumatic responses, and to adapt to loss and transition. In our experience helping children with their feelings of shame and self-blame are paramount.

Therapeutic work presents us with a number of challenges: (a) to involve the children as co-participants in the work so their voices are heard, and their contributions are recognised, by us, and others; (b) to help children use their imagination and playfulness constructively in the face of serious problems; and (c) to promote positive coping while dealing with upsetting and frightening situations. Children are engaged in therapeutic work by being listened to and taken seriously, while trying to get to know them, apart from their problems. A golden thread that runs through all our work with children involves discovering their abilities and preferences, and using these abilities as resources in solving problems. We can ask children what they have got going for them that will help in thinking about the present difficulties.

We try to find out what the child has been told about coming to see us, and what they understand about this first meeting. With younger children in child care proceedings, we make sure the child knows who is looking after them. With older children and adolescents we offer an opportunity to talk separately with us, and always look for appropriate opportunities to talk to younger children on their own, and with siblings. We are keen to draw on existing community resources and social support networks that children themselves find supportive. We have adapted some of the narrative therapy practices to the particular circumstances of children who experience domestic violence. For example, when thinking about how the child develops resilience and copes and adjusts, we help identify appropriate audiences, both real and imaginary, for the circulation of information about the child's knowledge and hard-won competence. We develop other ways of letting people know about children's dilemmas and abilities, that might involve letter writing, scrapbooks, art work, certificates, and so on. Finally we take action, along with the child and concerned others, to further develop and support the child's 'communities of concern', such as children's clubs, sports clubs, extended families, school staff, project work, and so on.[31]

The following vignette, illustrates some of the issues outlined above.

Vignette

In this example, we describe the Green family and focus on how we understood the family context both in the present and in the past. We paid attention to time—chronological time, individual time and family time— in an effort to understand the 'why now' question. The parents' question to us was 'How is it that our son who has always been easy to raise and of whom we are very proud, can treat us in this dreadful way?'

Mr and Mrs Green adopted Jim and Eve when the children were 3 and 5 years old. They had been taken into the 'looked after' system over a year earlier and had lived with a short-term foster mother for four months and long-term foster parents for eight months. They were placed with Mr and Mrs Green for three months before the adoption was approved. Jim and Eve had come into the looked after system because of extreme neglect, and violence by the birth father to the birth mother, her family and to the children. The trigger for the violence had most often been alcohol abuse. The children therefore, had suffered neglect and been victims of domestic violence and witnesses of violence to their mother and her extended family. The birth mother had found it very hard to relinquish the children for adoption and when the adoption was finally approved, Mr and Mrs Green had been through a long, demanding and tense court experience. Letterbox contact was arranged. There was a Green family story about how they had fought for Jim and Eve.

Mr and Mrs Green did not seek any extra post-adoption support because they saw themselves as self-sufficient and resilient. They were active members of a very supportive church group. They needed these qualities of resilience when they found Eve very difficult to settle and struggled to make her part of their family. Her behaviour was erratic, as she swung from attentive and cooperative, to kicking, hitting and punching her adoptive parents and her brother. They had to supervise her playtime with other children because her behaviour was so unpredictable. They reflected on how different the emotional development of Eve and Jim appeared to be. They would never underestimate the commitment and hard work that adoption requires but they both agreed that Jim seemed so much easier, tolerant and cooperative and because of that he made them feel like good parents.

Now Jim is 15 and Eve is 17 years old. There has been a recent family crisis. After many years with the same firm Mr Green was declared redundant. He diligently tried to find another job without success but as a consequence they had to sell their home and move to a much smaller house. Both Jim and Eve stayed at their schools but had long bus journeys. Mrs Green increased her working hours but her income was not enough to allow them to live with the same comfort. Mr Green continued to look for work and did part-time work and voluntary work at the church. The effect on the family was considerable although they all worked at adapting to their changed circumstances. Mr and Mrs Green met the challenge with their self-sufficiency and resilience, trying to make the best of what they had and encouraging Jim and Eve to do the same.

They were referred to us through the school as teachers were worried about Jim. His school work was falling behind and he was fighting with other young people during break times. This was uncharacteristic behaviour for him. The school's complaint startled Mr and Mrs Green into seeking help because they were also experiencing increasing levels of violent behaviour from Jim at home. Jim seemed overwhelmed by anger and hit out at the slightest provocation. Mr and Mrs Green thought his behaviour might be because of his age but their real fear was that of 'bad blood' and that Jim would grow up to be like his father who, the social work notes had said, 'terrorised' his family and his wife's family.

We offered therapeutic sessions to the family. Most often it was Mrs Green and Jim who came. Eve distanced herself from the problems, and in her mother's words, 'buried her head' in her other interests. It seemed Mr Green felt responsible and shamed and we could not really engage him, no matter how hard we tried. During the time we were seeing them Mr Green was re-employed. For him, this meant travelling considerable distances and so from time to time we would telephone him and from time to time he would attend meetings. By talking to us with Jim, Mrs Green could provide safety for Eve and we established a home no-violence contract and a school no-violence contract. We also sometimes saw Jim on his own. We referred him to a peer anger management group and liaised with his school. We tried to be flexible and cooperative and to acknowledge the beliefs and meanings about the importance of the family's self-sufficiency. We also worried about their missed appointments and how long we could keep our service open to them under these circumstances.

In talking to Jim and his mother a number of issues were discussed. Jim felt his behaviour was intolerable at home and at school. He felt guilty about his behaviour because it was making his parents even more worried. He had been proud that he had been the 'good boy' for a number of years and now he felt completely unacceptable. We asked about his memories of his birth father's violent behaviour. He was straightforward about his own anxiety that he was genetically linked to his father and like his father had a fatal flaw to his character. He also explored with us and his adoptive mother his fierce anger about the unfair treatment his adoptive father had received from his employers. This developed into a conversation about how this sense of unfairness linked with his own intense sense of fear and inability to protect those he loved when a little boy. He found our explanations and our insistence that he had the ability and the right to choose how he behaved, helpful. He also started seeing his response to the family crisis as unacceptable but understandable alongside the other responses that his family had experienced. In some ways Jim's extreme anger echoed all their angry feelings about what had happened to them.

Mrs Green acknowledged that she had been struggling with feelings of depression since her husband was made redundant. She shared many of the feelings of unfairness and outrage that Jim experienced. Mr and Mrs Green said they covered their feelings by a determination to get on with life. They had not wanted to talk or make themselves vulnerable to each other and their children by acknowledging their distress, sadness and fatigue. We thought that just at this moment their approach to resilience had got in their way and prevented them from being more nurturing, comforting and creative. We hypothesised that for Jim and Eve this unexpected house move reminded them of their foster carer moves.

Mrs Green and Jim sometimes brought messages back to us from Mr Green and Eve and so we felt we were communicating with them all at some level. The work stretched over a year in a rather fragmented way. However, a point of good enough stability was reached and we agreed to two sessions in the bank to be used at any time. We did not have any further contact with them. We often wondered how we could have done it better so it was a more coherent piece of work for them. However, we learnt such a lot from this family. They found systemic ideas useful to them in their thinking around the complexity of the crisis, and in particular, our three-generational focus. In addition, we were prompted to think further about the power of genetic 'bad blood' beliefs and domestic violence, and how these beliefs may lie dormant for many years and be held in different ways by different family members. (Names and details have been changed and permission for publication received from the family.)

Conclusion

Clearly the early years matter and early intervention matters. Children and young people need consistency, warmth and personal safety in their relationships with their caregivers. Both positive and negative experiences shape the development of children, so our task is to raise the awareness of caregivers and responders to the importance of prevention and early intervention when violence in the home is known, or suspected. Similarly, we need to try to influence the legal system of decision making, using our awareness of children's needs and the systemic implications of violent relationships, in how we write our reports and talk to judges. In planning and offering our services, we need to balance risk and protective factors, support mother and father figures in listening to their children, and support each other in our commitment to listen to what children have to say. This is the task that faces children's services and adult services: to offer help to families; help for the parents together with help for their children, using collaborative practices across agency boundaries.

So, as child and family practitioners, when we see in children a mixed picture of somatic symptoms, childhood depression, lack of interest in activities or a high activity level, numbing and inability to comfort self, repetitive play, and sleep difficulties and behaviour changes, we need to consider whether domestic violence may be the cause. Violence in intimate relationships is not a problem that requires a short-term solution. It needs a sustained community response dedicated to understanding the effects of transgenerational trauma, continuous trauma, and immediate trauma on children and their families—often endured in silence.

Endnotes

1. Council of Europe (1986). *Violence in the Family.* Strasbourg: Recommendation No R(85)4 adopted by the Committee of Ministers of the Council of Europe on 26th March 1985 and Explanatory Memorandum.

2. Moffitt, T. and Caspi, A. (1998). Annotation: Implications of violence between intimate partners for child psychologists and psychiatrists. *Journal of Child Psychology and Psychiatry, 39,* 137–44.

3. Vetere, A. and Cooper, J. (2003). Setting up a domestic violence service. *Child and Adolescent Mental Health, 8,* 61–7.

4. British Crime Survey (1996). *Home Office Statistical Bulletin,* Issue 19/96. Croydon: Home Office.

5. British Crime Survey (2000). *Home Office Statistical Bulletin,* Issue 18/00. Croydon: Home Office.

6. Browne, K. and Herbert, M. (1997). *Preventing Family Violence.* Chichester: Wiley.

7. Straus, M.A. and Gelles, R.J. (1990). *Physical Violence in American Families: Risk factors and adaptations to violence in 8,145 families.* New Brunswick, NJ: Transaction Publishers.

8. Renzetti, C.M. (1992). *Violent Betrayal: Partner abuse in lesbian relationships.* Newbury Park, CA: Sage.

9. Lie, G.Y., Schilit, R., Bush, J., Montague, M. and Reyes, L. (1991). Lesbians in currently aggressive relationships: How frequently do they report aggressive past relationships? *Violence and Victims, 6,* 121–35.

10. Shankleman, J., Brooks, R. and Webb, E. (2000). Children resident in domestic violence refuges in Cardiff: A health needs and health care needs assessment.

11. Rennison, C.M. and Welchans, S. (2000). *Intimate Partner Violence: Bureau of Justice Statistics Special Report.* Washington, DC: US Department of Justice.

12. Department of Health (1997). Local Authority Circular LAAC (97)15 *Family Law Act 1996 Part IV Family homes and domestic violence.* London: DoH.

13. Gelles, R. and Cornell, C. (1990). *Intimate Violence in Families.* Newbury Park, CA: Sage.

14. Osofsky, J.D. (ed) (1997). *Children in a Violent Society.* New York: Guilford Press.

15. Bowlby, J. (1984). Violence in the family as a disorder of attachment and caregiving systems. *American Journal of Psychoanalysis, 44,* 1, 9–27.

16. Koenen, K.C., Moffitt, T.E., Caspi, A., Taylor, A. and Purcell, S. (2003). Domestic violence is associated with environmental suppression of IQ in young children. *Developmental Psychopathology, 15,* 297–311.

17. Fonagy, P. (1999). The male perpetrator: The role of trauma and failures of mentalisation in aggression against women—an attachment theory perspective. The 6th John Bowlby Memorial Lecture, The Centre for Attachment-based Psychoanalytic Psychotherapy, 20th February, London.

18. Crittenden, P.M. and Ainsworth, M.D. (1989). Attachment and child abuse. In D. Cicchetti and V. Carlson (eds) *Child Maltreatment: Theory and research in the causes of child abuse and neglect.* New York: Cambridge University Press.

19. Fonagy, P., Target, M., Steele, M. and Steele, H. (1997). The development of violence and crime as it relates to security of attachment. In J.D. Osofsky (ed) *Children in a Violent Society* (pp. 150–77). New York: Guilford Press.

20. Fonagy, P. and Target, M. (1997). Attachment and reflective function: Their role in self-organization. *Development and Psychopathology, 9,* 679–700.

21. Osofsky, J.D. (1998). Children as invisible victims of domestic and community violence. In G.W. Holden, R. Geffner and E.N. Jouriles (eds) *Children Exposed to Marital Violence: Theory, research and intervention* (pp. 95–120). Washington, DC: American Psychological Association.

22. Hague, G., Mullender, A., Kelly, L., Malos, E. and Debbonaire, T. (2000). Unsung innovation: The history of work with children in UK domestic violence refuges. In J. Hanmer and C. Itzin (eds) *Home Truths about Domestic Violence.* London: Routledge.

23. Hester, M., Pearson, C. and Harwin, N. (2000). *Making an Impact: Children and domestic violence.* London: Jessica Kingsley.

24. Madhok, R., Hameed, A. and Bhopal, R. (1998). Satisfaction with health services among the Pakistani population in Middlesbrough, England. *Journal of Public Health Medicine, 20,* 295–301.

25. Minnis, H., Kelly, E., Bradby, H., Oglethorpe, R., Raine, W. and Cockburn, D. (2003). Cultural and language mismatch: Clinical complications. *Clinical Child Psychology and Psychiatry, 8,* 2, 179–86.

26. Mullender, A., Hague, G., Imam, U., Kelly, L., Malos, E. and Regan, L. (2002). *Children's Perspectives on Domestic Violence* (p. 214). London: Sage.

27. Onyskiw, J. and Hayduk, L. (2001). Process underlying children's adjustment in families characterised by physical aggression. *Interdisciplinary Journal of Applied Family Relations, 50,* 376–85.

28. Jouriles, E. and Norwood, W. (1995). Physical aggression towards boys and girls in families characterised by the battering of women. *Journal of Family Psychology, 9,* 69–78.

29. Vetere, A. and Cooper, J. (2001). Working systemically with family violence: Risk, responsibility and collaboration. *Journal of Family Therapy, 23,* 4, 378–96.

30. Sand-Pringle, C., Zarski, J.J. and Wendling, K.E. (1995). Swords into plowshares: Supervisory issues with violent families. *Journal of Systemic Therapies, 14,* 3, 34–46.

31. Freeman, J., Epston, D. and Lobovits, D. (1997). *Playful Approaches to Serious Problems: Narrative therapy with children and their families.* New York: Norton.

CHAPTER 9

Cybernetic Children:
How technologies change and
constrain the developing mind

GRACE E. JACKSON MD

Cybernetics
• from Greek: kybernetes helmsman (kybernan: to steer, govern)
• the science dealing with the comparative study of human control systems such as the brain and nervous system, and complex electronic systems

The subject of this chapter is the science of *cybernetics as it applies to children.* Two themes emerge: (1) new technologies are changing the human brain in ways that make children increasingly vulnerable to, and dependent upon, electronic systems; (2) pharmacological interventions (illustrated by the stimulant therapies given for so-called Attention Deficit Hyperactivity Disorder (ADHD)) are a destructive response to these developments. The outcome of both forces is the increasing construction of cybernetic (*electro-chemically* controlled) childhoods, and the destruction of children.

The *construction of childhood* is, for wealthy nations, in the context of television, video games, the Internet, text messages, mobile phones and computers. The *destruction of children* in these wealthy nations increasingly occurs through the prescription of psychiatric medications, specifically stimulants.

Today's children

In his book *Open Sky,* Paul Virilio[1] outlines three discrete phases in history. The First Interval, illustrated by the transportation revolution of the nineteenth century, represents the interval of space where the journey (geographic expanse) was conquered. The Second Interval, signified by the Transmission Revolution, has resulted in the abolition of time. In other words, television and radio have enabled simultaneous *reception*. In the Third Interval, signified by light speed and fiberoptic transmission (the world of the Internet), there exists only the world of the instantaneous. Virilio argues that technology has changed what it means to be human. He views mankind as evolving from active traveller to passive recipient of electromagnetic signals. On a social and cultural scale, he worries that new technologies have led increasingly to a distorted form of interactivity, whereby people have become so engaged with online pseudo-realities that they have lost touch with the realities around them.

Dromospheric pollution and the developing brain

Dromology is the study of speed (from dromos = race, running):

> Alongside air pollution, water pollution, and the like, there exists an unnoticed phenomenon of pollution of the world's dimensions that I propose to call dromospheric.[2]

Evidence that the dromosphere may be changing our children comes from three recent investigations.

Researchers at the University of Washington's department of pediatrics studied the impact of television exposure in early childhood.[3] The study design involved interviews with children (average age 7) in three different survey waves: 1996, 1998, and 2000. The main outcome measure used was the score each child received on a subscale of the Behavioral Problems Index. This score was then correlated with average hours of TV viewing, based upon interviews with the children's mothers that had been recorded in a separate database many years before.

Even after controlling for the influence of prenatal substance use, gestational age, maternal psychopathology, and socioeconomic status, the research found a strong association between early TV exposure and the development of attentional problems by early childhood: 10 percent increased risk of attentional decrements for every hour of television watched at age 1 or 3.[4] The investigators concluded that their findings were consistent with the recommendations of the American Academy of Pediatrics (urging caution in TV exposure for children under two) and with the findings of other researchers whose studies had confirmed links between television, reduced reading ability, and poor attention spans.

A second study, at the University of Rochester,[5] explored the impact of different types of video games upon four tests of selective visual attention. The study compared the performance of experienced video game players with non-players. A separate experiment involved training the non-video game players and re-testing for signs of improvement. In the first test, subjects were exposed to target symbols and distracting flankers (called a flanker compatibility effect). This test was designed to assess the capacity to ignore detractors on a target task. As the performance task increased in difficulty, experienced video game players were found to have much greater capacity to avoid irrelevant processing (i.e. able to remain on-task longer). In the second test, called an enumeration task, subjects were asked to identify the number of squares (1–10) that were presented in briefly flashed displays. Video game players remained highly accurate in their ability to track higher numbers of items at the same time (about 30 percent more items than non-video game players.) In the third test, subjects were expected to identify a localized target against a cluttered background. Video game players performed about 50 percent better than non-players on the task, which examined the processing of visual information over space. In the fourth test, subjects were presented with a list of letters flashed quickly one after another in the middle of the screen. On each trial, the subjects knew that all letters would be black except for one letter. Their task required the identification of the one white letter. They were also required to say whether or not the letter X had been presented (it was shown in only 50 percent of the trials). Findings revealed that the detection of the letter X depended upon how closely it was related to the appearance of the white letter. If X was flashed within several hundred milliseconds of the white letter, it was missed. Action game players outperformed non-video game players on this task, suggesting an increased ability to process visual information over time: increased task switching, decreased 'attentional blink'.

The investigators concluded that action video games (but not non-action games, such as Tetris) improve several elements of selective visual attention. They then performed a fifth experiment which exposed non-video game players to training (action vs. non-action video game, 1 hour per day for 10 days). All participants improved their scores on the video games on which they had trained. Action game training led to greater improvement on tasks of selective visual attention, spatial distribution, and temporal resolution. When interviewed about the possible implications of their research, the investigators conceded that video games probably 'do *not* cultivate the sustained attention needed for tasks such as reading,' (italics added) but they were optimistic that action games might be used for rehabilitating visually impaired patients (e.g. stroke victims) or for training military personnel.[6] *The possibility that action video games might over-stimulate attentional or visual systems in some age groups was not addressed* (emphasis added).

Researchers in London[7] investigated the effects of video game playing upon dopamine release in the brain. PET (positron emission tomography) scans were given to eight male volunteers during the first 50 minutes (learning phase) of a new video game. The game involved navigating a tank through a battlefield to collect flags and destroy enemy tanks, with higher scores leading to monetary reward. During a second PET scan, subjects stared at a blank screen. Changes in the binding of a radiolabelled ligand (raclopride, a drug which binds selectively to the D2 receptor) were used to infer differences in dopamine release in the striatum of the brain. The experiment revealed significant increases (at least twofold) in extra-cellular dopamine during video game playing, similar to that seen with intravenous injections of amphetamine or methylphenidate. Results appeared to validate the findings of electrophysiological studies in animals, suggesting a link between dopamine neurotransmission and sensorimotor functions related to reward, aversive conditioning, and stressful stimuli.

Dromospheric addiction

The possibility that new technologies might feed addictive patterns of behavior has become a topic of concern for several investigators.[8-11] In 1996, a psychologist at the University of Pittsburgh proposed a modification of the *DSM* (*Diagnostic and Statistical Manual of Mental Disorders*) criteria for pathological gambling and substance dependence to create a measure of Internet addiction. More recently, she has developed an Internet Addiction Rating Scale which—ironically—is available to the public online.[12] Other researchers have conducted studies which demonstrate 'excessive use' of the Internet among individuals with high lifetime rates of so-called psychiatric conditions, including anxiety and eating disorders, alcohol dependence, and manic depression. In one community survey of 169 Internet users, greater use of the Internet was associated with a decline in social involvement and mood.

The call for the inclusion of 'Internet Addiction Disorder' in the psychiatry lexicon has not been unopposed. At least one observer[13] has questioned the premature creation of a new diagnostic entity on the grounds of unclear construct validity. First, it is not at all clear what constitutes 'normal' versus 'excessive' computer use. Second, there are problems associated with the identification of the appropriate object of addiction: is it the computer use itself, or some other object—such as information, companionship, or online purchase—which is compulsively desired? While psychiatric researchers express an interest in identifying the biochemical aspects of compulsive computing, there is little discussion about the motivation which lies behind the behavior. To the extent that researchers focus narrowly upon reward systems and dopamine pathways, they will continue to miss the most important aspect of the phenomenon: the *meaning* which Internet connectivity has come to assume for each individual and for society.

The psychopharmacological destruction of children

New technologies—including television, video games, and the Internet—are changing the brain and changing the nature of human relatedness. Small wonder, then, that children have become increasingly prone to shorter attention spans, increased impulsivity, and hyperkinesis—features which are now understood in terms of the conditioning of dopamine pathways in key centers of the brain. To put it briefly, the dromospheric pollution is creating children who are addicted to novel stimuli, multitasking, and speed. What is most concerning, however, is the method which industrialized societies have adopted for dealing with the changed nature of childhood. Consider the following letter to the Editor which appeared in a 1971 issue of *Pediatrics*:

> I receive one or two calls a week about the first or second grade boy who is not sitting still in school, who is disturbing the other children, and whose parent or teacher or guidance counselor feels that my putting him on methylphenidate hydrochloride (Ritalin) or dextroamphetamine (Dexedrine) would be of value.
>
> Recently a mother called me with this typical case history. I explained to her ... I had detected no neurological abnormalities. I also pointed out that nothing in his prenatal or subsequent course had indicated neuro-logical impairment ... Further discussion centered around the fact that his hyperactivity would probably get better when he was around 9 or 10 years old, and it was worth waiting. It was also pointed out that, really, the long range effects of medication to make boys sit still are not well known.
>
> The boy's mother ended the conversation with a most heartwarming statement: 'In other words, Doctor, what you're telling me is that Ritalin wouldn't make my boy any better but would make the school better.'[14]

Such a letter would be unlikely to make it past peer review if it were submitted to the same journal today.

Stimulants and adverse events

Despite the precipitous increase in the use of stimulant medications to control childhood conduct, particularly within the United States, scant attention has been paid to the deleterious effects of these drugs. It is typical of the psychiatric literature to refer to stimulant side effects as 'mild, time-limited, and well tolerated'. For some children, this may indeed be true. For other children, however, the drugs have been harmful, even lethal. A closer inspection of both the acute and long-term effects of stimulant drugs suggests a more guarded appraisal of their safety.

In a double-blind, placebo-controlled crossover study,[15] researchers compared the reactions to Ritalin and placebo of 206 children between the ages of 5 and 15. Treatments were rotated on a weekly basis, and side effects were evaluated using the Barkley Side Effect Rating Scale. Overall response to Ritalin was quite poor, with just 62 percent of children demonstrating an improvement in their behaviors. Five side effects increased significantly with Ritalin therapy: appetite disturbance (19 times more likely than placebo); dizziness (8 times more likely than placebo); stomachache (7 times more likely than placebo); headache (5 times more likely than placebo); and insomnia (3 times more likely than placebo).

A study of ambulatory patients seen at the Melbourne Royal Children's Hospital[16] between 1995 and 1996 compared side effects experienced by ADHD diagnosed children (ages 5 to15) in a double-blind crossover trial. Subjects were randomized to Dexedrine (d-amphetamine) or Ritalin (methylphenidate) treatments for two weeks at a time; then, after a 24-hour drug washout period, they were continued for another two weeks on the other drug. Favorable response rates, as assessed by parents, were 69 percent and 72 percent for Dexedrine and Ritalin, respectively. Appetite reduction was a prominent side effect of both drugs. Insomnia was worsened by Dexedrine, but not by Ritalin. The investigators concluded that their results were fairly consistent with the side effects studies conducted by other researchers:

Barkley (1990) 83 children on Ritalin for 7–10 day study, side effects included insomnia, decreased appetite, headache, stomachache on both low and high doses of the drug

Borcherding (1991) 48 children on Ritalin and Dexedrine in crossover study, 83% experienced significant (mild to moderately severe) side effects, including decreased appetite, sleep disturbance, unhappiness

Millichap (1967) reviewed 15 different Randomized Control Trials of stimulants, 15–70% of Ritalin patients experienced adverse effects, 5–100% of Dexedrine patients experienced adverse effects

For many patients, it appears to be true that the somatic effects of stimulant therapy—such as appetite disturbance, headaches, and dizziness—may be mild and short-lived. However, the same cannot be said about endocrine, cognitive, and behavioral effects.

Endocrine effects of stimulants

The negative effects of stimulant drugs upon growth rates have been recognized for years. However, some researchers have inappropriately blamed the patient— suggesting that ADHD itself is the cause of growth retardation in stimulant-treated children. The evidence against this argument is abundant. In a recent study conducted by physicians in Australia,[17] none of the 52 ADHD diagnosed children treated in their practice were 'growth deficient' *until* stimulant therapy was initiated. Animal studies have confirmed the growth-impairing effects of Ritalin (methylphenidate).[18]

If anything, the most recent research has confirmed a far too cavalier attitude among physicians with regards to the growth suppressing effects of stimulant drugs. In the Australian study,[17] researchers found that stimulants were associated with progressive declines in both height and weight in 86 percent of their subjects. The decreases were especially prominent in the first 6 to 18 months of treatment but they did not stop throughout the course of treatment. (One patient, who stopped taking dexamphetamine for six months to see if it was still needed for behavioral reasons, experienced a fairly rapid weight gain of 16 pounds but no catch-up in height for another twelve months.)

Similarly, researchers at Yale University in a study involving 84 ADHD diagnosed children (ages 5–17) followed in two large pediatric practices, compared the growth rates of Ritalin subjects against their own unmedicated siblings.[19] Subjects had to have taken Ritalin for at least two years without interruption. Siblings had to be healthy, born within three years of the patients, and living within the same household. Using height standard deviation scores to compare subjects, the researchers detected significant effects of Ritalin upon mean height and growth velocity: 76 percent of the males and 90 percent of the females experienced significant height suppression after three years of therapy. These effects did not reverse or stabilize at any point during treatment. Growth suppression occurred over a broad range of doses, with boys and girls experiencing an overall height deficit of approximately 3–4 cm (1.2–1.6 inches) over three years.

What is most concerning about these findings is not only the growth suppression, but the fact that neuroscientists and physicians do not yet understand the mechanism which causes it. Many theories have been advanced, but all of them have weaknesses due to inconsistent evidence from clinical and physiological investigations.[20]

At least one research group[21] has detected a possible explanation for stimulant-induced height suppression in the *target* of growth hormone, rather than in the complex endocrine systems (hypothalamus/pituitary/adrenal axis) which control its synthesis and release. Investigators examining the effects of several stimulants (pemoline, methylphenidate, and methamphetamine) upon cartilage discovered that all three drugs inhibited the uptake of sulfate and impaired the formation of glycosaminoglycans. Although these findings have not yet been verified *in vivo* (live humans), they offer an important mechanism through which stimulants may impede the linear growth rates of children. Nevertheless, the possibility still remains that stimulants are disruptive to the regulation of *growth hormone homeostasis*. This has not yet been consistently disproven, and quite a few studies[22] *have* detected associations between stimulants and deficiencies in growth hormone and other growth-related proteins (such as IGF-1 and growth hormone binding protein). To the extent that they disrupt the body's formation of trophic factors or the cellular responses to them, it remains possible that stimulant medications exert an equally disruptive effect upon the *development of the human brain,* as they do upon the developing skeleton.

Cognitive effects

Most discussions of stimulant drugs emphasize their short-term effects upon cognitive functioning. Among the favorable effects noted by researchers and patients are improvements in sustained attention, reaction times, time on task, ability to switch mental sets, academic productivity, impulse control, and certain aspects of learning. Most long-term studies, however, have documented a *waning of drug benefits over time*, either because of tolerance to the effects of the drug, changes in the underlying condition (e.g. natural maturation of the brain, decrease in situational demands, or modification of stressors), or direct toxicities exerted by stimulants upon specific aspects of brain physiology and human performance.

The results of neuroimaging studies may provide an explanation for these long-term changes. In the 1980s, a team of researchers[23] performed computed tomography (CT) scans on twenty-two young males (mean age: 23.2 years) who had been diagnosed with ADHD and treated with stimulants in childhood (mean age at diagnosis: 8.7 years). The results of their head scans were compared to the findings of twenty-seven slightly older males (mean age: 28.7 years) with no history of neuropsychiatric difficulties. Even when compared to these *older* healthy controls, the stimulant-exposed subjects demonstrated significant sulcal* widening (58 percent of the ADHD group vs. 3.8 percent of the controls) and cerebellar atrophy** (25 percent of the ADHD group vs. 3.8 percent of the controls). The investigators concluded that 'more research was needed' to determine if the cortical atrophy detected in these ADHD subjects was the result of stimulant therapy or an underlying neuropathology.

In 1994 a team of investigators[24] published results from a neuroimaging study involving five healthy males between the ages of 21 and 40. Participants were injected with intravenous doses (0.5mg/kg) of methylphenidate (Ritalin) followed by PET (positron emission tomography) scans 5–10 minutes and 30 minutes after injection. The goal of the study was to identify the effects of Ritalin upon cerebral blood flow. Findings were significant for consistent, *global reductions in blood flow* compared to baseline: 14–36 percent reduction at 5–10 minutes, 10–30 percent reduction at 30 minutes. Because these changes were seen throughout the brain (unlike the regional effects detected by neuroimaging techniques which focus upon glucose metabolism), the researchers surmised that the findings reflected direct effects upon the cerebral vasculature rather than neurons. The investigators concluded:

> Though CBF [cerebral blood flow] changes after oral MP [methylphenidate] are probably smaller than with intravenous MP, its pharmacokinetics may be slower, and CBF decrements may last longer. The extent to which prolonged decrements in CBF with chronic MP occur needs to be evaluated.[25]

As of 2004, no such follow-up investigation had been performed. However, the lead author of this earlier study has reported that he has received funding from the National Institutes of Health for a project to address the 'long-term' (one year) effects of oral methylphenidate upon the dopamine system of drug naïve ADHD subjects.[26]

Sophisticated experiments have been developed to evaluate the functioning

---

*sulcal: pertaining to sulci, or invaginations of the brain surface; these furrows appear to widen as underlying brain tissue shrinks or recedes

**cerebellar atrophy: shrinking of the cerebellum, which is a posterior brain structure involved in balance, coordination, and cognitive functioning of different hemispheres of the brain. In one such experiment,[27] the responses of 26 ADHD children (ages 8–15) to tachiscopic tasks were compared under Ritalin and placebo conditions. (Tachiscopy is a test of visual field dominance which evaluates the speed of processing based upon the appearance of stimuli—dots or digits—to the left or right of a central fixation point.) Reaction times to stimuli producing left visual field advantages (right hemisphere processing) were slower than to stimuli producing advantages in the right visual field. The possibility that stimulant medications might provoke deficits in right hemisphere functioning has been noted by many other researchers as well.

The concern is that the ADHD literature has been so focused upon the left hemisphere effects of stimulants (such as verbal tasks and sustained attention) that the other half of the brain has been forgotten. *Right hemisphere deficits* have been linked to reductions in diffuse attentional mechanisms, emotional intensity, social responsiveness, and mood (depression and anxiety). Following right hemisphere lesions (such as strokes), patients may develop a 'semantic pragmatic disorder'[28] characterized by an impaired capacity to express themselves in language; flattened intonation; and an inability to perceive emotion, metaphor, humor, and subtleties in the world around them.

If stimulants induce a similar lateralized disorder in children, it is understandable that many ADHD subjects could experience the onset or worsening of deficits in eye contact, playfulness, spatial awareness, the perception of social cues, the use of imagery, the control of impulsive responding, and the holistic integration of feelings, context, and interpersonal relationships—all of which are predominantly right hemisphere functions.

The effects of stimulants upon driving and flying performance have raised additional concerns about their safety. While stimulants have long been used by pilots in the US military for their alerting properties during long-term missions, the self-administration of 'combat amphetamines' has provoked criticism in the aftermath of serious accidents involving medicated pilots. In the summer of 2002, two Air National Guard pilots mistakenly bombed and killed Canadian troops over Afghanistan, claiming that 'go pills' consumed before the mission had impaired their judgment.[29] According to a retired Navy Admiral,[30] 'the better warrior through chemistry field' is the focus of aggressive research. While Pentagon officials believe that the 'capability to operate effectively, without sleep' will 'fundamentally change current military concepts of operational tempo',[31] critics believe that it is hazardous to manipulate human sleep schedules artificially. Of particular concern in jet and bomber pilots is the possible induction of stimulant psychosis (hallucinations or delusions), as well as neurological side effects such as tremor, blurred vision, and dizziness.[32]

The topic is pertinent for children and adults with ADHD, almost all of whom receive treatment with stimulants. Several investigations conducted in the US and Canada have documented higher rates of motor vehicle accidents among ADHD drivers, relative to non-ADHD controls. In a study which evaluated the driving records and knowledge of 25 young adults with ADHD,[33] investigators found that ADHD subjects had no deficit in their understanding of road rules. However, ADHD drivers were more likely to have had their licenses suspended or revoked; more likely to have received repeated traffic citations (mostly for speeding); and more likely to have experienced car crashes while driving (four times more accidents than controls). Although the investigators attributed the accidents and reckless driving styles to the underlying condition of ADHD, rather than to its treatment, the experience of the US military should be instructive for more critical observers. Whatever else one concludes about ADHD drivers, it seems obvious that stimulant medications often fail to control impulsive habits and possibly exacerbate errors in judgment in the same way that amphetamines have been found to impair the performance of combat pilots.

Stimulant drugs and addiction

Beginning in the 1960s, central nervous system stimulants came under increasing regulatory control due to concerns about illicit manufacture and distribution. In 1971, the World Health Organization classified methylphenidate (Ritalin) as a Schedule II drug, due to its high abuse potential. Concerns about Ritalin abuse were relatively moderate for two decades. Curiously, production of the stimulant soared from less than three tons in 1990, to more than thirteen tons by 1997.[34] These developments were alarming to the international community. In 1996 and 1997, the World Health Organization issued press releases (and several letters to the US Drug Enforcement Agency) about the exponential rise in Ritalin, noting that the United States was responsible for 90 percent of the drug's production and consumption. The International Narcotics Control Board (INCB: the World Health Organization agency responsible for monitoring the production and use of controlled substances) explicitly identified a number of concerns about these American developments, including the dangers of inappropriate diagnosis of ADHD; widely divergent prescribing patterns; off-label prescribing to children under six; and excessive duration of treatment (many countries restrict Ritalin use to three years). The INCB was especially worried about the expanding black market for Ritalin, based upon increasing evidence of abuse by individuals who confiscate pills prescribed to others.

Despite the real-world concerns of regulatory authorities, the psychiatric literature has consistently minimized or ignored the addictive potential of psycho-stimulants. More alarmingly, the recent publications of several research teams have suggested that ADHD children should be *encouraged* to use stimulants, in order to *prevent* the emergence of cocaine or other substance dependencies.[35 36]

There are two critical points to be made about psycho-stimulants and addiction. First, although it is uncommon, it is possible for ADHD children to become directly dependent upon their prescribed therapies. Fortunately, this addictive liability appears to be rare as long as the drugs are consumed orally (rather than intravenously or intra-nasally) and in the amounts prescribed. Second, it is possible that stimulants change the human brain over time, so that the vulnerability to a variety of addictions is enhanced. A number of animal studies have documented the capacity of stimulant medications to *sensitize* the brain to cocaine.[37-39] The precise neuro-physiological mechanisms have not been identified, but hypotheses include the down-regulation of the dopamine transporter (a posited cause of craving), changes in post-synaptic dopamine receptor function or density, or the induction of genes and proteins (such as delta c-fos) which modulate long-term changes in neuronal activity.

If it is true that stimulant medications *prevent*, rather than *induce*, substance abuse, it should be possible to detect that link in epidemiological studies. A large-scale, prospective study of just this kind was performed with 492 ADHD children in Northern California[40] beginning in 1974. After two decades of follow-up, researchers discovered that stimulant-treated subjects developed higher rates of cocaine and nicotine dependence than unmedicated peers diagnosed with either ADHD or behavioral (conduct) disorders:

Percentage of Subjects Developing Addiction

	ADHD No stimulant exposure	ADHD Up to 1 Year of stimulant drug	ADHD 1 year or more of stimulant drug	Behavior Disorder No stimulant
	n = 81	n = 9	n = 84	n = 41
Tobacco	32.1%	38.5%	48.8%	32%
Alcohol	32.1%	33.3%	45.2%	39%
Marijuana	22.5%	23.1%	32.1%	34%
Cocaine	15.0%	17.9%	27.4%	12%

A second prospective study,[41] conducted by a different research team, followed 147 hyperactive children (diagnosed between ages 5–12) for approximately thirteen years. The subjects were interviewed at age 15 (78 percent follow-up) and again in early adulthood (mean age 21, 93 percent follow-up) to explore the use of various substances in relation to ADHD and its treatment. *Childhood exposure to stimulant therapy* was significantly associated with higher experimentation with cocaine (26 percent of stimulant treated vs. 5 percent of unmedicated subjects) by early adulthood. *Adolescent exposure to stimulant therapy* was significantly associated with greater frequency of cocaine use as young adults. Even after controlling for the severity of ADHD symptoms and the lifetime prevalence of conduct disorder features, the researchers detected a statistically significant relationship between prescribed stimulants during high school and a higher rate of cocaine experimentation ('ever use') by adulthood. Despite the limitations of this study (possibly underpowered, no consideration of association between stimulant medication and conduct disorder, and questionable validity of the assessment instruments and data analysis), several findings were consistent with the hypothesis of stimulant sensitization as a risk factor for illicit drug use.

Must we create cybernetic children?

Although Paul Virilio has been described by critics as overly pessimistic about the consequences of technology, his writings provoke a meaningful reflection about the speed of life in relation to our creations. Virilio proposes that there is a fundamental need within our species for movement through space and time. He worries about the consequences of the Transportation and Information Revolutions, attributing to them the progressive reduction of the human organism to a Brownian-motion existence within a cyberspace pseudo-reality.

Only recently has research within the fields of neuroscience and cognitive psychology caught up with the musings of social theorists like Virilio, expanding upon his ideas about machines and their effects upon the human body. Research on the impact of television, video games, and the Internet suggests that electromagnetic and digital technologies are re-wiring the brain, particularly during the most critical periods of neurodevelopment: childhood and adolescence.

As children have become increasingly exposed to a world of multitasking, immediate gratification, and electronic interrelatedness, their behaviors have come to reflect varying degrees of fitness to the real-time, three-dimensional environments around them. Regrettably, the response of many societies has been a call for the medical control of children, illustrated by the exponential rise in the use of stimulants. By ignoring or minimizing the dangers of these drugs, clinicians have contributed to the suppression of children's growth; the blunting of certain cognitive capacities; and the induction of brain changes associated with higher risks of substance abuse. As childhood continues to be transformed by electrochemical shaping and pharmacological degrading, Virilio's observations become ever more salient. Lived time is changing, to be sure, but there is still time for society to re-evaluate the forces and decisions which have led to the creation of cybernetic children.

Endnotes

This chapter summarizes a presentation at the Tavistock Clinic in London on June 5, 2004 at a conference entitled: *The Construction of Childhood and the Destruction of Children.* The author is grateful to the Psychotherapy Section of the British Psychological Society for the invitation to speak.

1. Virilio, P. (1997). *Open Sky*, (tr Julie Rose). New York: Verso.

2. Ibid., p. 22.

3. Christakis, D.A., Zimmerman, F.J., DiGiuseppe, D.L. and McCarty, C.A. (2004). Early television exposure and subsequent attentional problems in children. *Pediatrics, 113*, 708–13.

4. No author, 'TV "rewires" developing brains, researchers fear' *The Washington Times* (5 April 2004), accessed 26 May 2004 on-line at: http://www.washingtontimes.com/functions/print.php?StoryID=20040405-120940-2602r

5. Green, C.S. and Bavelier, D. (2003). Action video game modifies visual selective attention. *Nature 423*, 534–7.

6. Bavelier, D., personal communication, 25 May 2004.

7. Koepp, M.J., Gunn, R.N., Lawrence, A.D., Cunningham, V.J., Dagher, A., Jones, T., Brooks, D.J., Bench, C.J. and Grasby, P.M. (1998). Evidence for striatal dopamine release during a video game. *Nature, 393*, 266–8.

8. O'Reilly, M. (1997). Can users get addicted to the internet? *CMAJ, 157,* 785–6.

9. Griffiths, M.D. and Hunt, N. (1998). Dependence on computer games by adolescents. *Psychological Reports, 82,* 475–80.

10. Brenner, V. (1997). Psychology of Computer Use: XLVII. Parameters of Internet Use, Abuse, and Addiction: The first 90 days of the Internet Usage Survey. *Psychological Reports, 80,* 879–82.

11. Tazawa, Y., Soukalo, A.V., Okada, K. and Takada, G. (1997). Excessive playing of home computer games by children presenting with unexplained symptoms. *The Journal of Pediatrics 130,* 1010–11.

12. No author, 'Internet Addiction Test,' accessed 23 May 2004 on-line at: http://netaddiction.com/resources/internet_addiction_test.htm

13. Shaffer, H.J., Hall, M.N. and Vander Bilt, J. (2000). Computer addiction: a critical consideration. *American Journal of Orthopsychiatry 70,* 162–8.

14. Olsen, R. (1971). Pediatric practice: Whose mood are we altering? *Pediatrics 47,* 961.

15. Ahmann, P,A., Waltonen, S.J., Olson, K.A., Theye, F.W., Van Erem, A.J. and LaPlant, R.J. (1993). Placebo-controlled evaluation of Ritalin side effects. *Pediatrics 91,* 1101–6.

16. Efron, D., Jarman, F. and Barker, M. (1997). Side effects of methylphenidate and dexamphetamine in children with Attention Deficit Hyperactivity Disorder: A double-blind, crossover trial. *Pediatrics 100,* 662–6.

17. Poulton A. and Cowell, C.T. (1987). Slowing of growth in height and weight on stimulants: A characteristic pattern. *Journal of Paediatrics and Child Health 39,* 180–5.

18. Pizzi, W.J., Rode, E.C. and Barnhart, J.E. (1987). Differential effects of methylphenidate on the growth of neonatal and adolescent rats. *Neurotoxicology and Teratology 9,* 107–11.

19. Lisska, M.C. and Rivkees, S.A. (2003). Daily methylphenidate use slows the growth of children: A community based study. *Journal of Pediatric Endocrinology and Metabolism 16*, 711–18.

20. Lurie, S. and O'Quinn, A. (1991). Neuroendocrine responses to methylphenidate and d-amphetamine: Applications to Attention-Deficit Disorder. *Journal of Neuropsychiatry, 3*, 41–9.

21. Kilgore, B.S., Dickinson, L.C., Burnett, C.R., Lee, J. Schedewie, H.K. and Elders, M.J. (1979). Alterations in cartilage metabolism by neurostimulant drugs. *Journal of Pediatrics, 94*, 542–5.

22. Holtkamp, K., Peters-Wallraf, B., Wuller, S., Pfaaffle, R. and Herpertz-Dahlmann, B. (2002). Methylphenidate-related growth impairment. *Journal of Child and Adolescent Psychopharmacology 12*, 55–61.

23. Nasrallah, H.A., Loney, J., Olson, S.C., McCalley-Whitters, M., Kramer, J. and Jacoby, C.G. (1986). Cortical atrophy in young adults with a history of hyperactivity in childhood. *Psychiatry Research, 17*, 241–6.

24. Wang, G-J., Volkow, N.D., Fowler, J.S., Ferrieri, R., Schlyer, D.J., Alexoff, D., Pappas, N., Lieberman, J., King, P., Warner, D., Wong, C., Hitzemann, R.J. and Wolf, A.P. (1994). Methylphenidate decreases regional cerebral blood flow in normal human subjects. *Life Sciences 54*, PL 143–6.

25. Wang et al. (1994). p. PL 144.

26. Wang, personal communication, 12 October 2004.

27. Campbell, L., Malone, M.A., Kershner, J.R., Roberts, W., Humphries, T. and Logan, W.J. (1996). Methylphenidate slows right hemisphere processing in children with Attention-Deficit/ Hyperactivity Disorder. *Journal of Child and Adolescent Psychopharmacology 6*, 229–39.

28. Shields, Jane (1991). Semantic-pragmatic disorder: a right hemisphere syndrome? *British Journal of Disorders of Communication 26*, 383–92, accessed 20 May 2004 online at: http://www.mugsy.org/shields1.htm

29. Bonne, Jon (2003). Go Pills: A war on drugs? MSNC (9 January 2003), accessed 15 May 2004 on-line at: http://msnbc.msn.com/id/3071789/

30. Knickerbocker, Brad (2002). Military looks to drugs for battle readiness. *The Christian Science Monitor* (9 August 2002), accessed 15 May 2004 online at: http://www.csmonitor.com/2002/0809/p01s04-usmi.html

31. Ibid.

32. Berkowitz, B. (2002). Bombs and speed kill in Afghanistan. AlterNet.org (7 August 2002), accessed online 15 May 2004 at: http://www.alternet.org/story.html?StoryID=13791

33. Barkley, R.A., Murphy, K.R. and Kwasnik, D. (1996). Motor vehicle driving competencies and risks in teens and young adults with Attention Deficit Hyperactivity Disorder. *Pediatrics, 6*, 1089–95.

34. No author, 'United Nations' Warnings on Ritalin: Two Press Releases,' (28 February 1996), accessed 14 October 2004 at:
http://216.239.41.104/search?q=cache:6RroSjUcTPsJ:www.pbs.org/wgbh/pages/frontline/shows/medicating/backlash/un.html+ritalin+abuse+in+canada&hl=en

35. Biederman, J. (2003). Pharmacotherapy for Attention-Deficit/Hyperactivity Disorder (ADHD) decreases the risk for substance abuse: findings from a longitudinal follow-up of youths with and without ADHD. *Journal of Clinical Psychiatry 64,* Suppl. 11, 3–8.

36. Wilens, T., Faraone, S.V., Biederman, J. and Gunawardene, S. (2001). Does stimulant therapy of ADHD beget later substance abuse? Meta-analytic Review of the Literature, *Pediatrics, 111,* 179–85.

37. Schenk, S. and Izenwasser, S. (2002). Pretreatment with methylphenidate sensitizes rats to the reinforcing effects of cocaine. *Pharmacology, Biochemistry and Behavior 72,* 651–7.

38. Brandon, C.L., Marinelli, M., Baker, L.K. and White, F.J. (2001). Enhanced reactivity and vulnerability to cocaine following methylphenidate treatment in adolescent rats. *Neuropsychopharmacology 25,* 651–61.

39. Kollins, S.H., MacDonald, E.K. and Rush, C.R. (2001). Assessing the abuse potential of methylphenidate in nonhuman and human subjects. *Pharmacology, Biochemistry and Behavior 68,* 611–27.

40. Lambert, N.M. and Hartsough, C.S. (1998). Prospective Study of Tobacco Smoking and Substance Dependencies among Samples of ADHD and Non-ADHD Participants. *Journal of Learning Disabilities 31,* 533–44.

41. Barkley, R.A., Fischer, M., Smallish, L. and Fletcher, K. (2003). Does the treatment of Attention-Deficit/Hyperactivity Disorder with stimulants contribute to drug use/abuse? A 13-year prospective study. *Pediatrics, 111,* 97–109.

Part Three

Appreciating
Children

CHAPTER 10

Constructing Meaning
in the Lives of
Looked After Children

HELEN ROSTILL AND
HELEN MYATT

'I've got ADHD, Asperger's, Conduct Disorder, Post-Traumatic Stress and Special Needs and I don't care what you say; I'm not going back to hospital.' This was how 17-year-old David introduced himself to me [HR] at the start of our first meeting. Then, without stopping to draw breath, he went on to give me a detached but detailed chronology of his life in the care system.

By the age of three, David had suffered severe sexual, physical and emotional abuse at the hands of his stepfather. The Local Authority obtained an emergency protection order and David was removed from his mother and two sisters to be placed with foster carers. His stepfather was eventually convicted and sentenced to three years' imprisonment, but ongoing contact with the remainder of his family was inconsistent. After two years in care, Social Services took the decision to return David to his mother, without any warning or preparation. From his mother's recollections, David seemed to mourn for the loss of his foster parents and she found it impossible to cope with a 5-year-old who was all but unrecognisable to her. Shortly after his return home, David was diagnosed with ADHD and two years later his mother took the decision to return him to the care system.

Over the next ten years, David moved from one foster placement to another, with each one failing because his behaviour was viewed as uncontrollable and a risk to others. He then entered the arena of residential care and specialist treatment units, where he accrued multiple diagnostic labels. The longest settled period that David experienced in one placement was sixteen months. When I first met him, he had spent six months in prison, before being sectioned to a secure hospital. He presented with what was described as unexplained aggressive outbursts, fleeting attention, impoverished interpersonal functioning and behavioural rigidity. Professional agencies were at a loss as to what to do with David and how to make sense of him.

Unfortunately David's story is all too common within the public care system, where mental health needs are frequently unrecognised or masked by diagnosis and medication. This chapter aims to look beyond simple diagnostic labels that constrict the exploration of emotional experience by attempting to open up a dialogue that places children's lives in context. These broad conversations about children's emotional experiences can provide an arena in which they learn to represent, understand and give meaning to who they are. Such meaning provides opportunities for developing hopefulness and alternative ways of coping with negative experiences.

For children and young people living in care, the experience of emotional and psychological distress is very familiar. Within the last two years, both the Department of Health and the Mental Health Foundation have provided evidence indicating that looked after children exhibit higher rates of mental health problems than other young people and they call for a system of early mental health assessment and intervention for this vulnerable group.[1][2] However, assessing need within this group seems to have taken the form of psychiatric labelling rather than considering psychosocial explanations. There are a number of studies that demonstrate the high prevalence of psychiatric labels amongst children in public care.[3][4] Perhaps the most wide-ranging review of 'mental disorders' in the looked after population, has been that conducted by Meltzer et al. (2002).[5] Taking a diagnostic approach, they surveyed over a thousand children and young people across England using questionnaires based on *ICD-10* and *DSM-IV* diagnostic criteria. Forty-five per cent were classified with clinically significant conduct disorders, emotional disorders or hyperkinetic disorders (these prevalence rates are approximately four or five times higher than those found amongst private household children). Within the looked after group, children diagnosed with hyperkinetic disorders were more likely than any others to have had contact with a specialist in child mental health and a fifth of them (21 per cent) were taking psycho-stimulant medication (Methylphenidate, Equasym, Ritalin). Five per cent of this group were also prescribed anti-psychotics (Risperidone, Risperada). This worrying trend towards medicating our children is born out in a recent survey of psychiatric and paediatric practice, where 100 per cent of clinicians acknowledged prescribing psycho-stimulants for the routine management of ADHD symptoms.[6] Given this pattern of practice, it would follow that a higher level of diagnosis of mental health disorders in looked after children means generally higher prescription rates in this group.

Minimising the dangers of psycho-stimulants

For David, each new placement brought with it the promise of another psychiatric assessment, the possibility of a new diagnostic label or confirmation of an old one and, of course, the obligatory cocktail of psychiatric drugs. Over the years his 'ADHD' has been treated with a range of psychoactive medications including

Ritalin and Risperidone, amongst others. It seems surprising that no-one ever questioned this practice or considered how David's sense of self was being defined or constructed by the labels professionals attached to him. To this day, David is still searching for a drug to make everything better but he now prefers to self-medicate with cannabis, speed, crack and gear.

So do we follow blindly or are we being misled by multi-billion dollar drug companies and the mental health professionals? Warnings about using psycho-stimulant drugs are rarely given to parents or carers.[7] Instead we appear to be in a culture where professionals encourage those charged with the care and protection of children to medicate them without considering the long-term effects or the more immediate counter indications. Davy and Rogers[8] noticed that some children became very subdued and hypoactive when taking stimulant drugs. This zombie-like, robotic behaviour is one of the many side effects that have been noted. Others include obsessions and compulsions,[9] which impede learning due to narrowed attention, the development of tics,[10] and overstimulation, which is often mistaken for worsening of ADHD symptoms, rather than an effect of the drug.[7] Rates of diagnosis have continued to increase, despite questioning and legal proceedings.[11] It has been argued that society has evolved into the perfect context for this, with what has been perceived as the death of childhood,[12] where children have increased access to an adult world through media, adults control over what children learn is compromised and there is a growing sense that children pose a risk to society that requires ever-increasing state controls.

Psychological explanations

Do we discover meanings behind a child's difficulties, or create them? Timimi[13] argues that our understanding of what childhood is has become narrowed in order to define and fulfil our professional roles. Where the medical model dominates, it may be that childhood becomes pathologised and medicated. This can be seen in the comparatively high rates of psychiatric diagnosis amongst looked after children. It seems that the effects of early childhood experiences of abandonment and trauma are being sanitised through medical diagnoses without alternative explanations being given due consideration. Some child psychiatrists will say, 'I accept that there are signs of trauma but I also think there is ADHD.' By paying lip-service in this way the emotional and psychological trauma gets sidelined at a stroke, the medical diagnosis and treatment remains at the centre and, unless there is someone very determined, therapy is likely to get forgotten. In line with this observation, Dimigen et al.[4] noticed that whilst a significant proportion of children entering the care system received a psychiatric diagnosis, they were not then referred on for therapeutic work. Belief in ADHD as a medical disorder represents the dominant position but we need to recognise that there are other positions that must be privileged. Medical ideas about ADHD are readily expressed by professionals across multi-agency settings for the purpose of their own communication; a sort of professional shorthand. The dominance of these ideas should not be surprising as categorisation and labelling are an integral part of the way human beings process social information and form impressions about other people. The labels we attach to people act as a belief system that links the individual to a set of traits or behavioural characteristics. They can also provide a bridge to almost automatic emotional and behavioural reactions in the perceiver, which can then form the basis of misunderstandings, conflicts or emotionally constricted communication. In extreme cases discrimination and social rejection can follow. Attempts to classify and diagnose looked after children are often excused and justified as the only means of accessing resources or services,[5] with very little regard for the increasing stigmatisation of some of the most vulnerable young people in our society.

Understanding the mental health needs of looked after children is a complex process, as their problems may arise from a combination of interrelated causes. It is hard to disentangle the effects of family, social and environmental factors impinging on their lives. Risk factors such as placement stability, child temperament, parental and family functioning, social disadvantage, early abuse and neglect have all been shown to play a part in mediating psychological and emotional health.[2]

By far the largest proportion of children and young people are being looked after because of abuse and neglect (62 per cent); the next largest category come into the care system as a result of family dysfunction (10 per cent).[14] Research is demonstrating more clearly than ever before the detrimental effects of early abuse and neglect on children's psychosocial development.[15] Unfortunately the disturbed patterns of behaviour that these children exhibit are often misidentified and labelled as some sort of psychiatric disorder. Studies using DSM diagnostic criteria have found that children with a history of abuse and neglect by parents are more likely to be diagnosed with attention deficit hyperactivity disorder (ADHD), oppositional disorder, and post-traumatic stress disorder than age-matched controls.[16]

It is perhaps easy to see how this confusion occurs. Many abused and neglected children will exhibit behaviours typically associated with ADHD, such as inattention, impulsivity and hyperactivity. Children who have experienced significant trauma in their lives may display hyperarousal, hypervigilance, avoidance and numbing.[17] Sleep disturbance is also common, as is the tendency to actively seek highly stimulating environments. Unsurprisingly, these children find it difficult to settle and feel secure. They may also experience altered states of awareness, giving the impression that they are inattentive and easily distracted. Abused and neglected children have also been found to be less securely attached to their caregivers than non-abused children.[18][19] Attachment relationships act as a blueprint, allowing children to develop internal representations of interactional styles or patterns that they then apply to other relationships. Within this context they also develop a sense of self and the ability to regulate their emotional/ behavioural states. Children with insecure or disorganised attachments can be aggressive, anxious, impulsive, aloof, as well as socially manipulative and indiscriminate. They may develop a view of themselves as deserving maltreatment and see others as unpredictable or untrustworthy.

Cairns describes how many children within the care system, like David, have been 'radically changed by traumatic stress'.[20] For them trauma has become normality. She notes the tendency of different professional agencies to classify the signs and symptoms of trauma under manageable headings, whilst for the children themselves these divisions are meaningless. 'The child simply has the thread of their daily experience to live through'.[20] The tendency to fragment the child's needs and experiences to fit with the professional agenda leads us to 'ask the wrong questions. Is this a health problem? A mental health problem? An educational problem? A drugs problem? Or is it perhaps a problem for the criminal justice system? We go on adding to the number of ways the behaviours may be institutionally addressed, and in so doing we add to the burden of disintegration. Until we can achieve as a society a deep integration in our approach to trauma, we will continue to see children's problems multiply'.[20]

ADHD: narrow versus broad descriptions

As the cluster of behaviours described as 'ADHD' [21] is presented in an acontextual form, in isolation from situational information, it is possible to hypothesise many ideas about the possible meanings. Yet the biomedical explanation prevails and dominates. Maintaining a distance from a dominant idea can be achieved with the promotion of curiosity.[22] It is often better if this curiosity comes from within, otherwise it may be perceived as an attack upon the service or system. As professionals working with children we need to encourage conversations that give meaning to children's emotional experiences and look beyond the labels. However, it is important to have real and tangible interventions that come from this curiosity. Family therapy literature has many therapeutic techniques that help to gather contextual information, adding to a description of a child's behaviour. Positive connotation and reframing involve finding positive, purposeful meaning for a system in what is described as a child's negative behaviour.[23] These techniques acknowledge that the child's behaviour is meaningful, and in so doing shift the way that carers and professionals think about the child's behaviour.

David chose to share some of his life experiences with me but I was left wondering who this young man really was and how he made sense of what had happened to him. These questions seemed to challenge David and those working with him. Was it safe for our conversations to move beyond the constraints of the familiar psychiatric labels and search for a different meaning? Would David and those who worked with him be able to tolerate an alternative construction of his experiences? By inviting David to join with me in a conversation that emphasised aspects of his life that did not fit the dominant story he and others often told, we began to explore alternative constructions of his life experiences and relationships. I asked him about areas of his life that he regarded as his strengths, achievements that he remembered with pride, relationships that gave him a sense of warmth and hope, about his dreams for the future and what sense of himself these gave him. David visited his dreams of a loving relationship and a family of his own. He talked about his wish to nurture and protect his own child and we began to discover how David already displayed these qualities in his current relationships. We thought about David's journey through the care system and the strength he had gained by facing so much adversity in his life. Slowly he began to move from the position of passive victim towards that of active survivor. David's own curiosity about his life and his future had been aroused.

Exception talk was important for carers and professionals working with David. The thin, acontextual description of David's behaviour had left them feeling medication and a secure environment offered the only possible way forward. Acknowledging exceptions, where the thin description did not fit, resulted in a rich, thick description, placing David in the context of his life experiences, creating a fuller understanding of his behaviour and opening up many new ways of communicating. For example, acknowledging that David did not display risky behaviours when in the company of his sisters was important when determining meaning. Perhaps this was the only time David felt safe or got a sense of belonging. This made us curious about other ways of helping David to meet these needs. Exploring David's behaviours as a healthy and understandable response to his life circumstances evoked many possible meanings of the challenges he presented to workers. Professionals and carers were invited to begin noticing David's strengths and vulnerabilities.

For the non-prescribing professionals and carers, the ADHD description and other psychiatric labels seemed to have rendered them powerless. Alternative techniques and ways of working and thinking seemed to restore their sense of helpfulness. These broad descriptions of David added to the information gained and opened up opportunities for alternative explanations and action. Describing a child as intrinsically problematic and disordered constructs the system's reality and constrains movement. Using rich, contextual descriptions helps children to organise their experiences in a meaningful way and feel understood and secure. However, they can also evoke some degree of anxiety and discomfort. By not talking about David's ADHD we began to explore the multiple abuses that he had experienced within an under-resourced social and health care system. At times, for all involved in this work, it felt like the narrower psychiatric description was easier to tolerate.

Conclusion

Many children living within the looked after system have missed out on the normal, run-of-the-mill family conversations in which their sense of self and others is typically co-constructed and developed. Instead, like David, their lives and experiences are often reduced to a list of diagnostic labels and a chronology of events recorded by the Local Authority. Within the mental health arena, dialogues about these children take place against the backdrop of the dominant medical ideology and continue to disadvantage this already stigmatised and vulnerable group. In order to adopt a broad contextual view, there needs to be a cultural shift towards integrating children's experiences at the centre of our understanding, rather than allowing the professional agenda to dictate and fragment the treatment focus. We need to call for more research which specifically addresses the diagnostic labelling and administration of psycho-stimulants within the looked after population. This will serve to provide greater knowledge for service commissioners and clinicians about the prevalence of such diagnoses and medical interventions. There is also a need for non-biological accounts of those behaviours referred to as ADHD, in order to raise the profile of alternative methods of help. It may be that closer scrutiny will promote curiosity, encourage multi-modal assessment and explanations, therefore avoiding such narrow descriptions of these children's needs.

Acknowledgement

To David and all the other young people who have helped us move towards a position of curiosity and encouraged our search for meaning.

Endnotes

1. Department of Health (2002). *Promoting the Health of Looked After Children.* London: Department of Health.

2. Mental Health Foundation (2002). *The Mental Health of Looked After Children.* London: Mental Health Foundation.

3. McCann, J.B., James, A., Wilson, A. and Dunne, G (1996). Prevalence of psychiatric disorders in young people in the care system. *British Medical Journal, 313*, 1529–30.

4. Dimigen, G, Del Priore, C., Butler, S., Evans, S., Ferguson, L. and Swan, M. (1999). Psychiatric disorder among children at time of entering local authority care: Questionnaire survey. *British Medical Journal, 319*, 675.

5. Meltzer, H., Gatward, R., Corbin, T., Goodman, R. and Ford, T. (2002). *The Mental Health of Young People Looked After by Local Authorities in England.* London: HMSO.

6. Salmon, G and Kemp, A. (2002). ADHD: A survey of psychiatric and paediatric practice. *Child and Adolescent Mental Health, 7,* 73–8.

7. Breggin, P.R. (2001). *Talking Back to Ritalin.* Cambridge: Perseus.

8. Davy, T. and Rogers, C.L. (1989). Stimulant medication and short attention span: *Journal of Developmental and Behavioural Paediatrics, 10,* 313–18.

9. Castellanos, F.X., Giedd, J.N., Elia, J., Marsh, W.L., Ritchie, G.F., Hamburger, S.D. and

Rapoport, J.L. (1997). Controlled stimulant treatment of ADHD and comorbid Tourette's Syndrome: Effects of stimulant and dose. *Journal of the American Academy of Child and Adolescent Psychiatry, 36,* 589–96.

10. Lipkin, P.H., Goldstein, I.J. and Adesman, A.R. (1994). Tics and dyskinesias associated with stimulant treatment for attention deficit hyperactivity disorder: *Archives of Pediatric and Adolescent Medicine, 148,* 859–61.

11. Timimi, S. (2002). *Pathological Child Psychiatry and the Medicalization of Childhood.* Hove: Brunner-Routledge.

12. Hendrick, H. (1997). Constructions and reconstructions of British childhood: An interpretive survey, 1800 to the present. In A. James and A. Prout (eds), *Constructing and Reconstructing Childhood: Contemporary issues in the sociological study of childhood.* London: Falmer Press.

13. Timimi, S. (2003). The New Practitioner: The emergence of the post-modern clinician. *Young Minds Magazine 62,* 14–16.

14. Department of Health (2001). Children looked after in England: 2000-1. *Bulletin 2001/26.* London: Department of Health.

15. Dore, M. (1999). Emotionally and behaviourally disturbed children in the child welfare system: Points of preventive intervention. *Child and Youth Services Review, 21,* 7–29.

16. Famularo, R., Kinscherff, R. and Fenton, T. (1992). Psychiatric diagnoses of maltreated children: Preliminary findings. *Journal of the American Academy of Child and Adolescent Psychiatry, 31,* 863–7.

17. Berliner, L. (2002). The traumatic impact of abuse experiences: Treatment issues. In K.D. Browne, H. Hands, P. Stratton and C. Hamilton (eds) *Early Prediction and Prevention of Child Abuse: A handbook.* Chichester: Wiley.

18. Barnett, D., Ganiban, J. and Cicchetti, D. (1999). Maltreatment, negative expressivity, and the development of Type D attachments from 12 to 24 months of age. *Monographs of the Society for Research in Child Development, 64,* 97–118.

19. Toth, S.L. and Cicchetti, D. (1996). Patterns of relatedness, depressive symptomatology, and perceived competence in maltreated children. *Journal of Consulting and Clinical Psychology, 64,* 32–41.

20. Cairns, K. (2002). *Attachment, Trauma and Resilience. Therapeutic caring for children.* London: BAAF, pp. 111–12.

21. American Psychiatric Association (1999). *Diagnostic and Statistical Manual of Mental Disorders (fourth edition).* Washington: Division of Publishing and Marketing, American Psychiatric Association.

22. Mason, B. (1993). Towards positions of safe uncertainty. *Journal of Systemic Consultancy and Management, 4,* 189–200.

23. O'Brian, C. and Bruggen, P. (1985). Our personal and professional lives: Learning positive connotation and circular questioning. *Family Process,* 311–22.

CHAPTER 11

Taking a Positive, Holistic Approach to the Mental and Emotional Health and Well-being of Children and Young People

KATHERINE WEARE

Traditionally the focus of mental health work with children and young people, including those seen as having behaviour problems and Attention Deficit Hyperactivity Disorder (ADHD), has been on the individual child or young person, and specifically on the identification, referral and treatment of their problem. This is now changing, and child mental health work is starting to take a more holistic and preventive approach. There is fortunately a great deal of support for those who want to make this shift coming from many quarters.

In this short chapter I have only the space to outline the nature of that shift and recommend that mental health work makes this shift with as much speed as possible, working closely with some new developments in research and practice to do so. The research evidence to support the assertions of this chapter can be found in some recent publications,[1][2][3] which include case studies of five Local Education Authorities in England who are working with more holistic approaches in their work with children and young people, including work on child and adolescent mental health.

An overall positive framework for work

Traditionally the words 'mental health' have been used as a synonym for mental illness and are thus seen as the concern only of mental health professionals—the so-called 'pathogenic' model. Now broader and more positive models of mental health are developing, sometimes called the 'salutogenic' or wellness model.[4] The World Health Organisation has been in the forefront of encouraging a focus on positive health rather than just on illness, and the 'Ottawa Charter',[5] a WHO position statement which outlined the principles of health promotion, suggested that health is 'a positive concept, emphasizing social and personal resources, as well as physical capabilities.' A salutogenic approach to mental health sees the promotion of mental, emotional and social health as potentially being about more than the treatment or even the prevention of something conceptualised as mental illness. It is concerned with the promotion of positive wellness as the overall framework for mental health work, a framework within which the treatment of individuals and services for those classified as mentally ill can take their rightful place.

Many involved with mental health work are starting to 'unpack' the idea of mental health using non-specialist, positive and inclusive terms and to focus on people's positive capacities rather than their perceived deficits. Recent definitions of mental health have focused on positive characteristics such as: resilience and an inner sense of coherence; the ability to make relationships, to attach to others and to love; the ability to think clearly including about emotional matters; the ability to manage the emotions successfully and appropriately; the ability to be sensitive to one's own and other's emotions; and the capacity to have an accurate self concept and high self-esteem.[672] This is a useful way forward when working with non-specialist agencies, such as social services or schools, who can find the idea of 'mental health' work unnerving and alien. It echoes work which is happening in many contexts, such as the workplace and educational establishments, on what is called 'emotional intelligence', 'emotional literacy', or 'emotional and social learning', which will be discussed later in this chapter.

An holistic approach

At the same time as mental health work is becoming more positive it is also becoming more holistic. Across all types of social and health related research there is a growing tendency to take a more 'joined-up approach'. This involves looking at environments rather than only at individuals, as a way both to understand and also to address problems. It promotes a concern with the relationships between problems rather than with single problems, and encourages us to look at clusters of risk factors rather than single causes. Terms commonly used to describe holistic approaches include 'settings', 'universal', 'ecological', 'environmental', 'comprehensive', 'multi-systemic' and 'multi-dimensional'—depending on which discipline and which agency are involved, but they all refer essentially to thinking and working holistically.

Shifting to a positive, holistic approach

If we make this shift to a more positive and holistic view of mental health, it has huge implications for how we tackle mental health problems in children and young people. The goal changes from a concern to address the pathology of individuals only, to the creation of an overall framework to promote the positive emotional well-being of all, including the learning of mental health skills and competences for everyone. The emphasis is on ensuring an embedded, coherent, congruent and coordinated approach across all parts of the service, working in partnership with schools and families. Mental health work becomes the concern of everyone for everyone—as relevant to the needs of children without overt behaviour problems, and to professionals, as it is the people with problems who have been its traditional concern.

To look for example at education, there the mental health perspective is gaining support from the growing tendency to take a 'whole school' approach to most of the issues that concern schools, including learning, behaviour and health.[8] Within the school the focus is increasingly not just on individual pupils and classrooms but on the totality of the school as an organisation, embedded in its community. The school is seen as a jigsaw or organism, which includes a myriad of aspects of school life, all of which have an impact on mental health. Some key facets include school ethos, relationships, communication, management, the physical environment, teaching and learning, special needs procedures and responses, and relationships with parents and the surrounding community. The school is also seen as including everyone, not just pupils, but also teachers and support staff.

Focusing on contexts

Focusing on the setting rather than just on individuals also helps us to identify ways in which the contexts in which the children and young people find themselves shape behaviour, for good or ill. It is important to realise that these contexts are not always benign, and that the adults who care for children may be, usually unwittingly, contributing to the very 'problems' they claim to be trying to address, for example through their own responses and behaviour.

The ethos of an organisation is one of the most powerful determinants of the behaviour of those in it, and in particular the approach taken to dealing with difficult behaviour. Many settings in which children can be found continue to focus mainly on poor behaviour and use sanctions and punishment as their main strategy for improving behaviour. A classic conundrum emerges, whereby adults (such as parents, carers or teachers) pay most attention to the kind of disruptive and difficult behaviours they claim not to want—focusing at length and with great emotion on that child, allowing their behaviour to dominate proceedings and take up all the available air time. Indeed difficult behaviours are sometimes 'rewarded' directly, for example by sending that child to a special class or unit where they get even more attention and, in the eyes of their fellows, even better conditions. Sometimes a reward system is created just for the difficult children. Such attention and paradoxical reward has the effect of inadvertently fostering more of the unwanted behaviour—both among those children who are inclined to it anyway and see the attention as the only recognition they are likely to get, and those who might not naturally be so inclined but who find that being quiet and behaving well is a sure way of being overlooked and not getting any rewards. When children conclude that realistically the only attention they are likely to get is for being difficult, many will naturally opt for that.

A general climate of negativity and punitiveness alienates children and does nothing to build up trust that is the bedrock of relationships. It helps create a climate of violence, aggression and fear, which frightens more timid children and feeds the inclination to violence in aggressive children. It reinforces the problems of those who come from backgrounds where violence and punishment are the norm, supporting their tendency to repeat these behaviours, and making them feel comfortable and 'at home', rather than giving them an alternative model.

There is now a good deal of work on the kind of positive, emotionally and socially healthy environments that help promote good behaviour and the growth of mental and emotional well-being—helping both 'troublesome' children to reduce their inclinations to disruption, aggression and violence, and encouraging 'troubled' children to open up and express their fears and anxieties and stand up for themselves. Such environments are those that get the right balance between warmth, participation, the encouragement of participation and autonomy, and the setting of clear boundaries and expectations—where the ethos is positive and the focus is on good rather than bad behaviour.[8][1] This has been accompanied by a growth in attempts to develop and teach emotional and social skills to children and the adults (such as parents, carers and teachers) who look after them. Many such projects have proved to be very effective.[9]

Taking a positive, holistic approach

It may be thought that a positive, holistic approach to mental health work simply gives more to the 'haves' while neglecting the needs of those with problems. However, there is strong evidence that taking a holistic and positive approach can serve a preventive function to reduce the onset of problems or reduce their severity or longevity, provide a context which helps to meet the needs of children more effectively than targeting alone, and provide sound support for the specialist services that those with more severe problems need.

There is now a good deal of work on what factors in a context help everyone to be more effective, to experience emotional and social well-being, and to feel part of that context. These factors include starting any programmes or interventions early, being clear about what outcomes are preferred, active listening, counselling, building warm relationships, setting clear boundaries, and participation. Interestingly, exactly the same factors have been shown to be especially helpful in helping those seen as having emotional and behavioural problems.[10][11][12] Children with special needs may need *more* of certain approaches, but they do not need *different* approaches.

Emotional, behavioural and social problems are extremely widespread—they are by no means minority problems. The same risk and protective factors predict more or less the whole range of problems in children and adolescents, from teenage pregnancy to school failure. Problem behaviours tend to cluster together, and reinforce one another.[9] Most behavioural and emotional problems exist on a continuum and affect a very high percentage, sometimes the majority of the population, so where we decide to have the cut-off (e.g., '20 per cent have problems') is, for most conditions, arbitrary. If we target an arbitrary percentage, the very many people who suffer from a problem to some extent will be ignored. Constructing the climate and procedures has a preventive function, making it both less likely that children will have problems in the first place, and enabling us to spot any problems early and deal with them before they become engrained.

It is in any case less stigmatising to work with everyone, as it means that those with problems are more likely to use the services offered and feel positive about them than if they feel they are being treated differently. For example, a child identified as having problems is more likely to seek a session with a school counsellor if that counsellor is also engaged in routine work in the school, teaching lessons to all and advising staff—rather than risk being seen going into the office of someone known to work only with 'nutters' and 'sad' people. Parents too are likely to be reassured if they feel that their child is not being singled out, and likely to be more supportive of any programme suggested.

The principle of 'herd immunity' means that the more people in a community, such as a school, who are emotionally and socially competent, the easier it will be to help those with more acute problems.[13] The 'critical mass' of ordinary people has the capacity to help those with problems, and peer group support has proved to be a very effective form of intervention to help those with difficulties. Those who are given extra help will be able to return to the mainstream more easily, as the way they are dealt with in terms of special help is then congruent with what happens to them in the mainstream when they return and they are not so likely to get into difficulties in future.

So projects and interventions which aim to promote mental and emotional well-being and which focus on developing the kind of overall climates which foster the mental and emotional well-being of everyone in that context, have been shown to be more effective in helping those with problems than those which concentrate on those with problems alone.[14] The ideal would seem to be to provide a basic level of help for all, while giving increased help to those who need it—this is the norm in the many successful US-based projects to improve emotional and social well-being and skills.[15] There are two new initiatives to develop social, emotional and behavioural skills which are now being introduced into all English primary[16] and secondary[17] schools also taking such an approach.

Putting emotions at the centre

As well as taking a positive, holistic approach to services and organizations, there is a complementary tendency (which some of us would see as a welcome return!) to take a more holistic and positive view of the person, and in particular to recognise the centrality of emotion in all aspects of life, including in shaping and explaining behaviour. The emotions have long been a neglected area in psychology; they are now moving centre stage. Work is developing at an extraordinary pace, in psychology, neuroscience, and education to name but three disciplines, which is demonstrating that emotions are at the heart of how we think, how we learn, how we behave, and how we attribute meaning and value. This work has part of its roots in child psychology, particularly in work on attachment, developed initially by Bowlby, which has recently been the subject of a major revival.[18] This work is underlining how important the making of primary emotional attachments to carers is to the subsequent healthy growth of children's minds and cognitive abilities. This work is now starting to be recognised as having widespread applicability, not just for emotionally neglected children but for everyone. It suggests that our feelings for others, our sense of trust in them and concern for them, are the foundation for sound cognitive as well as emotional development.

Links with work in education

The interest in the role of the emotions also finds support from recent work on learning. Those who work in educational contexts are recognising that the emotions are educable, that we all have the ability to do far more than respond blindly to feelings; we can think about them, organise them, modulate them, moderate them, and shape them through reflection and learning, and help others to do so.[19] As a consequence schools are starting to take an interest in understanding and educating the emotions—work which tends to be known in school contexts as work on emotional intelligence,[20] emotional literacy[21] or emotional and social learning. There is the promise of some useful alliances between education and mental health under such banners.

Implications

This chapter has attempted to show that these developments are helping to change approaches to child mental health in fundamental ways, and paving the way for the introduction of forms of intervention that are more humane, less stigmatising and divisive, and above all, work better. For example, they are encouraging:

- those who work in mental health to make more links with those who work in other sectors, such as social services and education, and to link with positive intervention programmes, for example to promote the mental health of looked after children, emotional health and well-being in organisations, and programmes to develop social and emotional skills/emotional intelligence.

- those who work in schools and the community services to seek positive and preventive advice and support, rather than just end-of-the-line diagnosis and treatment, from the specialist mental health services.

- all who work with children to consider some fundamental principles that underlie all effective work—such as focusing on the meaningfulness of behaviour and on the contexts in which it is created, the need to build on strengths, capacities and skills rather than focus on pathologies and deficits, and the need for all the services to work in 'joined up' ways which promote teamwork and which place the needs and interests of the child and their family, not the needs and interests of the services, at the centre.

Endnotes

1. Weare, K. (2000). *Promoting Mental, Emotional and Social Heath: A whole school approach.* London: Routledge.

2. Weare, K. (2004). *Developing the Emotionally Literate School.* London: Sage.

3. Weare, K. and Gray, G. (2003). *What Works in Promoting Children's Emotional and Social Competence and Well-being?'* London: Department of Education and Skills.

4. Antonovksy, A. (1987). *Unravelling the Mystery of Health: How people manage stress and stay well.* San Francisco: Jossey Bass.

5. World Health Organisation (1986). *Ottawa Charter For Health Promotion.* Geneva: WHO.

6. Mental Health Foundation (1999). *The Big Picture: Promoting children and young people's mental health.* London: The Mental Health Foundation.

7. Health Education Authority (1997). *Mental Health Promotion: A quality framework.* London: HEA.

8. NHS Health Development Agency (2004). *Promoting Emotional Health and Well-being Through the National Healthy School Standard.* London: Department of Education and Skills and the Department of Health.

9. Catalano, R.F., Berglund, L., Ryan, A.M., Lonczak, H.S. and Hawkins, J. (2002). *Positive Youth Development in the United States: Research finding on evaluations of positive youth development programmes. Prevention and Treatment, (5),* article 15.

10. McMillan, J. (1992). *A Qualitative Study of Resilient At-Risk Students: Review of literature.* Virginia: Metropolitan Educational Research Consortium.

11. Cohen, J. (1993). *Handbook of School-Based Interventions: Resolving student problems and promoting healthy educational environments.* San Francisco: JosseyBass.

12. Rutter, M., Hagel, A. and Giller, H. (1998). *Anti-social Behaviour and Young People.* Cambridge: Cambridge University Press.

13. Stewart-Brown, S. (2000). 'Parenting, well-being, health and disease'. In A. Buchanan and B. Hudson (eds) *Promoting Children's Emotional Well-being.* Oxford: Oxford University Press, p. 28–47.

14. Wells, J., Barlow, J. and Stewart-Brown, S. (2004) A systematic review of universal approaches to mental health promotion in schools. *Health Education* (4).

15. Zins, J.E., Weissberg, R.P., Wang, M.C. and Walberg, H. (2004). *Building Academic Success on Social and Emotional Learning.* Columbia: Teachers College.

16. Department for Education and Skills (2005). *Developing Children's Social, Emotional and Behavioural Skills: A whole curriculum approach.* London: Department for Education and Skills.

17. Department for Education and Skills (2005). *Developing Social, Emotional and Behavioural Skills Using a Whole School Approach.* London: Department for Education and Skills.

18. Cassidy, J. and Shaver, P.R. (eds) (1999). *Handbook of Attachment: Theory, research and clinical applications.* London: Guilford Press.

19. LeDoux, J. (1998). *The Emotional Brain.* London: Phoenix.

20. Goleman, D. (1996). *Emotional Intelligence.* London: Bloomsbury.

21. Elias, M., Zins, J., Weissberg, R., Frey, K., Greenberg, M., Haynes, N., Kessler, R., Schwab-Stone, M. and Shriver, T. (1997). *Promoting Social and Emotional Learning.* Alexandria, Virginia: ASCD.

CHAPTER 12

Empowering Vulnerable Children and Families

RAJA BANDAK

Raising a child who is physically and psychologically healthy and is able to realise their potential is the hardest challenge that can be tackled in most adults' lifetime. A more successful outcome is ensured if the carer has a partner and there is a wide personal social network of support available to them.[1] The single most important factor, which makes raising a child significantly harder, is poverty. This exerts its influence in many spheres, including poor housing[2,3] homelessness,[4] unemployment,[5] dependence on benefits,[6,7] living in a deprived area,[8] material resources,[9] depression[10,11] and increased social isolation.[12] Twenty years ago poverty in our society was shared equally between the elderly and families[13] but is now mainly represented by families with young children[14] and especially by lone-parent families.[6] Poverty damages not only the health and longevity of the children from these families[15] but also affects the parenting problems that can be encountered and the likelihood of conflict between the child and parent.[16]

The interaction between stressful life events, which lead to a greater incidence of depression and anxiety and a greater likelihood of these occurring in the lives of single parents, especially of women,[10,17] adversely compounds the parenting behaviour and leads to a downward spiral in their children's behaviour and performance.[18] Other factors leading to adverse outcomes for children include poor parental educational attainments[19] and parental unemployment[5] but lone parenthood in its own right is more significant.[20] Currently almost a fifth of British mothers are single parents and a half live below the poverty line.[21] A child of a lone parent is twice as likely to be involved in an accident as one from a two-parent family.[22] The death rate of children from single-parent households is 42 per cent higher than those from the poorest socioeconomic group, social class V.[6] However the provision of additional support to lone parents can reduce the number of accidents to their children.[23,24,25]

Lone-parent families living in Western societies are often supported by a variety of welfare benefits but the dilemma of raising a family under these systems is either accepting welfare dependency or low paid work, neither of which lifts the family out of poverty.[20] A currently used definition of poverty is household income below 60 per cent of median income after housing costs.[26] Between 1979 and 1996 the proportion of people living in households below the poverty line rose from 9 per cent to 24 per cent. Child poverty in the United Kingdom showed an increase from one in ten to around a third giving us one of the highest child poverty rates in the industrialised world.

The government in 1999 pledged to end child poverty within a twenty-year timescale. A broad range of measures have been introduced resulting in higher financial support for families with children, targeted programmes for children up to school leaving age and a range of changes to the tax and benefit system to allow families to work themselves out of the poverty threshold. The flagship of the targeted programmes to reduce child poverty is the Sure Start program, which has had a total of £4,253 million between 1998 and the end of the financial year 2005 allocated to it.[27] It aims to provide support for families and parents with home visiting (outreach) teams, good quality play, learning, and childcare in local nurseries, and extra services according to local needs, such as skills training for parents, personal development courses, and practical advice and support such as debt counselling, and language or literacy training.[28]

Lessons from family support interventions

Vulnerable children and families are more likely to derive lasting value from interventions that lead to greater empowerment.[29] Specifically the intervention should lead to an improvement of self-esteem, a reduced sense of isolation and increased feelings of self-efficacy, which is associated with a feeling of greater control over their lives. Poverty leaves low-income families with limited choices in all spheres of their lives.[30] It can lead to feelings that impair an individual's ability to improve their situation[31] and that their future is in the hands of others.[32] Poverty is also associated with a sense of isolation from the rest of society that is perceived not to care about them.[33] The sense of isolation, sometimes combined with feelings of shame[34] or guilt,[33] can exclude them from opportunities to improve their circumstances through support and networks of friends.[35]

Studies with low-income women suggest that those with the most negative self-images tended to blame external factors for their situation, considered that they had no control over their circumstances and this led to feelings of hopelessness and helplessness.[36] Self-efficacy,[37] a sense of having some control over external events that influence your life, is associated with resilience, which allows an individual to find ways of coping with difficult situations that face them.[38] Individuals with high self-esteem may be able to handle poverty better than those with low self-esteem.[39] Self-esteem seems also to be linked to positive feelings of self-worth, empathy and nurturing of others.[39] Maternal self-esteem may be challenged by the demands of motherhood and a fall is associated with dissatisfaction with the perceived social support the mother has in the early months postpartum.[40] A positive relationship has been identified between maternal age and self-esteem.[40] Out of 5,820 mothers attending kindergartens in inner city areas of the USA[41] depression affected 40 per cent. The strongest associations were with a maternal chronic health problem, homelessness, and the lowest income level. A similar percentage of depression was confirmed in a study[42] of 279 mothers with young children living in an American inner city area using the Psychiatric Symptom Index (PSI). Seventy-one per cent were unmarried. The PSI scores did not vary by age, race, birthplace, educational level, employment, marital status, or family composition. Mothers' self-reports of poor financial status, health status, or activity limitation because of illness was associated with higher levels of depressive symptoms.

Depression is particularly important in mothers of young children, as shown in one recent study.[43] Having a mother who has been diagnosed with depression, has low education, or is an immigrant, and living in a household with low-income adequacy, increases the risk of poor developmental attainment in children aged 1 to 5 years.[43] Broadly focused interventions that address not only parenting deficits, but also family stress, depression, poverty and lack of social support are clearly needed. Vulnerable families may not only need to improve parenting skills, but also interpersonal skills, communication and problem solving.[44]

Seminal research interventions for children and families

The seminal work that led to the national Sure Start program was the longitudinal study over 27 years of the High/Scope Perry Pre-school program. David Weikart developed this program in 1962 in the Ypsilanti Public Schools, in the state of Michigan, USA. In the High/Scope model, teachers help children plan, carry out, and review their own educational activities. The teaching staff from High/Scope Perry, whilst still in the first years of their experimental program in 1965, found themselves in demand throughout the nation as teacher trainers for the Head Start program. This initiative developed out of President Lyndon B. Johnson's 'War on Poverty' and offered pre-school children from low-income families, high quality nursery provision and a variety of family support.

During the late 1960s and early 1970s, the research examining the effectiveness of pre-school programmes was inconclusive, although it did show that the pre-school program children had greater readiness for school. An evaluation[45] of the Head Start program published in 1969 after the children had been in school for three years showed no sustained improvement from the intervention and led policy makers to believe that it had been a failure. However by the late 1970s the follow-up studies for the High/Scope Perry School program were beginning to show dramatic benefits when the children were re-evaluated at

15 years of age.[46] Further follow-up studies at the age of 27 years continued to show dramatic differences.[47]

This longitudinal study had recruited its participants between 1962 and 1965 to assess the outcome of the High/Scope Perry School program, by randomly assigning 123 poor African American children (from 100 families) either to a pre-school program group or a no-pre-school program group. The program teachers conducted daily 2½-hour classes for children on weekday mornings and made weekly 1½-hour home visits to each mother and child on weekday afternoons. It is worth looking in detail at this study for four reasons. Firstly, it was close enough to true random assignment to inspire confidence that group differences are due to the effects of the pre-school program, although younger children in the same families were put in the same group as their older siblings to prevent the spread of the program effects to the no-program group. Secondly, the longitudinal follow-ups through to age 27 had very little missing data—an average of only 5 per cent per measure, minimising attrition as a potential source of design contamination. Thirdly, a cost-benefit[48] analysis was performed, which showed that it saved $7 for every $1 invested. Fourthly, the home visiting component brings it into the category of a family support program as well as an educational intervention. By the age of 27 years the following significant differences were found between the pre-school group and the no-pre-school group:

- Incidence of crime. Only 7 per cent of adults who had participated in the High Scope/Perry Pre-school program had been arrested five or more times, compared with 35 per cent of those who had not participated in a pre-school program. Of those in the pre-school program group, 7 per cent had ever been arrested for drug-related offences, compared to 25 per cent of those in the no-program group.

- Earnings and economic status. Adults in the program group were four times more likely (29 per cent) to earn $2,000 or more per month than were adults in the no-program group (7 per cent). Almost three times as many (36 per cent) owned their own homes, compared to those in the no-program group (13 per cent). More than twice as many (program 30 per cent, no program 13 per cent) owned a second car. As adults, 59 per cent of those in the program group had received welfare assistance or other social services at some time, compared to 80 per cent of those in the no-program group.

- Educational attainment. Seventy-one per cent of those in the program group graduated from regular or adult high schools or received General Education Development certification, compared with 54 per cent of those in the no-program group. Earlier in the study, the pre-school program group had significantly higher average achievement scores at age 14 and literacy scores at age 19.

- Marriage and single parenthood. Forty per cent of women in the program group were married at the time of the age-27 interview, compared to 8 per cent of those in the no-program group; and 57 per cent of women in the program group were single parents, compared to 83 per cent of those in the no-program group.

Other research brought together by a consortium of researchers from many longitudinal studies has also shown clear long-term effects for children who had attended diverse early childhood programmes—some focusing on parents, some on children, indicating that fewer were placed in special education programmes and that more graduated from high school.[49]

Two particular studies stand out for being well designed, pre-school, randomised, longitudinal studies following the participants into adulthood. These are the North Carolina Abecedarian Project and the Chicago Child-Parent Centres Study. The North Carolina Abecedarian Project randomly assigned children to one of four intervention conditions: educational treatment from infancy through three years in public school (up to age 8); pre-school treatment only (infancy to age 5); primary school treatment only (age 5–8 years), or an untreated control group. The study[50] followed the participants up to age 21. Researchers found that about 35 per cent of the young adults in the intervention groups as opposed to 14 per cent in the control group had either graduated from or were at the time of the assessment attending a four-year college or university. However there were not significant differences regarding a reduction in crime although this was seen in the Chicago Child-Parent Centres Study.[51]

This study began in 1986 and tracked 1,539 pre-school children from low-income families across a wide variety of pre-schools and schools in Chicago. Participation was associated with significantly higher levels of school readiness, achievement, and educational attainment, and with lower rates of child maltreatment, juvenile delinquency, special education placement, and grade retention. Every dollar invested in the pre-school program returned $7.14 to society at large. The Chicago Longitudinal Study showed a high school completion rate of 50 per cent compared to 39 per cent for the group that did not have the benefit of quality early care. The High/Scope Perry, the North Carolina Abecedarian Project and the Chicago Child-Parent Centres Study show the potential lasting effects of good pre-school programmes on young children living in poverty, despite the variability in contexts, pre-school programmes, and populations served.

However, caution about generalising their claims to all pre-school programmes, let alone family support programmes, needs to be taken. They were all model programmes, adequately supported and professionally run, with the active support of scientists and expert program developers or attentive administrators. The specific educational intervention used is also of significance. A study found that children in Head Start programs that used the High/Scope model experienced statistically significant gains on the Woodcock-Johnson test of letter and word recognition[52] over a six-month period. This was over and above the effects of other teacher and child characteristics, and High/Scope was the only model for which such a gain was found.[53] This is significant[54] as only one-fifth of Head Start programs were still following this validated educational model in 2002.

Child and family support projects in the UK and Ireland

The implications of some of the above factors contributing to the success of a program are of relevance when examining interventions in the United Kingdom that have proliferated, especially from the late 1980s, offering support to children and families.[55] [56] Some of these have been longstanding such as Newpin[57] and Portage.[58] Newpin (New Parent and Infant Network) was started in 1980 and introduces parents wanting or thought to need support, to a befriender at a Newpin centre. The befrienders are often parents who have been supported themselves in the past and have subsequently developed their own skills and confidence. Portage supports parents whose children have special needs. The range of other programmes in the UK varies from helping parents to enhance the development of children with intellectual disability[59] to dealing with behavioural problems.[60]

The Parent Adviser Scheme[59] is a community-based early intervention psychology service for pre-school children with emotional and behavioural problems. Homestart recruits and trains volunteers, who are usually parents themselves, to visit families at home.[61] Mellow Parenting is a program aimed at engaging hard-to-reach families with children under five, and in helping them make changes in their relationships with their children. One-year follow-up has shown lasting gains in maternal well-being, parent-child interaction, child behaviour and child development.[62] Parenting skills are increasingly the focus of programmes to reduce the need for future specialist remedial work. Examples of this include the Parent-Link courses of Parent Network[63] and Parents in Partnership-Parent Infant Network (PIPPIN). PIPPIN offers training to professionals who can then lead classes for new parents to support their emotional health through the period surrounding the birth of a new baby.[64]

Despite some evidence for the effectiveness of UK interventions, there are few adequate studies conducted to evaluate outcome. An early evaluation of Newpin found a high rate of depression in those referred for befriending but that approximately a third of women referred did not sustain involvement in the scheme.[65] A later study found that nearly half the women referred to four Newpin centres went on to make use of its services but a larger proportion did not. It was not clear why there was such a high loss of referrals and whether it was due to inappropriate referrals, a perceived lack of support from joining the scheme or poor administration. It was argued that voluntary sector initiatives should be subjected to the same rigorous scrutiny for cost-effectiveness as the statutory sector.[66]

In 1997 an overview of parenting programmes[67] aimed at reducing child behaviour problems identified a considerable number of studies conducted since

1969 in both the USA and UK. Only randomised control trials and studies containing measures of child behaviour were included. Out of 250 studies, only 18 were judged to be methodologically adequate. From these it was concluded that such programmes worked, particularly behaviourally orientated programmes focused on children with conduct problems. The study concluded that further investigation is needed to evaluate the relative costs and benefits of the programmes that are available and their acceptability to parents.

Two well-evaluated interventions have relevance to current Sure Start programmes. They point to the possible benefits of an increased role for health visitors, working in co-operation with Sure Start outreach workers in supporting families in need. One study was followed up over a fifteen-year period.[68] It was set in a semi-rural population in New York State and women who had no previous live births were randomised to either a home visiting group or no visits. Families received a mean of 9 home visits during pregnancy and 23 home visits from the child's birth until the second birthday. The study participants were followed up for 15 years and it was demonstrated that home visitation reduced the number of subsequent pregnancies, the use of welfare, child abuse and neglect, and criminal behaviour on the part of low-income, unmarried mothers for up to 15 years after the birth of the first child.

The second study was the 'community mothers' program which took place in Dublin.[23] In the community mothers program 30 experienced mothers from the same community were recruited as community mothers. They received some training on feeding, managing children's routines and encouraging the development of the infant. The program was randomised to first-time mothers who lived in a deprived area of Dublin. All the first-time mothers received standard support from the public health nurse. In addition, those in the intervention group received the services of a community mother, who was scheduled to visit monthly during the first year of the child's life. At the end of the study, children in the intervention group were more likely to have received all of their primary immunisations, to be read to, and to be read to daily, to have played more cognitive games, and to be exposed to more nursery rhymes. The diet of the infants in the intervention group was also more appropriate than in the control group. Mothers in the intervention group also had a better diet than controls. At the end of the study they were less likely to be tired, feel miserable, and want to stay indoors; had more positive feelings; and were less likely to display negative feelings.[23] As Sure Start outreach workers that perform home visits are generally not medically qualified, this study's findings are of particular relevance.

Family support interventions—should there be controlled studies?

Clearly the need to have well-conducted research into the effectiveness of programmes is essential, especially in the UK, which has not conducted rigorous studies that will help to guarantee that on-going investment by future governments will continue. The cost-benefit of these interventions is crucial, especially when you look at the scale of the Sure Start investment of £4,253 million over an 8-year period from 1998. It is not enough to show that Sure Start can be demonstrated to lead to benefits, unless these can be shown to be greater than simply alleviating poverty in the target population by giving them the money directly, which would relieve the stress of poverty and lead to some long-term benefits.

The Sure Start program has been designed and costed with evaluation as a central feature of its budget and it has a national evaluation structure linked to a number of universities. However Sure Start is not undertaking any random controlled trials. Some of the possible reasons behind this and concerns of independent researchers about this omission[69] were outlined in 2003. Communities with similar indices of deprivation that are geographically close to Sure Start programmes but not within their boundaries could be used as controls within ethically approved protocols. The power of good research cannot be overstated as neither the Sure Start program, nor the Head Start program in the USA, would be available to families now if the long-term evaluation and cost-benefit studies had not taken place into the High/Scope Perry Study from 1965.

Lessons from a grass-roots family support project

There are many challenges to developing interventions that make a lasting difference to children living in deprived families in the UK. The issues of the acceptability of the programmes to these families, access and being of relevance to hard-to-reach families are certainly crucial. Developing a structure for the intervention to aid empowerment is also a challenge; especially if the program has to meet external targets, which are set by the government for the Sure Start programmes. Empowerment and increased self-efficacy are more easily achieved by the engagement of vulnerable families in setting the agenda for the intervention.

This has been a central feature of the Sutton Hill Families Project,[70] which developed from the needs of the population that I work with, as a GP in a deprived area, with relatively high numbers of single mothers and teenage pregnancies. A striking feature noted at the first visit of the outreach worker to families, referred by the health visitor for parenting problems, has been that debt is the first concern of most families setting their own agenda. The behavioural problems of the children noted by the health visitor are of secondary concern to these families who are preoccupied by their financial difficulties. The agendas for the groups and workshops run by the project are also set by the users every three months and include activities that they would like to learn to do with their children. This leads to high attendance rates at these events and emphasises to the users that the groups belong to them. A further benefit seen in the project comes from combining mothers in the same (large) space as their children, who are led by play-focus workers, which allows opportunities for the mothers to absorb effective behavioural approaches to child discipline from them. The combination of outreach work for some families until they have developed their own self-confidence to attend group meetings has also been an essential component that has contributed to involvement of some hard-to-reach families. The attendance at groups allows users to have a safe place to explore asserting themselves and developing their confidence. This coming together of vulnerable families frequently leads to them supporting each other outside of the groups. It is also the first step that can lead to community building which has been argued to be the most important challenge in the next century to the future of children and families at risk.[71]

The latest edition of the Hall report,[72] which analyses the current evidence base for the screening and health promotion needs of children, recommended a greater allocation of health visitors to deprived neighbourhoods and a community-based response to meeting the needs of children and families. The Sutton Hill Families project[70] has used health visitors in this capacity, working jointly with outreach workers and group facilitators with play-focus worker support since 1995. Without these extra resources the health visitors in our practice area would have been bystanders to the unmet needs of vulnerable families. The skills of health visitors in managing families with child protection concerns have been crucial to directing and managing the involvement of the outreach workers and group facilitators in the Sutton Hill Families Project. This model could be valuably integrated into Sure Start programmes, with the health visitor providing a consultancy role for any casework that is undertaken. For many areas with health visitors not experienced in multidisciplinary working and management, training will be needed to promote this new role.

Current challenges

The National Services Framework (NSF) for Children has set new challenges for future interventions targeted at children in need.[73] This is a 10-year program and includes 11 standards, which relate to both community and hospital services. The standards refer to the following areas:

- promoting health and well-being, identifying needs, and intervening early
- supporting parents or carers
- child, young person, and family centred services
- age appropriate services as children grow into adulthood
- safeguarding and promoting the welfare of children and young people
- children and young people who are ill
- children and young people in hospital
- disabled children and young people and children with complex health needs
- mental health and psychological well-being of children and young people
- drugs management for children
- maternity services

Five of these standards should lead to greater provision for children and families in need and a sixth for disabled children or those with complex health needs. The framework also aims to integrate health, social, and education services in children's centres. Most of these are likely to be developed jointly with local Sure Start programmes.

The NSF for Children hopes to encourage early intervention for vulnerable families. If this is to be effective there is a need for future integration of the primary health care team, who are in frequent contact with vulnerable families (including those that other agencies find hard to reach) with multidisciplinary support programmes, as has been accomplished in the Sutton Hill Families Project.[70] The pooling of skills and knowledge from a wide variety of professionals including health, education and social services must be accomplished. To be successful this process requires interagency joint training that helps us understand each other's terminology, concepts, capacity, resources and perspective. This cannot be achieved in understaffed departments or organisations that are already straining from the burden of work. Without the staff capacity to enable joint training and working we cannot develop contacts between the individual service providers.

Vulnerable families and children are more likely to be empowered by interventions of multidisciplinary teams who share a philosophy to empower each other's capacities and knowledge. Cynicism in public services, fuelled by repeated well-publicised failures, such as documented in the Victoria Climbié report[74] leads to poor recruitment, morale, effectiveness and retention of staff in some of the caring professions.[75] The momentum for change from the combination of the NSF for Children, the Sure Start programmes across the country and hopefully extra training for health visitors to manage teams of multidisciplinary workers in deprived areas, will lead to tangible improvements. There are many challenges which must be faced at all levels of our society for these changes to succeed, but support from the media and local and central government is vital if we are to stop squandering the potential contributions of children who are excluded from life's opportunities.

Endnotes

1. Waterston, T., Alperstein, G. and Brown S. (2004). Social capital: a key factor in child health inequalities. *Archive of Diseases in Childhood 89*, 456–9.

2. Platt, S.D., Martin, C.J., Hunt, S.M. and Lewis, C.W. (1989). Damp housing, mould growth and symptomatic health state. *British Medical Journal, 298*, 1673–78.

3. Lowry, S. (1991). *Housing and Health*. London: BMJ Publishing.

4. Health Visitors Association and the British Medical Association (1989). *Homeless Families and Their Health*. London: BMA.

5. MacClure, A. and Stewart, G.T. (1984). Admission of children to hospitals in Glasgow: relation to unemployment and other deprivation variables. *Lancet. ii*, 682–5.

6. Judge, K. and Benzeval, M. (1993). Health inequalities: new concerns about the children of single mothers. *British Medical Journal, 306,* 677–80.

7. Bryson, A., Ford, R. and White, M. (1997). *Making Work Pay: Lone mothers, employment and well-being.* Layerthorpe: York Publishing Services.

8. Reading, R., Jarvis, S. and Openshaw, S. (1993). Measurement of social inequalities in health and use of health services among children in Northumberland. *Archive of Diseases in Childhood 68,* 626–31.

9. Shepherd, M. (1996). Poverty, health and health visitor. *Health Visitor 69,* 141–3.

10. Hall, L.A., Williams, C.A. and Greenberg, R.S. (1985). Supports, stressors, and depressive symptoms in low-income mothers of young children. *American Journal of Public Health, 75,* 518–22.

11. Chung, E.K., McCollum, K.F., Elo, I.T., Lee, H.J. and Culhane, J.F. (2004). Maternal depressive symptoms and infant health practices among low-income women. *Pediatrics, 113,* 6, 523–9.

12. Oakley, A., Hickey, D. and Rigby, A.S. (1994). Love or money? Social support, class inequality and the health of women and children. *European Journal of Public Health, 4,* 265–73.

13. Hedstrom, P. and Ringen, S. (1987). Age and income in contemporary society: a research note. *Journal of Social Policy, 16,* 227–39.

14. Graham, H. (1994). The changing financial circumstances of households with children. *Children and Society, 8,* 98–113.

15. Roberts H. (1997). Socio-economic determinants of health: children, poverty and health. *British Medical Journal, 314,* 1122–5.

16. Long, N. (1996). Parenting in the USA: Growing adversity. *Clinical Child Psychology and Psychiatry, 1,* 3, 469–83.

17. Harrison, J., Barrow, S., Gask, L. and Creed, F. (1999). Social determinants of GHQ score by postal survey. *Journal of Public Health Medicine, 21,* 283–8.

18. McLoyd, V.C. and Randolph, S.M. (1984). The conduct and publication of research on Afro-American children: A content analysis. *Human Development, 27,* 65–75.

19. Considine, G. and Zappalà, G. (2002). The influence of social and economic disadvantage in the academic performance of school students in Australia. *Journal of Sociology. The Australian Sociological Association, 38,* 2, 129–48.

20. Walter M. (2002). Working their way out of poverty? Sole motherhood, work, welfare and material well-being. *Journal of Sociology. The Australian Sociological Association, 38,* 4, 361–80.

21. Child Poverty Action Group. Available at: www.cpag.org.uk/

22. Roberts, I. and Bless, P. (1995). For debate: social policy as a cause of childhood accidents: the children of lone mothers. *British Medical Journal, 311*, 925–8.

23. Olds, D.L., Henderson, C.R., Chamberlin, R. and Tatelbaum, R. (1986). Preventing child abuse and neglect: a randomised trial of nurse home visitation. *Pediatrics, 78*, 65–78.

24. Johnson, Z., Howell, F. and Molloy, B. (1993). Community mothers' programme: a randomised controlled trial of non-professional intervention in parenting. *British Medical Journal, 306*, 1449–52.

25. Kitzman, H., Olds, D.L., Henderson, C.R. Jr., Hanks, C., Cole, R., Tatelbaum, R., McConnochie, K.M., Sidora, K., Luckey, D.W., Shaver, D., Engelhardt, K., James, D. and Barnard, K. (1997). Effect of prenatal and infancy home visitation by nurses on pregnancy outcomes, childhood injuries, and repeated childbearing. A randomized controlled trial. *Journal of the American Medical Association, 278*, 8, 644–52.

26. Department for Work and Pensions: Available at: www.dwp.gov.uk/asd/recent.asp

27. Department for Education and Skills: Available at: www.dfes.gov.uk/deptreport2004/sure_start/index.cfm

28. Glass, N. (1999). Sure Start: The development of an early intervention programme for young children in the United Kingdom. *Children and Society, 13*, 257–64.

29. World Health Organisation. (1985). *Targets for Health for All*. Geneva: WHO.

30. Callahan, M. and Lumb, C. (1995). My check and my children: The long road to empowerment in child welfare. *Child Welfare, 74*, 795–819.

31. Bandura, A. and Locke, E.A. (2003). Negative self-efficacy and goal effects revisited. *Journal of Applied Psychology, 88*, 1, 87–99.

32. Lochead, C. and Scott, K. (2000). The dynamics of women's poverty in Canada. Accessed at: www.swc-cfc.gc.ca/pubs/0662281594/200003_0662281594_7_e.html

33. McIntyre, L., Officer, S. and Robinson, L.M. (2003). Feeling poor: The felt experience of low-income lone mothers. *Affilia, 18*, 3, 316–31.

34. Garbarino, J. (1998). The stress of being a poor child in America. *Child and Adolescent Psychiatric Clinics of North America, 7*, 105–19.

35. Raphael, D. (2001). *Inequality is Bad for our Hearts: Why low income and social exclusion are major causes of heart disease in Canada*. Toronto, Canada: North York Heart Health Network.

36. Goodman, S.H., Cooley, E.L., Sewell, D.R. and Leavitt, N. (1994). Locus of control and self esteem in depressed, low-income African-American women. *Community Mental Health Journal, 30*, 259–69.

37. Bandura, A. (1994). Self-efficacy. In V. S. Ramachaudran (ed.), *Encyclopedia of Human Behavior*. 4: 71–81. New York: Academic Press. (Reprinted in H. Friedman (ed), (1998).

Encyclopedia of Mental Health. San Diego: Academic Press.

38. Bachay, J.B. and Cingel, P.A. (1999). Restructuring resilience: emerging voices. *Affilia. 14*, 162–75.

39. Brody, G.H. and Flor, D.L. (1997). Maternal psychological functioning, family processes, and child adjustment in rural, single-parent, African-American families. *Developmental Psychology, 33*, 1000–11.

40. McVeigh, C. and Smith, M.A. (2000). Comparison of adult and teenage mother's self-esteem and satisfaction with social support. *Midwifery, 16*, 4, 269–76.

41. Lanzi, R.G., Pascoe, J.M., Keltner, B. and Ramey, S.L. (1999). Correlates of maternal depressive symptoms in a national Head Start Program sample. *Archives of Pediatric Adolescent Medicine 153*, 801–7.

42. Heneghan, A.M., Silver, E.J., Bauman, L.J., Westbrook, L.E. and Stein, R.E.K. (1998). Depressive symptoms in inner-city mothers of young children: who is at risk? *Pediatrics, 102*, 6, 1394–400.

43. To, T., Guttmann, A., Dick, P.T., Rosenfield, J.D., Parkin, P.C., Tassoudji, M., Vydykhan, T.N., Cao, H.J. and Harris, K. (2004). Risk markers for poor developmental attainment in young children: results from a longitudinal national survey. *Archives of Pediatric Adolescent Medecine, 158*, 7, 643–49.

44. Webster-Stratton, C. (1997). From parent training to community building. Families in society. *The Journal of Contemporary Human Services, March/April*, 156–71.

45. Westinghouse Learning Corporation (1969). *Impact of Head Start: Evaluation of the effects of Head Start on children's cognitive and affective development*, 2 vols. Washington, DC: Clearinghouse for Federal, Scientific, and Technical Information.

46. Schweinhart, L.J. and Weikart, D.P. (1980).*Young Children Grow Up: Effects of the Perry Pre-school Program on youths through age 15 .*Ypsilanti, Michigan: High/Scope Press.

47. Schweinhart, L., Barnes, H.V. and Weikart, D.P. (1993). *Significant Benefits: The High/Scope Perry Pre-school Study through age 27*. Ypsilanti, Michigan: High/Scope Press.

48. Barnett, W.S. (1996). *Lives in the Balance: Benefit-cost analysis of the Perry Preschool Program through age 27*. Monographs of the High/Scope Educational Research Foundation. Ypsilanti, Michigan: High/Scope Press.

49. Lazar, I. and Darlington, R. (1982). *Lasting Effects of Early Education: Report from the Consortium for Longitudinal Studies*. Chicago: University of Chicago Press for the Society for Research in Child Development.

50. Campbell, F.A. and Ramey, C.T. (1994). Effects of early intervention on intellectual and academic achievement: a follow-up study of children from low-income families. *Child Development, 65*, 2, 684–98.

51. Reynolds, A.J., Temple, J.A., Robertson, D. L. and Mann, E. A. (2001). Long-term effects of an early childhood intervention on educational achievement and juvenile arrest: a 15-year

follow-up of low-income children in public schools. *Journal of the American Medical Association, 285,* 2339–46.

52. Woodcock, R.W. and Mather, N. (1989). WJ-R test of achievement: examiner's manual. In R.W. Woodcock and M.B. Johnson, *Woodcock-Johnson Psycho-Educational Battery—Revised.* Chicago: Riverside.

53. Zill, N. and Resnick, G. (2002). Relationship of classroom quality and type of curriculum to children's progress in Head Start. Presentation at the National Head Start Research Conference, Washington, DC.

54. McKey, R.H. (2003). The Head Start Family and Child Experiences Survey: what are we learning about program quality and child development? *Children and Families: The Magazine of the National Head Start Association, Winter,* 62–4.

55. Pugh, G., De'ath, E. and Smith, C. (1994) *Confident Parents, Confident Children: Policy and practice in parent education and support.* London: National Children's Bureau.

56. Smith, C. (1996). *Developing Parenting Programmes.* London: National Children's Bureau.

57. Pound, A. (1994). *NEWPIN: A befriending and therapeutic network for carers of young children.* London: HMSO.

58. Shearer, M. and Shearer, D. (1972). The Portage project: A model for early childhood education. *Exceptional Children, 39,* 210–17.

59. Davis, H. and Rushton, R. (1991). Counselling and supporting parents of children with developmental delay: a research evaluation. *Journal of Mental Deficiency Research, 35,* 89–112.

60. Sutton, C. (1992). Training parents to manage difficult children: a comparison of methods. *Behavioural Psychotherapy, 20,* 115–39.

61. Van der Eyken, W. (1990). *Home-Start: A four year evaluation.* Leicester, UK: Home-Start Consultancy.

62. Puckering, C., Rogers, J., Mills, M. and Cox, A. (1994). Process and evaluation of a group intervention for mothers with parenting difficulties. *Child Abuse Review, 3,* 299–310.

63. Davis, H. and Hester, P. (1996). *An Independent Evaluation of Parent-Link: A parenting education programme.* London: Parent Network.

64. Parr, M. (1995). *Why PIPPIN was Developed: Some research findings.* Stevenage, UK: PIPPIN.

65. Cox, A., Pound, A., Mills, M., Puckering, C. and Owen, A. (1991). Evaluation of a home visiting and befriending scheme: Newpin. *Journal of the Royal Society of Medicine. 84,* 217–20.

66. Oakley, A., Mauthnes, M., Rajan, L. and Turner, H. (1995). Supporting vulnerable families: an evaluation of Newpin. *Health Visitor, 68,* 188–91.

67. Barlow, J. (1997). *Systematic Review of the Effectiveness of Parent-Training Programmes in Improving Behaviour Problems in Children aged 3–10 years*. Oxford, UK: University of Oxford.

68. Olds, D.L., Eckenrode, J., Henderson, C.R. Jr., Kitzman, H., Powers, J., Cole, R., Sidora, K., Morris, P., Pettitt, L.M. and Luckey, D. (1997). Long-term effects of home visitation on maternal life course and child abuse and neglect. Fifteen-year follow-up of a randomized trial. *Journal of the American Medical Association, 278,* 8, 637–43.

69. Oakley, A., Strange, V., Toroyan, T., Wiggins, M., Roberts, I. and Stephenson, J. (2003). Using random allocation to evaluate social interventions: three recent UK examples. *The Annals of the American Academy of Political and Social Science, 589,* 170–89.

70. Henderson, C. (2000). Helping parents to help themselves and their children. *Community Practitioner, 73,* 1, 801–3.

71. Barter, K. (2000). Building Community: A conceptual framework for child protection. Paper presented at the British Association for the Study and Prevention of Child Abuse and Neglect, The Millennium Congress 2000: Meeting Children's Needs—The opportunity for change in Child Protection. University of York.

72. Hall, D.M.B. and Elliman, D. (2002). *Health for All Children*. Oxford: Oxford University Press.

73. Department of Health. *National Service Framework for Children, Young People and Maternity Services*. The Stationery Office. September 2004. Available at: http://www.dh.gov.uk/PolicyAndGuidance/HealthAndSocialCareTopics/ChildrenServices/ChildrenServicesInformation/fs/en

74. Laming, W.H. (2003).*The Victoria Climbié Report*. London: Stationery Office. Available at: www.victoria-climbie-inquiry.org.uk/finreport/finreport.htm

75. Harlow, E. (2004). Why don't women want to be social workers anymore? New managerialism, postfeminism and the shortage of social workers in Social Services Departments in England and Wales. *European Journal of Social Work, 7,* 2, 167–79.

CHAPTER 13

The Family Well-being Project: Providing psychology services for children and families in a community regeneration context

CARL HARRIS

This chapter has been adapted from a presentation to an audience of clinical psychologists, trainee clinical psychologists and assistants at a community psychology conference.[1] The presentation was designed to demonstrate some of the ways in which a focus on community can be helpful to clinical psychologists and how clinical psychologists can operate in a community regeneration context. Sometimes critical and community psychology ideas are persuasive, but ways of applying them are not always immediately apparent.

This chapter aims to describe some characteristics of a service response in a particular context without making any claims for its overall relative value. There is a question of 'better for whom?' as for some children and families they would simply have wanted a direct clinical psychology service delivered as quickly as possible and with as much input as they required. For them, the indirect work of the project raising the profile of research on the patch, or generating a broader range of hypotheses to use as a guide to investigating local problems, are likely to have a lower priority.

For the project, having the opportunity to work with a community-wide organisation meant a different ethical context, as there were now opportunities to have a more direct influence on some of the environmental factors which many psychologists see as relevant to the well-being of the children and families with whom they work. Having these opportunities meant that it would have been more ethically questionable than usual to have followed a strictly individualistic model of treatment. In the end a balance was struck between delivering 'normal clinical psychology' and becoming involved in other areas of work on a more community level.

The Family Well-being Project

The Family Well-being Project (FWP) is a partnership project between a New Deal for Communities (NDC) programme and a Clinical Psychology Department within a UK NHS Trust (with responsibility for children's services). NDC is a complex community regeneration project which aims to address a wide range of issues across twelve theme areas including: health, education, housing, employment, community safety, etc. When residents were asked to prioritise themes, health was rated eleventh out of twelve. The FWP is located within the health theme.

NDC has approximately £50 million at its disposal over a ten-year period. It has to address a range of issues (defined by central government) in a 'cross-cutting' manner, acknowledging that the difficulties it aims to address are not the sole concern of any one organisation or agency. NDC aims to encourage providers from a wide range of services to 'come out of their silos' and develop new partnerships to assist each other in addressing the issues which present themselves in the area it covers.

The NDC area itself is comprised of three council estates which are clustered together on the outskirts of the city. There are around 10,000 people living on the estates. The residents are 90 per cent white British with about 10 per cent black and ethnic minorities. There are three primary schools in the area and one secondary school.

The city council had originally focused attention on this area several years ago, as there were high levels of mobility in two of the estates in particular (20–25 per cent per annum). This was causing difficulties in terms of service delivery, as people became 'lost' to services, and was disrupting communities, with impact, for instance, on turnover of pupils in schools.

The housing in the two estates with high mobility is of a poor quality and was built in the 1950s and 60s. The housing in the estate with lower mobility (around 10 per cent per annum) is of a better quality and was built in the 1970s.

NDC has a budget which is significant but which represents approximately an extra 2–3 per cent of public expenditure on the area as a whole per annum. It is not, therefore, in a position to provide bespoke services itself as this would be neither affordable nor sustainable. It aims instead to 'bend the mainstream' so that public services are delivered in a way that better suits local requirements.

The FWP performs two main functions in this context. Firstly, it carries out action research designed to promote mutual understanding between residents and service providers. Secondly, it supports local stakeholders, services and initiatives that promote emotional well-being. The FWP works with families with children under 16.

For the larger part of its existence the FWP has been made up of one full-time clinical psychologist and three sessions of administrative support (paid for by NDC). The clinical psychology department have contributed management support and clinical supervision. In the last nine months a third-year specialist trainee has also provided input to the project through a six-month placement, and an exchange of resources has been in place between the FWP and the clinical psychology department which has traded one session of the clinical psychologist's time for two sessions of an assistant psychologist's time.

The FWP developed from a previous project funded by NDC, a 'Community Psychologist' (October 2001–April 2003). This post had been designed as part of a Family Health Team, which had been intended to include a clinical psychologist, a health visitor, a community nursery nurse, a school nurse and a social worker. The recruitment to the other posts had failed to progress with NDC being unwilling to fund the Family Health Team for longer than a year and the respective organisations being unwilling to attempt to recruit to a post with only twelve months of funding.

The FWP is based in a health centre on one of the three estates and has become part of the local primary care network. The FWP has also built up partnerships including the local schools, charities and specialist mental health providers.

The influences on the Family Well-being Project

Personal and professional experiences

The psychologist who has provided the bulk of the input to the project is a white, middle-aged male who grew up in a middle-class environment on the edge of a Coal Board estate on the outskirts of a nearby town. The psychologist has a BA in Political Economy and an MPhil in Political Theory and Philosophy. From this perspective there is a clear class-base to the theory and practice of clinical psychology.

NHS clinical psychology, as a working context is professionally organised and provides secure employment. It is easier to take risks when you know that you can always find another job and that your pension is unlikely to be affected.

The profession has a good track record of governance. It is, however, inclined to take an individualistic perspective on people's difficulties and interprets evidence-based practice as identifying which mode of therapy works best with which class of problem (this factor contributes 15 per cent of the variance in therapeutic outcome). This neglects the other factors which contribute to variance in 'therapeutic outcome' such as client expectancies (15 per cent), environment (40 per cent) and therapeutic relationship (30 per cent).[2]

Nevertheless, the practice of clinical psychology is generally useful to many individuals and families. It is also, however, unavailable to large sections of the population, partly because of resource issues and partly because of the obstacles that prevent some sections of the population from using such services.

The post-holder had previously worked for five years in a 'life-span' Primary Care Psychology service which had a significant 'direct-access' component. Through this direct-access work, children and families could drop in to the service during one session per week and could phone in to book an hour-long consultation. Adults could also self refer to a 'Self-Help Clinic', through which they would gain access to up to three individual sessions.

This service also had a strong systemic orientation, which allowed for the identification of social, economic and cultural factors in people's circumstances. The systemic focus also allowed for the identification of how and where knowledge was constructed. Much clinical psychology knowledge is created in specific locations, which are frequently populated by only mental health personnel, with a consequent influence on the nature of the understanding which develops.

The National Health Service context

A number of central government and National Health Service publications support the approach of the FWP, for example, the Acheson Report[3] and *Saving Lives: Our Healthier Nation*[4] which argued that the solutions to major health problems require interventions that break through the normal sector barriers to take account of inequalities and the environmental factors that impact upon well-being. Within health the concept of social capital has also received attention.[5] With regard to children and families in particular, the standards of the National Service Framework for Children, Young People and Maternity Services[6] focus attention on the mental health and psychological well-being of young people.

There is of course a limit to how far such publications will go. While it is recognised that social inequalities impact adversely on the population's health[7] and most severely on those in the most deprived socio-economic groups[3] no government publication has advocated differential taxation as a health intervention. Instead the arguments are for services to try and take these differences into account. A danger here is that social capital, for instance, could become another means of blaming communities for their own ill-health because they just aren't cohesive enough.

New Deal for Communities

The New Deal for Communities programme involves an 'across the board' approach to community regeneration, as opposed to initiatives like Single Regeneration Budgets (SRBs) which generally focus on one issue, such as health or housing. NDC has created new local networks of service providers (e.g., Local Stakeholders), although with costs to the previously existing local networks (e.g., the Under-8s Forum). The new local networks can create new connections and new understandings as they bring together agencies which have had little contact in the past. One such example is 'Local Stakeholders', a meeting of any and all service providers to the NDC area. The meeting takes place in the same community hall on the first Wednesday of every month. Below is an example of a piece of dialogue between two service representatives at a local stakeholders' meeting.

At a local stakeholders' meeting a police representative was describing the recent increase in burglaries in the area.

The nurse manager present asked whether this was due to the release from prison of a particular individual. The police representative confirmed that it was.

The nurse manager then asked whether that person had a drug-related problem. The police representative confirmed that the person did.

The nurse manager then asked whether the police had been given notice locally of this person's impending release. The police representative said that they would normally be informed but that on this occasion the person had been released to a different part of the city.

The nurse manager asked why the person had come to this part of the city. The police representative said that this area is often targeted by people intent on criminal activities as there is a high proportion of lone female parents who are vulnerable to exploitation by people intent on criminal activity.

This conversation is reported as an example of how a shared understanding (of a relationship between crime and drugs) can be rehearsed in a public meeting (with possible increases in understanding for those present) and then be amplified through questioning (to enhance our understanding of the processes which affect the safety of our client group).

The programme is largely target-driven, so projects within the programme are required to show how their 'outputs' and 'outcomes' relate to the 18 'strategic objectives' laid down by central government. This involves a considerable bureaucratic demand from government partners. This demand also represents a shift from the original ethos of the NDC programme which was to emphasise collaboration with the local community as the key to gaining the extra resources, rather than compliance with a centrally-determined set of objectives. The process of change and service delivery within NDC is informed by a community development approach.[8]

The UK Community Psychology Network

The UK Community Psychology Network has been a significant influence upon the project. Community psychology focuses on the 'person in context'. This is an approach which focuses on neither the person nor their social setting in isolation from the other but which explores the transaction between the two.[9]

There have been expectations from within clinical psychology and the NDC organisation that the project would adopt the approach of seeing individual families and children. Adopting a different approach has required support from others who have been more used to taking a community perspective and a significant degree of tolerance and understanding from NDC and clinical psychology department members (particularly line management).

Members of the network have provided mentoring, external appraisal and informal supervision to the project. These have all been invaluable in maintaining a community approach. The network has been supportive both emotionally and practically (see micro-neighbourhood analysis below).

Examples of Family Well-being Project activity

There are a number of examples of the work of the FWP. These are listed below.
- enhancing the shared understanding between residents and service providers of the influences on family well-being
- a 'drop-in' at a local primary school
- consulting to individual families and children
- providing psychology supervision to local worker
- analysing micro-neighbourhood referral pattern
- supporting a Parental Mental Health and Family Well-being Network
- supporting NDC evaluation of the effectiveness of projects and their impact on well-bein
- supporting local understanding of the human context of service delivery and change

The remainder of this chapter will focus on three of these activities: enhancing the shared understanding between residents and service providers of the influences on family well-being; a 'drop-in' at a local primary school; and, analysing micro-neighbourhood referral patterns.

Shared understandings

This work, which is the principal function of the FWP, is an action research project intended to investigate the different understandings of the factors influencing family well-being on the three estates. Although various elements of the FWP activities inform these understandings, the work is being carried out primarily through a qualitative research process, exploring the views of residents and service providers. This begins by inviting residents to participate in individual interviews and service providers to fill in a questionnaire. Residents are paid for the time they contribute to the project. The participation of children depends upon a parent being willing for the project to approach children within their family.

Those agreeing to participate are then invited to meet as a resident group and as a service provider group to discuss the views they have expressed individually and the views expressed by the other group. When agreed by those participating, the two groups will come together. At this point we will be asking them to use their 'more shared understanding' to develop a strategy to promote family well-being in the area. The process is currently at the stage of feeding back the results so far to the separate groups.

This work will influence the development of the NDC strategy which will, in turn, influence the delivery of mainstream services to the area, which will help to shape the context of families locally so that it better promotes their well-being.

A 'drop-in' at a local primary school

This followed an offer by the FWP at a Local Stakeholders meeting, to deliver psychology services to any local agencies who wished to make use of them. The school was the only organisation to take up the offer.

Through consultation with two deputy heads within the school a 'drop-in' was set up on a wednesday afternoon. Three half-hour slots are available to families and children, who self-refer or are referred by members of the school teaching or classroom support staff.

Approximately 35 different children and families have accessed this service. In seven instances these have been children who were also referred to the clinical psychology department via the Child and Adolescent Mental Health Services for this part of the city. The referrals received via the 'drop-in' have been appropriate for a child psychology service. This reflects the degree to which potential users of clinical psychology services are prevented from doing so, as well as the significant unmet need in the community.

During the third-year specialist placement we had the capacity to evaluate the delivery of psychology services to the school and an audit of satisfaction with psychology input to the school was carried out among staff. As a consequence of this, a fourth slot, for staff, was added to the end of the afternoon. A request was also made for some information on what a psychological problem was, and so a 'teaching' session was arranged for the staff in the foundation stage of the school (i.e. reception and year one).

A more informal impact on school culture has been reported. The staff, without being prompted, and prior to the training, have often spoken about how much they now discuss psychological or mental health issues in the school, 'now that there are psychologists about'. It has become possible to move freely in and out of the staff room and to be greeted in a way that is not dissimilar to the way the rest of the staff greet each other. Educational Psychologists had already been providing a highly-valued service to the school but did not have the resources to establish such a regular presence.

Teachers have invited psychologists into the classroom where it is possible to see a number of children who have been referred to the service interacting with each other and with other classmates. This also provides the opportunity to support a teacher who may be supporting a number of referred children.

A number of the school staff are local residents who are becoming classroom assistants and learning support staff. For many of them this is their first experience of formal learning in some time. For a number of them it is an experience which makes them think about the way they parent their children and the way they were parented themselves. From time to time they visit the drop-in to talk through their experiences, the concerns these raise and the solutions they are developing. These issues are normally related to their parenting of their own children.

By supporting these residents the drop-in contributes to the capacity-building of the staff in the school. This, in turn, contributes to the capacity-building of the school itself, as the staff in training enable the school to include children who would otherwise be excluded.

These capacity-building exercises support the children's and families' relationships with the school and education. This is one way for residents, particularly children, to enhance their health and that of their children. This is based on the premise that they will be better able to move up the socio-economic scale. This is, of course, problematic when applied to a broader context than the local one, as, if these children do better, they will probably have been competing with others from other areas, who will then do worse.

Analysing micro-neighbourhood referral patterns

Within NDC there are specialist community development workers. These workers had drawn up, in collaboration with a small group of residents, a new map of the area. This map grouped sections of the estates into 'micro-neighbourhoods'. Fifty-seven micro-neighbourhoods of varying shapes and sizes were constructed. Some are long and narrow, stretching along a road; others are compact, incorporating a number of defined 'closes' or 'groves'; others group together rows of high- and low-rise blocks of flats. On average there are around 200 people in each micro-neighbourhood.

The micro-neighbourhoods were intended to provide a way of mapping meaningful communities onto the area. This would then allow the community development arm of NDC to recruit representatives from each of the micro-neighbourhoods. This could then support a two-way flow of information between community and the central NDC team.

In the same way that a service can look at the source of their referrals, the micro-neighbourhoods can also be used to see which parts of the area referrals are coming from. The FWP used them to analyse the referrals to the community psychology post which had existed in the 18 months prior to the funding of the current project.

There were 58 referrals to the community psychologist between October 2001 and March 2003. An analysis of the referrals by their micro-neighbourhood shows that five (out of the 57) micro-neighbourhoods accounted for 29, or half, of the referrals. Two micro-neighbourhoods had four referrals, two had six and one had nine. One of those with six was adjacent to the micro-neighbourhood with nine, meaning that between them they accounted for over a quarter of the referrals to the community psychologist over that period.

The level of referral from this area can be accounted for partly by the impact of one family contributing three referrals and by the fact that the project provides a service close to this particular area through the in-school drop-in. Even taking these factors into account, however, the levels are still significantly higher for that patch than for the rest of the estates.

These results fitted with information gathered from a health visitor who had been working in this area for ten years. She was asked to put crosses on a map to indicate which parts of the patch she felt were most in need of support. She put five crosses on the map of the whole area, two of which were in the two micro-neighbourhoods identified through this process.

Looking at a map of the NDC area, which shows the way that houses are laid out in relation to each other, there are differences between the different estates. In the most modern estate, which is only separated from the area of high referral by a single-carriageway road, the houses are grouped in clusters which tend to face each other, which are enclosed by themselves, frequently facing in towards a central (sometimes green) area, and which appear to have a shared identity.

In the areas with the high referral rate the houses are arranged in a Radburn formation. That is in straight rows with the front doors of one row facing the back gardens of the next row or 'grove'. These houses also have an unusual layout inside, with bedrooms, garages and front door all at street level, while the living rooms and kitchen are on the first floor. Furthermore, since the houses are built on a slope the back garden is higher than the street onto which the front door faces and so the back door is on a mezzanine between the ground and first floors in some of the houses.

The UK Community Psychology Network, via the British Psychological Society, hosted a visit from a professor of community and urban psychology from a university in Mexico in September of 2004.[10] This person visited the project during his time in the UK and was shown the data that had been collected. He was then taken on a drive around the estates and shown the houses in question. He provided a commentary on the houses in the context of their landscape and the houses' relationship to each other in their respective formations. His analysis was, of course, influenced by having seen the data prior to his viewing the houses but it demonstrated an awareness of the relationship between the person, their habitat and the environment that a clinical psychology training cannot currently provide. The two paragraphs which precede this one are strongly influenced by the analysis he provided.

The micro-neighbourhood analysis has an effect on the hypotheses we might generate to attempt to understand the pattern of referrals the community psychologist received. The nature of the hypotheses will also be influenced by the person or persons generating them. The information gathered so far was taken to a Neighbourhood Management meeting within the NDC organisation.

The Neighbourhood Management Team within NDC are a team of theme coordinators who each have a strategic responsibility for a different part of the programme (e.g. health, housing, education, employment, etc.). At the meeting in question the data were presented and a discussion followed. During the discussion a number of hypotheses were generated with the overall proviso that any explanation was likely to be made up of a combination of different factors.

The hypotheses included:

- the hard-to-let nature of the housing
- the consequent desperation of those who were likely to accept it
- the difficult histories which some people may bring to the location
- the reputation attached to the location
- failure of services to deliver to those living there
- the unorthodox, 'difficult' layout of the houses themselves
- the environment surrounding the houses (which is an expanse of grass with no 'cues', e.g., paths or benches, as to how it should be used)
- the 'unsupervised' or 'un-overlooked' nature of a significant section of the rows of Radburn houses (which may then become a locus of behaviour which is difficult to manage)
- the absence of play facilities for young people
- the 'barrack-like' nature of the housing layout which may not promote the development of a sense of community
- the low levels of 'resources' of those living there, which will make it unlikely that they will be in a position to provide support to each other

These hypotheses have implications for the project's response to the referrals from this particular area. Should the project respond to each individual referral as a mental health referral or should we consider a response in collaboration with a different partner (e.g., community development) or at a different level (e.g. housing services management)?

This discussion supplemented the work that other organisations and agencies in the area had done using the micro-neighbourhood tool for analysis, and of which the FWP had been unaware. The neighbourhood management team confirmed that the results mirrored those of the other analyses in other areas of activity, e.g. strategies to increase employment. The team were also reminded that the community development team had planned to provide an intensive input to a particular street in that area but that this had not taken place due to a variety of factors. They expressed an intention to follow that work up.

The hypotheses generated confirm that psychological awareness is not the sole preserve of professional psychologists. They also demonstrate that collaboration with different workers can produce a wider range of ideas and possible explanations than would be likely from a uni-professional or uni-disciplinary perspective.

Is this better for children? There are those who would argue that each child should receive individual attention from the project and that anything that diverts resources from this process is unhelpful. In this instance, outlining the likely significance of the environment in terms of the presentation of these children and families to the project seems to be helpful for a variety of reasons.

First, the analysis may have gained extra, targeted resources for this part of the NDC area, which should benefit the children and families referred both directly and indirectly. Second, by broadening the target of intervention to an area, any stigma may be reduced for the children and families concerned. Third, intervention from community development and/or housing may be more appropriate and helpful than delivering clinical psychology services alone to individual children and families (while also being potentially less stigmatising and more empowering). Finally, raising the potential significance of the environment in terms of explaining reasons for referral and consequently encouraging other agencies to help in addressing pertinent issues has helped to identify and strengthen partnerships. This should lead to a more effective intervention (any failure in which is consequently less likely to be simply put down to intra-personal issues such as 'lack of motivation').

Indeed, agreeing to intervene with a particular family or child in the context of our current understanding of the area with no attempt to engage other organisations or agencies which have a responsibility for the well-being of those in the area could be seen as unethical. An intervention on a solely individual basis could amplify any 'child-blaming' beliefs.

On the other hand, there may be those who experience any broader input as less helpful. Families who are managing well in this setting could experience input from community development to their grove as stigmatising in itself.

Person in context

The project and the post within it have been a demonstration of the impact of context on the person. The project, existing as it does as a partnership between a community regeneration programme and a mainstream NHS provider, provides contrasting sets of expectations for a worker within it. This tension can be productive, as the micro-neighbourhood analysis demonstrates, combining orthodox referral analysis with a tool that has been developed by a different agency, i.e. community development.

The project and post have also been a demonstration of the impact of the person on their context. It has taken time for relationships and partnerships to develop. The eighteen months of the community psychologist post were a helpful 'lead-in' to the Family Well-being Project.

In trying to have an impact on the context, the project's shortcomings in terms of the narrowness of clinical psychology training in its focus on individuals, with little or no reference to social context, has been apparent. Support from a number of sources has been helpful in the attempt to overcome these limitations: the community psychology network, providing mentoring and supervision; line-management within the clinical psychology department; and, those local workers with whom there has been interaction on a daily basis.

As outlined in the original presentation of this information to the audience of psychologists at the conference, much of what is done in this project is familiar to clinical psychologists, especially those working with children, and educational psychologists. This refers to activities such as classroom observations, building relationships with colleagues from other agencies, analysing referral patterns and delivering services in on-site settings.

The differences described in this chapter can be seen largely in terms of the context of this service delivery. In this case the context is a cross-cutting community regeneration programme. This context has significant implications in terms of the range of agencies with which the project interacts, the possible range of interventions which can be used in response to the issues identified and the understandings which these activities generate.

The context of many community-based programmes, aimed at developing services in collaboration with communities, is subject to alteration from time to time as central government priorities shift. The significance of community participation within the NDC programme was downgraded in the first couple of years of its existence. Centrally determined strategic objectives became the main criteria by which all projects should be judged.

The Sure Start programme appears to be experiencing similar shifts, with the priority of supporting early-years development possibly being diluted by the goal of providing child care so that parents can get back to work. This shift reflects the movement of oversight of the programme between government departments.[11][12]

It takes time for programmes like Sure Start and New Deal for Communities to engage successfully with local communities. Programmes have to establish themselves as trustworthy. Communities need to be in a position to engage with such programmes. This tentative drawing-together requires a supportive political context on both a local and a national level.

In terms of the impact of the Family Well-being Project on its broader context, i.e. national policy and practice, it is important to recognise that the FWP is not widely replicable in its current form, as it requires too high a level of resources. The same, however, is true of many other interventions which inform best practice.[13]

This piece of work has, nevertheless, demonstrated the importance of families' contexts to our understandings and practices. It has helped to broaden services' views of what constitutes evidence. It is also an example of how a different context can help practitioners step outside the clinic and form partnerships with other agencies to the benefit of children and families.

Endnotes

1. Programme for Community Psychology Conference (2004) Lancaster University.

2. Lambert, M.J. (1992). Psychotherapy outcome research: Implications for integrative and eclectic therapists. In J.C. Norcross and M.R. Goldfried (eds) *Handbook of Psychotherapy Integration*. New York: Basic Books.

3. Acheson, D. (1998). *Independent Inquiry into Inequalities in Health Report*. London: Stationery Office.

4. Department of Health (1999). *Saving Lives: Our healthier nation*. London: Stationery Office.

5. Health Development Agency (2004). *Social Capital for Health: Issues of definition, measurement and links to health*. www.hda.nhs.uk

6. Department of Health, Department for Education and Skills (2004). *National Service Framework for Children, Young People and Maternity Services*. London: Stationery Office.

7. Wilkinson, R. (1996). *Unhealthy Societies: The afflictions of inequality*. London: Routledge.

8. Barr, A. and Hashagen, S. (2000). *Achieving Better Community Development*. London: Community Development Foundation Publications.

9. Orford, J. (1992). *Community Psychology: Theory and practice*. Chichester: Wiley and Sons Ltd.

10. Bernardo Jiminez-Dominguez, Professor of Urban Psychology, University of Guadalajara, Mexico, personal communication.

11. Glass, N. (2005). Surely some mistake? *Guardian*, 5 January 2005

12. Craig, J. (2005). Gone but not forgotten. *Guardian*, 7 January 2005

13. Carr, A. (ed) (2000). *What Works with Children and Adolescents? A critical review of psychological interventions with children, adolescents and their families*. London: Routledge.

CHAPTER 14

Imagine Chicago:
Cultivating hope and imagination

BLISS W. BROWNE

Living is more than submission; it is creation. We can begin now to change this street and this city. We will begin to discover our power to transform the world.

Thomas Merton, a Trappist monk and social activist

In Chicago, the city in which I live, many people are so isolated within segregated communities and mindsets that they can't imagine themselves as meaningfully connected to others who are different. Patterns of discrimination by race, economic status and ethnicity, have become institutionalized in housing, neighborhood demographics, and political boundaries. Isolation leads to a loss of imagination about what is possible. Furthermore, there is a well-acknowledged 'confidence gap' with respect to institutional life. Due in part to shifts in corporate loyalty to employees, and continuing misbehavior by leaders, there is a high degree of skepticism about whether institutions will act ethically. Cynicism, which erodes hope and creativity, passes for sophistication. Apathy, addiction and violence are symptomatic of the loss of hope and the cancerous internalization of images of disorder and decay. Without confidence in a viable future, personal investment makes no sense.

How can we deal effectively with the challenges at hand? How can we create the learning environments necessary for a worthy and just future? How can we use those environments to help develop critical intergenerational and intercultural connections and empower democratic community building? How can we re-envision our economic relationships so they promote justice rather than deepen the divide between rich and poor? How can we re-imagine the work of schools so they invigorate community learning, rather than foster competition and support consumption of curricula and hierarchical social structures that do not serve the common good?

Imagine Chicago[1] has been attempting over the past fourteen years to engage these questions through collaborative projects that challenge individuals and institutions to understand, imagine and create the future they value. At the heart of the work has been the development of learning communities where structured exchanges of ideas, resources and experiences bring hope alive and expand what's possible to imagine and create.

We think of learning as a generative dialogue in which what we already understand is reordered and expanded by the encounter with new ideas, perspectives and experiences that open us to life and reveal and develop our own capacities. Learning changes us as we appropriate what we have learned. Ongoing dialogue with people, ideas, and our own inner teacher deepens our questions and capacity for wonder, stretching our ability to see and understand from multiple perspectives, and helping develop our talents into skills so we can make a worthwhile public contribution. Ideally, education encourages us to think critically, giving us tools to evaluate a multiplicity of approaches and disciplines that shed light on important questions. We learn to order random encounters and information into helpful categories and ideas. Increasing mastery of necessary personal and professional skills enables us to be productive. We bump into the fullness of life in ways that are disturbing and joyful, that reveal our personal and cultural limitations. Since learning involves risk taking, it happens best in a community with others who are open to the unknown, and can help build our confidence and willingness to encounter the mystery of life without fear.

The need for intergenerational learning communities

Life is an unimaginably rich learning environment. Part of the richness of life is the dissonance provoked in us by patterns we observe that run counter to our own deeply held values and therefore move us to action. Ten years ago, I was working simultaneously as a corporate banker, Anglican priest, mother, and civic activist. These worlds shared little common vocabulary and held each other in great suspicion. I began to be increasingly unsettled by the waste of human life and the persistent injustices obvious in terms gaining public usage like 'underclass' and 'lost generation'. Ronald Marstin, a philosopher, once defined justice as fundamentally a matter of who is included and whom we can tolerate neglecting. The prevailing social structures of our city seemed to tolerate the neglect of many, including most people of color, all of the poor, and most people under or over a certain age—in short, the most vulnerable populations. As a person of faith, I believed in the priority of an economy in which *everyone* has a place at the table, a share of what's on the table, and an opportunity to shape the common good by virtue of what they uniquely bring. What would it take for the city in which I lived and was raising our children, to learn to think of itself as a whole rather than in divided terms, to expect more from all its citizens, and give its young people, and others whose contribution had been discounted, a place to belong and a way to contribute?

I needed a learning community within which to struggle with this question. For months, I asked the question to friends and colleagues, many of whom shared helpful insights and led me to others wrestling with these issues. Hoping to think through the question in a more structured way, I organized a conference on 'Faith, Imagination and Public Life', gathering in more than 50 well-known city pioneers and social innovators. People introduced themselves by describing a hopeful image that had particular authority in their life—a religious symbol, the face of a beloved relative, a waterfall in the rainforest that spoke of the abundance of life. Together we worked to understand the imagination that had shaped Chicago over the last century and discussed how to stimulate a broad group of civic entrepreneurs to re-imagine the city as a whole. The highlight of the conference was an exercise in which people imagined visions of Chicago's future ultimately worthy of their commitment, and identified what would be necessary for those dreams to come to birth.

The image of a worthy future that propelled me was the recycling symbol as an image of God's economy. I was seized by a vision of a city in which nothing and no one was wasted. I imagined a city where young people and others whose visions have been discounted develop and contribute their ideas and energy. It was seeing this vision as possible that caused me to give up a sixteen-year banking career to launch a new civic initiative. What, I wondered, would it take to design and create such a city?

Addressing that question has, so far for me, taken ten years and the creation of many new learning communities. My initial study consisted of reading about and listening to first-hand accounts of Chicago history. One-on-one interviews followed in which I discussed with city leaders and with many local neighborhood residents what might constitute an effective visioning and economic development process in Chicago. An informal network of Chicago leaders began to gather around the questions at the heart of the inquiry. In September 1992, twenty of them—educators, corporate and media executives, philanthropists, community organizers, youth developers, economists, religious leaders, social service providers—were convened as a design team for the project which became Imagine Chicago.

A conversation with the future

From September 1992 to May 1993, the design team created a process of civic inquiry as the starting point for engaging the city of Chicago in a broad-based conversation about its future. Two ideas emerged from the design phase which shaped the ultimate process design: first, that the pilot should attempt to discover what gives life to the city (as opposed to focusing on problems), and second, that it should provide significant leadership opportunities for youth, who most clearly represent the city's future. It was hoped from the outset that positive intergenerational civic conversation could provide a bridge between the experience and wisdom of seasoned community builders, and the energy and commitment of youth searching for purpose, yielding deeper insights into the collective future of the community.

Two types of pilot studies were designed and implemented in 1993–94: a citywide 'appreciative inquiry' process to gather Chicago stories and commitments, and a series of community-based and led processes. In each case, the intent was to give young adults and community builders in Chicago opportunities to share their hopes and commitments in a setting of mutual respect. The process was designed to use intergenerational teams, led by a young person in the company of an adult mentor, to interview business, civic, and cultural leaders about the future of their communities and of Chicago, using a process of appreciative inquiry. Appreciative Inquiry[2] is a form of study that selectively seeks to locate, highlight, and illuminate the life-giving forces of an organization or community's existence. It seeks out the best of what is to help ignite the collective imagination of what might be. The aim is to generate knowledge that expands the realm of the possible and helps members of the group envision a collectively desired future and successfully translate images of possibility into reality. In the case of Imagine Chicago's intergenerational interview process, the youth would both conduct the interview and distill the content for public view in ways that would help build their skills, inspire public action, and reinforce commitment. The premise was that young people could be effective agents of hope and inspiration, if they were released from the negative stereotypes in which many held themselves and were held by others.

The citywide interview process involved approximately 50 young people who interviewed about 140 Chicago citizens who were identified by members of Imagine Chicago's design team as 'Chicago glue'. These included artists, media executives, civic and grassroots leaders, politicians, business and professional leaders, and other young people. The interviewees represented over half of Chicago's neighborhoods.

Once the interviews had been completed, several groups of young adults distilled the data for public view. This summary was shared in three public events including a citywide 'Imagination Celebration' to which all interviewers and their interviewees were invited. The room was organized into small intergenerational table groupings with interactive, arts-based activities that further developed themes coming out of the interviews. The culminating activity of the day was the completion of a large (8 foot x 8 foot) Chicago dream tree. The 'leaves' of the tree were drawn in advance by young interview interpreters who read several interview transcripts and inscribed on the canvas the core vision they caught from each interviewee. The 'trunk' border was defined by common themes emerging from the interviews as interpreted by another group of young people who read all the interview transcripts. The categories included *inner strength, the power of commitment, common life,* and *livelihood for all.* At the end of the Imagination Celebration, each participant was invited to summarize their commitment to their expanded vision for the city by writing on a small piece of paper one thing they would do to move the city in the direction of their own vision. Those commitments were then shared and stuffed into fruit pods sewn onto the tree canvas, becoming the seeds for spreading the ideas and vision even further.

Three community-based interview pilots followed, in which Imagine Chicago worked as a collaborator with local organizations. The young mentors from one neighborhood supported a similar process in a different community, and also facilitated a large suburban conference investigating the future of Chicago. That event changed the image that many of the adult attendees carried of 'inner-city kids from tough neighborhoods' and what they were capable of accomplishing. Once the interview pilots were completed, an evaluation of the process was done, which showed three outcomes as potentially important in reconstituting a shared sense of civic community:

1. Shared identity

The conversations brought people together across boundaries of age, race, experience, and geography to reflect together on their relationship to the city as a whole. The meetings were grounded in mutual respect and appreciation, and solicited positive visions and stories which people were eager to share. Participants found their Chicago citizenship provided common ground. The conversations prompted a mindset shift among many participants. Participants, who may have expected to feel separated from their conversation partners by age, culture, or background, instead experienced powerful and positive relationship connections. This, in turn, shifted their sense of possibility about their own and their community's future. They began to understand the commonalities between their visions for the city's future, and be encouraged by their respective commitments. Experiencing an 'undivided Chicago conversation' seems to have nurtured hope in the possibility of sharing ownership of the city's future. The process itself modeled the hope held by many participants, and expressed by one, of 'a new Chicago in which all people can (and would) participate'. As another commented, 'it was helpful to pull together all of our visions and create understanding for those who had not shared your experiences'.

2. Intergenerational partnership and accountability

Both the young people and the adults involved commented that they gained an appreciative understanding of the other generation. As one adult shared, 'Yes, I gained hope too. The thing we lived for ... hopefully will be shared by the young person and enhanced through them.' A young person commented, 'It has made me think about the youth and how much people care about us.' The adults talked about their understanding that youth are vital partners in creating a vision of the city's future, and that youth need to be viewed as community organizing partners. In the citywide interview process, a frequent interview response to the question, 'What image captures your hopes for the city's future?' was for the adult interviewee to point to the young person and say 'You!' Several of these young people, ten years later, have become leaders in youth development nationally.

3. New possibilities and methods of civic conversation

In addition to gaining a shared hope and identity across a well-documented intergenerational divide, many participants benefited from learning the power of intergenerational appreciative inquiry. Shifting civic conversation away from problem solving to collective visioning about a shared future created energy and opened new ways of thinking. Learning to ask and answer positive questions, and to engage in active listening, was a subtle and welcome shift for many participants. A significant by-product of the process was an obvious collective ease and goodwill among all those who had participated, which was evident in the May gathering of all those who had participated in the citywide interview process. Constructive civic conversation, in a diverse group, created momentum and interest in making commitments to bring the visions to life.

It was suggested that these results were propelled by the contagious mindset of positive question/positive image/positive action embedded in the appreciative inquiry process. It brought to the surface deeply held hopes and values, and created trustworthy connections between people who could band together to bring the hopes to fruition. An adult participant from one of the community pilots summarized the power of the process thus: 'It has gotten community people, activists, youth centers, police, churches, all stirred up about something positive that can become a reality. People who have never been together have come together to do something positive ... to bridge a gap between young people and adults. It has sparked energy ... It has sparked hope ... We have worked together; we have collaborated, young and old. It took all of us. We know it's going to happen, because we've become one family, everyone encouraging one another. Now it's going to become a reality. This has formed respect for our young people, that they can get an idea and bring it to life.'

But the intergenerational interviews only took the first step—of understanding what was possible, and imagining where that could lead in the future. There was no structure within which to create that future. Imagine Chicago learned that the appreciative intergenerational interview process needed to be embedded within structures that could move more readily to action.

Moving from dialogue to action

> An unanswered question is a fine traveling companion. It sharpens our eye for the road.
>
> Rachel Remen

Imagine Chicago has designed its subsequent initiatives to give participants a chance to be creators in concrete and sustained ways and move from dialogue to action. Imagine Chicago has now developed over 100 learning partnerships with schools, churches, museums, community groups, and businesses. The work has involved a wide range of individuals and institutions: grassroots leaders who want to improve their neighborhoods and learn from the innovations of other committed citizens; public schools who want to forge deeper museum connections; teachers trying to make sense of their vocations and of education; immigrant and faith communities who want to explore the promise of democracy and American pluralism; school children and parents trying to understand and impact the systems and communities of which they are a part. Rather than putting itself at the center as a source of knowledge and expertise, Imagine Chicago creates frameworks for learning exchanges and then acts as an active listener for what is practical and possible. New possibilities emerge out of constructive dialogue in partnerships that bridge generational, cultural, racial and geographical boundaries.

Central to all the initiatives emerging in Imagine Chicago is a common approach to learning that moves from idea to action:

- *Understand* what is (focusing on the best of what is)
- *Imagine* what could be (working in partnerships with others)
- *Create* what will be (translating what we value into what we do)

Understand

All projects begin with and are grounded in asking and teaching others to ask open-ended, asset- and value-oriented questions about what is life-giving, what is working, what is generative, what is important. The focus is on asking positive questions that encourage sharing of best practices, articulation of fundamental values, and which reveal the positive foundation on which greater possibilities can be built. For example, what is something your child has accomplished that you are especially proud of? What about your family, this school, is especially effective in encouraging children to learn? What questions interest you most right now?

Imagine

New possibilities are inspired by hearing questions or stories that cause us to wonder and stretch our understanding beyond what we already know. When we are invited to articulate and hear from others what is important and working, we readily imagine how even greater transformation and innovation can happen. In a learning community, our collective imaginations continually envisage more. Grassroots leaders discussing what they have helped change on their block inspires others to try and make a difference. Young parents sharing stories of how they are caring for their children leads others to good parenting practices. Oliver Wendell Holmes suggested long ago that 'a mind once stretched by a new idea never regains its original dimensions'. This stretching of our imagination happens naturally. I still remember vividly a powerful image offered by an elderly interviewee in the original Imagine Chicago intergenerational interview process, who said, 'I imagine a city where critical thinking is so common that politicians can never capitalize on ignorance.' Hearing it started me thinking about the connections between education and democracy in a way I had not earlier considered.

Create

For imagination to help create community change, it needs to be embodied in something concrete and practical—*a visible outcome* that inspires more people to invest themselves in making a difference. In one Imagine Chicago program, Citizen Leaders, grassroots leaders are invited to articulate their visions for community change and then create an imaginative community development project of their own design. In the course of four months of interactive forums, they learn to recruit volunteers, design and organize a project, prepare a proposal, and implement, evaluate and sustain their projects. Learning occurs largely through sharing experiences as community change agents interact with each other within a common framework of organizing questions captured in a Community Innovation Guide created by Imagine Chicago. Participants use this guide, which builds appreciative inquiry questioning into step-by-step worksheets to organize the project planning process. Examples of questions include: 'What's made you willing to invest yourself in this process?' 'What small change on your block could make a big difference?' Over the course of four months, Citizen Leaders structure their idea into a sustainable, low-cost community project, working with at least six other neighborhood volunteers. In the Citizen Leader workshops, they are active learners; in their neighborhoods, as head of a project team, they are leaders.

Participants cite a number of challenges they have to overcome to become a community innovator including:

• Sustaining a volunteer commitment

Community development requires a substantial commitment of time and a willingness to take risks and get involved. Other priorities may intervene and pre-empt the involvement of the leader or of team members. Participants discover that sharing leadership makes it more possible to achieve progress.

• Recruiting a project team

Forming a project team is an essential, yet difficult step. Leaders are new at trying to organize their neighbors and are usually not in the habit of asking appreciative questions. Many are afraid of being rejected if they reach out. Citizen Leaders discover they can begin most easily by reaching out to those looking for a way to get involved, especially friends and those they know personally. Teams can be built from interested people on the block, family and friends of the leader, fellow church members, pastors, teachers, and other active people in the community who bring their own community connections to the project.

Citizen Leaders: Tina Brumfeld

When I first met Tina Brumfeld, she had just finished an alternative high school and was living in public housing in Uptown Chicago. Tina was brought to Citizen Leaders, a program Imagine Chicago was running for emerging local leaders who wanted to make a difference in their community. Someone in the business community had heard about our program and brought Tina to participate. But they lacked confidence in her ability to do so and let me know that.

Tina was very shy. She didn't open her mouth in the first three meetings. By the fourth meeting, everyone was supposed to have an idea of the project they wanted to create and who might work with them. Tina cared that there were lots of young men in the neighborhood who were unemployed and in gangs and who needed something worthwhile to do. She wanted to help but she didn't really know what to do. She knew guys liked to play basketball but the Park district said they didn't have a league because nobody was interested.

So Tina did something very simple. She put up a notice asking young men (18–24 years old) to sign up if they wanted to play basketball. She said she would help organize a team as her Citizen Leaders project. Over 200 people signed up the first week. Tina then had to get donations from local businesses—uniforms, balls, court time from Park, and find referees. Suddenly she had a good kind of problem. As she recounted, 'Now, I can't hardly walk down the street anymore 'cause of people yelling "Tina, Tina" … Now everybody wants to talk to me …'

By the end of the summer, there were hundreds of people playing basketball in the Uptown league. Rival gangs played together without fighting. The league led into a leadership development and job-training program for the young men. The Park district built it into their program. It inspired the starting of other leagues. Tina, who had been unemployed, got job offers from the Park district and a local high school as a community outreach worker because the project had brought out in her and made visible to so many other people her commitment and leadership skills. I remember vividly in one of the last classes of Citizen Leaders, another one of the participants listening to Tina bubbling in astonishment at all that was happening and just saying to her, 'You go girl!' There was no stopping her. A year later, she was a featured interview on the Osgood Files on National Public Radio. As Goethe once said, 'Whatever you can do, or dream you can, begin it. Boldness has genius, power and magic in it'.

Where had Tina begun? With the simple hope that she could make a difference to some young men who were friends of hers. As it turned out, she made a difference that transformed the neighborhood as well as her. She discovered gifts in herself she didn't know she had. She brought out gifts in others. Her own commitment was leveraged many times over by other people, who were inspired by her enthusiasm and got involved themselves. Being in a learning community of other Citizen Leaders encouraged her to take the necessary risks that making a difference requires.

Recreating schools as community learning centers

Citizen Leaders has stimulated community innovation around low-cost high-impact community development projects. Imagine Chicago has also developed partnerships to invigorate learning within schools. The Chicago Public Schools have 450,000 students; educational outcomes are poor and clearly correlated with poverty demographics. In 1995, Imagine Chicago, with the Center for Urban Education at DePaul University, created the Urban Imagination Network. The network linked seven Chicago public schools in very low income communities with each other, with Imagine Chicago and with six museums: a botanic garden, an aquarium, a museum of Natural History, a museum of indigenous culture, a children's museum, and an urban history museum. The central goal was to redevelop schools as centers of community learning for the benefit of students, their parents and teachers. It proved a formidable challenge.

In Chicago, many students have 'checked out' of school because they are bored by passive teaching practice and a lack of connection between academic content and life issues of concern to them. They lack vocabulary and critical thinking skills to organize and express their own ideas. The primary focus for student development in the Urban Imagination Network was therefore to build reading and thinking skills by encouraging students to research content area topics, and develop exhibits that showed others what they discovered. This simple hands-on approach helps reconnect children to their own creativity, develops critical thinking skills, and increases vocabulary, knowledge, skills and self-esteem. Making their learning visible requires students to think through their ideas; the exhibits become centers for increased in-school and school-community learning. In one elementary school, for example, the older children worked with the Botanic Garden to create a garden in their school courtyard, learning extensive natural science in the process. Much younger children then went into the garden, and found a plant for each color they wanted to learn. They prepared their own description linking object and color, which was compiled into a 'color' book (now used for the incoming kindergarten class). In another school, each class created an illustrated quilt for the school hallway around a focused question like 'How did pioneers live?' or 'How does the economy work?' Now, students moving up and down the corridors see learning connections, inspired by the work of their peers.

Not all schools were equally successful in implementation. The sheer weight of bureaucratic requirements in a large standardized system dragged down people's energy and availability to participate in developing a creative learning community. We found over time that it was more productive to focus on areas within the schools where voluntary commitment rather than mandatory commitment could be leveraged. The two on which we came to focus most attention were engagement of families interested in creating a culture of learning in their homes and personal renewal of teachers.

The parent connection was an obvious one though it was not added until three years into a six-year development program. Public schools tend to be quite pessimistic about the possibility of engaging parents in voluntary personal development. But educators universally agree that families have the largest impact on a student's interest in and ability to learn. So a primary component of Imagine Chicago's work with schools has been to engage public school parents in forums that bring learning alive within a broad community context.

The parent development component, called *'Reading Chicago and Bringing It Home'* focuses on core computer and 'civic literacy' skills necessary to connect families (usually living in isolated low-income Chicago neighborhoods) to the life of the larger city. 'Civic literacy' implies the ability to take information from any source and translate it into ideas that make sense, expand our understanding of life and enable us to act as citizens. Monthly *'Reading Chicago'* workshops, held at area museums, engage parents in researching and discussing content at the heart of a family's budget and a city's life—food, housing, energy, communication, transportation, work, financial management, water, education, recreation, public health, cultural identity, etc. Through focused reading, reflecting on life experience, visiting museum exhibits, listening to public presentations, and discussions with parents from other cultures and neighborhoods, participants think through what makes a family and city work. They develop life skills like budgeting and saving and basic reading skills essential to making sense of information from any source.

'Bringing It Home' monthly workshops are also held at each participating school. These concentrate on applying what parents learn in the monthly 'reading a city' workshops to facilitating children's learning at home. Parents design family activities to do with their children that reinforce the key ideas and learning methodologies. Each month focuses on one core competency essential to city living (map skills, budgeting, résumé writing, using public transportation, primary health care, reading a bill, computer literacy, working with people from other cultures). Parents especially skilled in a given core competency serve as coaches to other parents. Parent participation is rewarded with books and additions to a Chicago 'tool kit' (atlases, public transportation maps, calculators, museum passes, tickets to cultural activities) that encourage and enable family learning and city participation.

The parent program's different elements help develop systems thinking in multiple ways. Parents learn about city systems in a location outside their neighborhood; they design activities at a local school location; they teach those creative activities to their children at home. Parents become aware of the city's complexity as a system, and of key vocabulary and practices in major systems. They build up an understanding of how systems change over time. For example, when parents studied transportation, they did so at the Chicago Historical Society, beginning with an exercise deciding what items they would have put in their wagon as a pioneer (an exercise in setting personal priorities). They heard first-person narratives of a pioneer journey to help build a more personal connection to the artifacts in the exhibit hall on pioneer life in Illinois. They discussed why studying history matters. They thought through the relationship of refrigerated railroad transportation and farming to the development of Chicago as a stockyard and mail order center. They examined the citizen action transportation plan currently being debated in the state legislature. They began to understand that individuals and communities both create and are shaped by the systems of which they are a part.

Participation in this civic learning community changes the consciousness of participants from being 'objects' of city life, in a city which is an 'It', to being 'subjects' (I decide, I create, I connect, I think) within a city which is a 'We'. Imagine Chicago *treats* parents as subjects by respecting their intelligence and interest in learning and their commitment as involved parents and *equips* them with skills that increase their ability to act as such. By learning to read their city, parents re-envision themselves as educators, community leaders, thinkers, parents, citizens, not objects or victims. Acting as agents of change within their families, their schools and their communities engages them and reshapes their self-understanding as citizens. Re-imagining, reorganizing their relationship to the city and its systems shifts power from unresponsive bureaucratic structures to parents who act on behalf of what they value.

The program faces multiple challenges. External funding bodies focused on school reform have been reluctant to support learning communities for parents they often view as 'beyond hope', unless the links can be clearly drawn to how such support will improve performance on standardized tests by their children, or directly change the political equation within schools. As one exasperated foundation officer commented, 'This program is just too interdisciplinary. You are actually trying to get people to think. That defies our program categories!' Many potential supporters are skeptical of the possibility of even attracting parents into a learning community when so many parents are drop-outs from the educational system. Recruitment is indeed a challenge. Most schools do not have effective technology to support ongoing communication with students' families. Most parents rarely show up on the school's premises except to collect report cards or when their child has misbehaved. Furthermore, principals who could allocate discretionary funds to parent development are reluctant to support a program that empowers parents because of the likely threat such parents can pose to school administrators who currently have little community accountability. To continue the program will require continuing to build broad financial and political support for family learning as a culture in the city, open to all income levels.

Imagine Chicago's other major arena of work with public schools has been professional development of teachers. Great teachers bring energy, concern, a meaningful connection to their subject and to their students, and an openness of mind and heart that helps them be present to their students and colleagues and facilitate their learning. Currently, many teachers are overwhelmed by the cumulative stress of working in a failing system of education. They need space within which to deepen their own vision for and commitment to learning, and to gain perspective on the inevitable fears and stresses that arise within a standardized and depersonalized education system.

Imagine Chicago's teacher renewal program is structured around quarterly weekend retreats held over a two-year cycle at the Chicago Botanic Garden. Holding it in a public place gives teachers a way to revisit this 'sacred ground' with their students if they choose. Content connects to seasonal themes. Large group, small group and solitary activities, involving multiple arts and outdoor experiences:

- 'give teachers time' to build trust and learn to speak from their hearts rather than simply accepting conventional images of 'being too busy' to attend to their own development;
- provide opportunities for teachers to articulate and explore their own experiences as teachers—and the gifts and understanding they bring to those challenges;
- offer ways for teachers to 'reframe' their experience so they can understand and respond to it more deeply (not as a problem of technique but as an opportunity for personal integrity);
- help teachers develop their *own* language and images and methods with which to explore 'spiritual' development with each other and their students;
- reconnect teachers to natural cycles so they appreciate what supports life, and recognize that the teaching vocation offers opportunities for entering daily into a cycle of renewal and growth that is an organic and not mechanistic process.

This program differs from other professional development efforts because it is not focused on professional competence or teacher retention, though it supports both. While it involves substantial natural science content, it assumes that content alone is not sufficient to create an environment for learning. The program engages and impacts teachers' intellectual, affective and spiritual lives, challenging them to revision the purposes and practices of education, to rediscover the 'heart' of teaching including their own inner strength, balance and resiliency. Engaging in arts and play fuels their innate creative capacities, and reminds them of the importance of play for their students. Developing habits of reflection and awareness helps teachers realize that silence may be as important to learning as speech. What often results is a spiritual reawakening in which joy and love are discovered at the heart of learning.

Securing ongoing funding has again been a challenge. Funders prefer to support professional competence development in prescribed content areas, not recognizing that the chronic shortage of public school teachers will never be addressed without addressing the matter of will and interest in learning, and the priority of ongoing participation in vibrant learning communities. The Urban Imagination Network had the great advantage (but associated risk to its long-term future) of financial support from a single private foundation that acted as a partner in mission. In six years of development, schools created dynamic learning connections among teachers, students, parents, community members and museums, connections that continue to enliven teaching and influence our city. But there is not yet broad enough support for learning initiatives that go beyond school boundaries, that challenge the current culture of education as being too narrow, that thrive on collaborative inquiry around questions rather than organized dissemination of answers. So we must continue to work at all levels, connect the dots, develop much broader support for learning communities that are inclusive and participative, help people create vital connections that change what's possible.

Harnessing hope

Imagine Chicago attracts participation because it inspires hope and offers living proof that peoples' highest aspirations are possible to translate into action. It builds competence by providing learning frameworks and networks and from these come ideas which create community change. Some of our practices and tools for the development of hope include:

- Offering a confident vision of human (and life) possibilities and learning
- Involving the 'public' in learning communities that motivate change, make information available in an accessible way, and respectfully engage marginalized participants, including children
- Tapping into the lived experience of community members, finding ways for them to enlarge their vocabulary of how to approach the experience and participate in collaborative inquiry about it
- Asking provocative, constructive questions and listening to responses with respect, delight, confidence, commitment and relaxed high expectations
- Looking at the past as an inventory of possibilities for the future
- Encouraging the participation and leadership of multiple generations so a vision of the future is present and highly visible
- Connecting individuals, institutions and systems with common values and goals that otherwise might not be working together and can benefit each other—and sustaining the networks
- Minimizing models of control and dependence through lateral structure, encouragement of personal initiative, validation of the skills, knowledge and values each individual and organization brings
- Encouraging exploration through action research (learning via experimentation) within projects that have community impact
- Integrating artistic expression into school and community development projects so people's confidence and self-understanding as creators is strengthened
- Acknowledging the importance of spirituality and the inner teacher as a primary resource for hope and learning

- Re-enchanting and expanding the language of citizenship to include civic imagination, civic literacy, education for public life
- Deconstructing language in which people are objects in a depersonalized politics and reclaiming our creativity as subjects concerned with reconstituting a common life
- Deconstructing the mindset of division (race, gender, class, culture) in favor of the language of inclusion (from 'we/they' to 'we the people')
- Deconstructing discourse grounded in cynicism and judgment in favor of the language of hope and possibility
- Deconstructing the culture of professionalism and isolated expertise in favor of the culture of community
- Celebrating and communicating lessons learned so the inventory of 'what's possible' expands

These tools have proven helpful in many places throughout the world, in dealing with a range of community challenges. Common to many places is the need and struggle to shift from single sector problem solving to focusing on what communities value and how to organize productive partnerships within which those values can be shared and lived. This involves helping professionals shift from an identity as competent experts with answers, to community partners with questions. Community partnerships invite us to be vulnerable together, to depend upon one another, not to have all the answers ourselves. They evoke our commitment and provide us with an opportunity not only to give of ourselves, but also to broaden and deepen the community to which we belong and from which we can learn. Working in partnership with uncommon partners, in a way that is natural and productive, we discover that our learning communities are much bigger than we thought.

A concluding reflection: living and learning from the inside out

Earlier this year, our older daughter, who is a first-year university student, talked with me about how to keep from taking into herself the rather overwhelming culture of violence and despair that pervades our world. She wants to keep her heart and mind open, not to be dominated by fear, to get an education that will make a difference. In mulling over her questions over the course of several days, the phrase 'inside out' lodged in my consciousness and I realized it summarized well my aspirations about learning. The best learning, and living, happens 'from the inside out' for both individuals and institutions. We learn most powerfully when education begins with what's inside—with our questions, innate talents, ways of seeing rather than with preprogrammed answers by experts to someone else's questions. Our lives have integrity when decisions flow from our values and spiritual understanding, not from what others expect from us. Action is most effective when we take time to reflect before we act. We enrich public life when we are willing to create images of hope and possibility rather than consume pre-packaged media images of violence and despair.

Living from the 'inside out' suggests that we must *act* to really learn, validate what we believe by experimenting with what works, taking risks, learning for ourselves. Spiritual introversion has to give way to living the values we have chosen, being accountable to the hope that is in us. We have to take who we are and get involved with what's around us, without taking on issues and responsibilities that rightly belong to others. When we operate from wholeness and hope, our lives radiate outward. They become sources of healing and inspiration to others. We learn to trust people to own their own issues and resources, to do our share but not more than our share, to encourage everyone to play their part in a way that gives life to the whole.

People find hope and inspiration by being connected to things that are bigger than they are. As meaning-making people, we need transcendent connections and a sense of purpose. Imagine Chicago helps people connect to bigger 'wholes' that are a place from which they can learn, draw courage and recognize that their individual effort is leveraged and exalted when put together with others.

Hope alone is realistic because it perceives the scope of our real possibilities

Hope does not strive after things that have no place but after things that have no place as yet but can acquire one. What will it take for us to believe that we can create a just economy, a global community in which no one is wasted, in which children are cared for and well educated, in which violence and addiction have lost their power to control? Are we willing to renounce cynicism and live out of a rich imagination for the flourishing of human life and community?

Hope is a choice not a feeling. We must tune ourselves into the frequency of hope by the questions we ask and the questions we live. What dreams or whispers are at the heart of your own life that may be seeking your commitment? What do you want to learn? What impresses your heart right now? What small change could you make that might make a big difference? How could you make solidarity with the stranger a daily practice? Who might stand with you? Hope, the willingness to celebrate what can be, brings with it remarkable resources for creative connections. I draw courage from being in the company of others who are committed to transforming institutions and communities through learning and who are working to create a future worthy of our hope. Take the risk of living into your questions and commitments without needing all the answers. Actively seek the company of others willing to learn and to hold you accountable to your highest hopes. Live from the inside out. And you will discover blessing.

Endnotes

'Cultivating Hope and Imagination' has been published in the *Journal of Future Studies* (August 2002) as well as in a special issue entitled *Unfolding Learning Societies* published by Shikshantar (available at www.swaraj.org/shikshantar)

1. IMAGINE CHICAGO is eager to identify and expand its partners in this work:
   IMAGINE CHICAGO
   910 Castlewood Terrace Chicago, IL 60640
   Phone: (1)773-275-2520
   www.imaginechicago.org (email: bliss@imaginechicago.org)

2. The most resources about Appreciative Inquiry are available at: ai.cwru.edu.

CONTRIBUTORS

Dr Elina Baker is a clinical psychologist working at the Devon and Cornwall Forensic Psychiatry Service. Her interests include promoting user involvement in secure mental health services.

Dr Raja Bandak qualified in medicine at Southampton University in 1978. He became a GP in Telford, Shropshire in 1984. He is married with two children and living in a timber-framed house has developed some experience in DIY, cabinetmaking, woodcarving and breadmaking. His GP practice area covers two of the ten per cent most deprived wards in England and this led to him developing a family support project in 1995. This project now is a registered charity with three group facilitators and four playfocus workers. Since 1999 it has attracted attention as an NHS Beacon and in 2002 was awarded the Health and Social Award in the category of Primary Care Partnerships. In November 2002 Dr Bandak succeeded with a National Lottery Bid for the project of £270,000 and is currently developing a second bid to continue the work of the project after the three-year funding finishes. He is on the local Sure Start board and hopes to be closely involved in the development of a Children's Centre built near the local surgery.

Geraldine Brady is a Research Assistant in the Centre for Social Justice at Coventry University. Her doctoral studies, funded by the ESRC at Warwick University, explored the experience of ADHD from the perspective of children/young people, their parents and mental health professionals. At present she is working on a number of projects (both research- and activity-based) focusing on the experience of pregnant teenagers and young parents.

Freddy Jackson Brown is a clinical psychologist working with children with disabilities and developmental delay in Bristol. He has previously published papers on the philosophy of science and the validity of psychiatric nosology.

Bliss W. Browne is an Episcopal priest, mother of three, director of many non-profit organizations, and former Division Head of the First National Bank of Chicago where she served as a corporate banker for 16 years. She founded Imagine Chicago in 1991. Imagine projects have been organised on six continents in the last five years. She was a member of the Saguaro Seminar on Civic Engagement in America, convened by the Kennedy School at Harvard University. Bliss is a graduate of Yale University (BA, History 1971), Harvard University (MDiv 1974) and the Kellogg School of Management of Northwestern (MM, 1978).

Jonathan Calder has degrees in philosophy and Victorian studies and writes on politics and the environment.

Jan Cooper is Co-director of Reading Safer Families, and a UKCP Registered Family Therapist.

Carl Harris is a white, British, middle-class, Midlands-male, clinical psychologist in his forties with a partner and two children. He works in the Family Well-being Project, an action-research post in a community regeneration project in Birmingham, UK. After an extended period of study of social sciences and philosophy at the universities of Kent, Glasgow, Cork and Birmingham, he qualified in clinical psychology in 1996.

Grace Jackson is a board certified psychiatrist who graduated from the University of Colorado School of Medicine in 1996. She has lectured widely in Europe and the United States about the limitations of drug therapies. An independent researcher and consultant, Dr. Jackson's interests include bioethics, neuroscience, and philosophy.

Helen Myatt works as a clinical psychologist with children and families in the care system. She is particularly interested in the use of medical labels for this group and the lack of psychological explanations for behaviour in services.

Craig Newnes is a dad, gardener and Director of Psychological Therapies in Shropshire. He won the 2005 Citizens Commission for Human Rights (CCHR) award for speaking out for 25 years about the state of psychiatry and psychology. He regards much of psychology as, in Anthony Burgess' words, no more than 'a mouthful of air'. Craig is editor of the *Journal of Critical Psychology, Counselling and Psychotherapy* and commissioning editor for the Critical Division of PCCS Books. He has edited a number of books including *This is Madness, This is Madness Too* and *Spirituality and Psychotherapy*. He is editor of *Clinical Psychology* and is the longest serving member of the Division of Clinical Psychology's National Executive Committee. Nowadays he tires easily.

Nick Radcliffe works as a consultant clinical psychologist in child and family mental health in Telford, England.

Helen Rostill, BSc, ClinPsyD, is a lecturer in clinical psychology at the University of Birmingham, researching and lecturing on the impact of early relational trauma on child and adolescent development. She is also a Consultant Clinical Psychologist working with looked after children and young offenders in Dudley.

Dorothy Rowe is an author, broadcaster and psychologist. She is famously Australian and notoriously outspoken. Her latest books are available from http://www.dorothyrowe.com.au/

Gerrilyn Smith has a degree in Psychology and English Literature from Canada. She moved to London in 1976, where she obtained an MPhil in Clinical Psychology. She has worked in a number of settings including voluntary agencies, the health service, local authorities and the private sector. Gerrilyn currently works as a freelance trainer, consultant and clinician. With Dee Cox she is the author of *Women and Self Harm* (The Women's Press).

Sami Timimi is a consultant child and adolescent psychiatrist who works full time in the National Health Service in Lincolnshire. He has published many articles on various subjects and two books: *Pathological Child Psychiatry and the Medicalization of Childhood*, and *Naughty Boys: Anti-social behaviour, ADHD and the role of culture*.

Dr Arlene Vetere is Co-director of Reading Safer Families, and Deputy Director of the Surrey University PsychD Programme.

Katherine Weare is Professor of Education at the University of Southampton. Her interests are in the mental, emotional and social health and well-being of children and young people. Her recent publications include *Promoting Mental, Emotional and Social Health: A whole school approach* (Routledge), *Developing the Emotionally Literate School* and *What Works in Promoting Children's Emotional and Social Competence* (DfES). She has helped various national and international agencies to develop their mental health services, including the European Union, the WHO in Eastern and Central Europe and Russia and the DfES. She is currently working on the links between children's wellbeing and their ability to learn.

INDEX

PCCS Books

Committed to reflexive, radical and critical contemporary psychology theory and practice

www.pccs-books.co.uk

• browse by subject and author •

• pre-publication offers •

• discounts on all orders •

• free p&p in the UK •

• low cost shipping worldwide •

• useful links •